Dangerous Pe

Dangerous People

Edited by

Nigel Walker

BLACKSTONE
PRESS LIMITED

First published in Great Britain 1996 by Blackstone Press Limited,
9–15 Aldine Street, London W12 8AW. Telephone: 0181-740 1173

© Blackstone Press Limited, 1996
The contributors hold the copyright for their respective chapters.

ISBN: 1 85431 518 8

British Library Cataloguing in Publication Data
A CIP catalogue record for this book is available from the British Library.

Typeset by Montage Studios Limited, Tonbridge, Kent
Printed by Livesey Limited, Shrewsbury, Shropshire

Contents

Preface

During most of the last three decades 'dangerousness' was regarded as a dirty word, or at least as a politically incorrect term. Probation officers seldom used it when describing offenders to courts. Psychiatrists preferred to talk of 'vulnerable' patients. Judges disliked using their special sentencing powers to order detention for indefinite periods, or, indeed, for longer than the 'tariff' recommended.

The last few years have seen a change. The news media have given increasing coverage to cases in which men, women and children have suffered serious and lasting harm from offenders who were known to have done similar harm on earlier occasions. Legislators have provided the courts with new powers, for example to impose long, precautionary sentences for violent or sexual offences. The Parole Board's role has been redefined so that risk to others is now its only important consideration. Probation services have been told not to mince words in their reports to courts, and to pay special attention to the supervision of offenders who have shown themselves capable of serious personal harm. In 1995 there were at least 20 official inquiries into the release of patients or prisoners who subsequently caused grave and preventable harm — often fatal — to others.

It seemed to me that there was a need for a book which would cover the main aspects of the subject in a way which no single person could. I have persuaded nine experts to contribute to it. It will be clear from the List of Contributors that their experience and backgrounds qualify them to write with authority.

As its title indicates, the book is about dangerous people, not about dangerous industries or organisations. To deal with them would call for another team of experts and another book.

Nigel Walker
The Institute of Criminology,
The University of Cambridge
March 1996

vii

List of Contributors

Paul Bowden is Consultant Forensic Psychiatrist at Bethlem Royal and the Maudsley Hospital, founding editor of the *Journal of Forensic Psychiatry*, joint editor of *Principles and Practice of Forensic Psychiatry*, and author of other contributions to the subject.

John Crichton is an honorary registrar in psychiatry at Addenbrooke's Hospital, Cambridge, and was research assistant to the Robinson inquiry. His publications include *Psychiatric Patient Violence: Risk and Response*. He is a former Nightingale Researcher at the Cambridge University Institute of Criminology.

Elaine Genders is a lecturer on criminal law and criminal justice at University College, London. Before that she was a research fellow at the Oxford University Centre for Criminological Research. She was co-author, with Elaine Player, of *Race Relations in Prisons*, and *Grendon: a study of a therapeutic prison*. Together with Shona Morrison she is writing a book on the social and legal realities of violent crime.

John Gunn is Professor of Forensic Psychiatry at the Maudsley Institute of Psychiatry. His publications include *Psychiatric Aspects of Imprisonment* and *Forensic Psychiatry: clinical, legal and ethical issues* (with Pamela Taylor). He is the Editor of *Criminal Behaviour and Mental Health*, and was a member of the Royal Commission on Criminal Justice.

David Hirschmann was an independent member of the Parole Board from 1989 to 1994. He has also been a member of the Board of Visitors at HM Prison, Shepton Mallett. In his professional life he is a Senior Lecturer and Head of the Philosophy Department at the University of Bristol.

Shona Morrison is a senior research officer with the Australian Commonwealth Law Enforcement Board's Office of Strategic Crime Assessments. Before that she was a research officer at the Oxford University Centre for Criminological Research. She was co-author, with Ian O'Donnell, of *Armed Robbery: a study in London*.

Nicola Padfield is a Fellow of Fitzwilliam College, Cambridge, author of *Texts and Materials on the Criminal Justice Process*, and co-author of the second edition of *Sentencing Theory, Law and Practice*.

Roger Shaw is Chief Probation Officer of Powys Probation Service, and before that one of HM Inspectors of Probation. He has twice held teaching appointments at the Institute of Criminology, Cambridge, and is the author and editor of books about prisoners' children.

Nigel Walker was Director of the Institute of Criminology and a Professorial Fellow of King's College, Cambridge. He was a member of the Butler and Floud Committees, and the author of books about sentencing, psychiatric defences, criminological explanations, and theories of punishment. He is an Honorary Fellow of the Royal College of Psychiatrists.

Donald West is Professor Emeritus of Clinical Criminology at the University of Cambridge, a Mental Health Act Commissioner, and a member of the Government's Advisory Committee on Mentally Disordered Offenders. His books include *Sexual Crimes and Confrontations* and (as Editor) *Sex Crimes*.

1

Ethical and Other Problems

Nigel Walker

People who are labelled as 'dangerous' present a humanitarian society with a moral dilemma. We want to prevent the harm such people may do to others, yet we feel guilty when prevention entails drastic interference with their lives. The horns of the dilemma are sharpest when the harm feared is of a kind that destroys life or the quality of life, and when the only effective means of prevention is detention. The horns are blunter when the harm is merely financial and the risk of it can be reduced by non-custodial measures, such as disqualification or supervision. But, the questions remain. How serious must the harm be to justify preventive measures? How drastic should the measures be?

Such questions hardly matter when prison sentences and compulsory stays in mental hospitals are so lengthy that by the time inmates are released their age, condition or circumstances make them unlikely to repeat their crimes. It is when periods of detention are shortened — whether because of pressure on resources or as a result of penological optimism — that dangerousness becomes a subject of public debate.

The debate arises because there are people who are prepared to tolerate — or demand — retributive punishment for harmful behaviour but are likely to object if detention is used for any other purpose. Others may accept the justification for incarceration as a deterrent or corrective yet insist that it should last no longer than is necessary for these purposes. A third group argues that the aim of protecting the public is a justification which can, in certain circumstances, override desert-based justice. It is fair to call this a debate between 'protectionists' and 'anti-protectionists'.

The Retributive Fallacy

It is retributive assumptions that create most of the tensions about precautionary measures which involve interference with individuals' liberties. As a
Swedish working-party uncompromisingly put it:

> The ethical problem is that incapacitation as a reason for penal intervention
> means that a person is punished not for what he has done but for what it is
> believed he may do in the future. A person exposed to a sanction that is more
> severe than that which that crime he committed usually entails, and justified
> by the fact that he is to be prevented from recidivating will thereby serve a
> sentence for a crime he did not commit and which in addition it is doubtful
> if he will ever commit. This conflicts with essential demands for legal
> security and can be compared to the sentencing of an innocent person.[1]

The rhetoric is persuasive, but begs an enormous question. It tries to smuggle
past us the assumption that the *only* respectable aim of a 'penal intervention'
— or, as we might say, 'a disposal by a criminal court' — is to inflict a penalty
which is proportionate to guilt. Some people of course would not accept this as
a respectable function. But, even those who would could hardly maintain that
it is the *only* respectable function, unless they were retributivists of an extreme,
ultra-Kantian sort. I cannot think of any jurisdiction which does not recognise
other functions of criminal sentences. An obvious example is the placing of
offenders in surroundings where treatment or regimes have a chance of
improving their behaviour; another example is the deterrence of potential
imitators. Why should not yet another example be the protection of other
people? The Swedish fallacy, however, dies hard, as we shall see.

Origins

Anti-protectionism originated in the United States as a reaction against the very
long periods for which violent or sexual offenders were detained in penitentiaries or mental hospitals. Even when such people became eligible for parole, or
appeared to have responded well to treatment in hospital, parole boards and
psychiatrists were sensitive to public opinion which held them responsible for
mistaken releases, and, consequently, 'played safe'. Their caution was attacked
from two directions. One of the tenets of 'labelling theory' was that calling
people 'killers' or 'rapists' because of a single crime misled us into ascribing

---

[1] From *A New Penal System* (1978) (the English summary of a report by the Working Group for
Criminal Policy of the National Swedish Council for Crime Prevention), Stockholm.

non-existent propensities for such behaviour. This glossed over two facts: that a murder or a sexual assault at least shows what a person is capable of; and that a capability is something that can be exercised more than once. There were even etymological attempts to discourage the use of the label 'danger' — at least when applied to human beings. It was pointed out that in the middle ages 'danger' meant 'being within someone else's power'.[2] This is nice to know; but the modern meaning has been in use for at least five centuries. In any case, the debate between protectionists and anti-protectionists is not over the use of a word, but over policies.

More impressive were accidental experiments like the Baxstrom case. Baxstrom was an inmate of a New York State institution for insane criminals. In 1961 his sentence expired, but his detention was continued under provisions of the Correction Law. He managed to convince the Supreme Court in 1966 that these provisions were unconstitutional. It followed that he and others in a similar position had to be dealt with under civil procedure, and in that year 969 such patients were transferred to civil hospitals. Although previously they had been denied this transfer by experienced psychiatrists on the grounds that they were too disturbed or potentially dangerous, the staffs of the civil hospitals were said to have found them no more alarming than their other patients. Within months 147 had been discharged into the community, and only seven had been found difficult enough to warrant a judicial commitment to special security. One year later only one of the released patients had been rearrested, which was only for a minor offence. Although a one-year follow-up is not long enough (longer follow-ups revealed that about one in four of those released eventually committed assaults), the effect on penological opinion was profound, and was reinforced by similar follow-ups, for example of the 'Dixon' patients in Pennsylvania.[3] In fact, the value of these *causes célèbres* as a basis for sound estimates was doubtful. The male Baxstrom patients, for example, had been detained for an average of 13 years (the women for 17 years) and most were in their late forties when released. Half had remained in or had been returned to hospital, and one in 10 had died by the end of the four-year follow-up. Only a genuine experiment in which all had been released when they were much younger, and after shorter periods of detention, would have allowed a sound estimate of the percentage of cases in which their psychiatrists' pessimism was mistaken.

The Baxstrom case, however, popularised what I have called 'the sinful mistake fallacy'. Anti-protectionists argued that detaining offenders for purely

---

[2] See Sarbin, T. R., 'The Dangerous Individual: an Outcome of Social Identity Transformation' (1967) *British Journal of Criminology*, 7 pp. 285–95.
[3] See Thornberry, T. P. & Jacoby, J. E. (1979) *The Criminally Insane: a community follow-up of mentally ill offenders*, Chicago: University of Chicago Press.

3

precautionary purposes involved too many mistakes, because their number exceeded the number that would have been made if the offenders had been released. If offenders who will repeat their offences are in a minority, a policy of precautionary detention will result in more unnecessary detentions than avoidable repetitions. The argument relies on the rhetorical use of the term 'mistake' to refer both to unnecessary detentions and to avoidable reoffending. This makes it plausible to use arithmetic to advocate a policy that minimises the number of 'mistakes'. The dishonesty of this sort of arithmetic, which ignores the difference between prolonging detention and failing to prevent another grave crime, should be obvious.

Underlying the arithmetical rhetoric, however, is something of more psychological interest: the assumption that there is something morally wrong about any mistake that has a regrettable effect on someone's life. That may well be so if the mistake could have been avoided by greater professional competence, or by a more diligent effort to obtain relevant information (a search, which is discussed below). Otherwise, moral condemnation is inappropriate. Nevertheless, there is such a thing as neurotic guilt.[4] 'Survivor guilt' is common amongst those who have been saved by mere luck from, for example, a battle, a shipwreck or a natural disaster. 'Decision-maker's guilt' is sometimes the result of a situation in which any of the possible choices has serious and irremediable consequences for some of those involved. What is important is that this should be recognised as irrational, and not an intuition of genuine blameworthiness.

Could decision-makers be given better information which would make some mistakes avoidable? This hope encouraged the application of prediction research to the problem, which had proved useful in estimating the probability that convicted offenders would be reconvicted. Gender, age, type of offence and previous record could be combined to produce 'prediction-scores'. Statistical prediction was recognised as more accurate than non-statistical — often called 'clinical' — forecasts.[5]

Even statistical prediction, however, had limitations which needed (and still need) to be emphasised. Essentially, all that it does is to use one or more (usually more) variables to subdivide a sample of individuals into subgroups, with different frequencies of the relevant outcome. Thus, insurance companies' actuaries assign smokers and non-smokers to subgroups with different death-rates, but complicate the variable by distinguishing cigar- and pipe-smokers from cigarette-smokers. The assumption underlying all prediction

---

[4] See Morris, H., 'Non-moral Guilt' in (1987) *Responsibility, Character, and The Emotions* (ed. Schoeman, F., Cambridge: Cambridge University Press.

[5] See, for example, Meehl, P. E. (1954) *Clinical versus Statistical Prediction*, Minneapolis: University of Minnesota Press.

studies is that the rates for future populations will be close to those of the subsamples.

Difficulties of Prediction

Prediction studies encounter major difficulties, however, when they are applied to violent or sexual offences, or, indeed, to any sort of offence which is relatively uncommon.

(a) The less frequent the outcome which has to be predicted the less accurately will samples predict. From the actuarial point of view the optimum frequency is 50 per cent, and frequencies of three or four per cent make for considerable inaccuracy. The reconviction rates for young male offenders are near the optimum, but reconviction is a miscellaneous criterion, covering many types of offence — from shoplifting to arson. Personal violence or sexual molestation) is much less frequent and, however large the sample, errors of prediction, especially 'false positives', will be far more common.

(b) The graver the offence the longer the offender is likely to be detained, whether for the sake of retribution, deterrence, treatment or the reassurance of the public. It would be unthinkable (politically at least) to release all such offenders after uniformly short periods in order to establish scientific conditions for discriminating more accurately between those who repeat their offences and those who do not. Accidental experiments of this kind have occasionally been made possible by court decisions in the United States, as we have seen; but even in such circumstances, inmates are released at different stages of their detention — some after months, some after years. Nor are researchers sufficiently forewarned to carry out thorough case-studies of the cohorts.

(c) Some outcomes are uncertain until long follow-ups have been completed. Most follow-ups are short, since they are used to compare the effectiveness of different ways of dealing with offenders: two years being a common length. However, if the question is how many violent or sexual offenders *ever* repeat their offences, a much longer follow-up is needed, which in theory, should last until the death of the offender. In practice, since research is expected to produce findings, follow-ups of more than five or six years are rare. If an offender does reoffend, it is usually within five years of freedom, but not always.

(d) Whether short or long, all follow-ups are subject to another serious difficulty: a violent or sexual offender may be rearrested and imprisoned for a non-violent, non-sexual offence; or, if suffering from some mental disorder, the offender may be readmitted to hospital, voluntarily or compulsorily, as a result of his behaviour or symptoms which are not violent or sexual. These are by no means uncommon eventualities. Violent and sexual offenders are by no means always 'specialists', and can commit offences of other kinds, usually dishonesties (as can many mentally disordered offenders). The result is custody, which sometimes (we cannot know how often) forestalls another act of violence or sexual molestation. The researcher does not know whether to classify the offender as a repeater or a non-repeater: the only honest thing to do is to discard him or her from the sample.

These are not reasons for completely dismissing attempts to identify predictors of the sorts of violence or sexual molestation which cause most alarm; but they are reasons for mistrusting arguments or policies which assume the accuracy of estimates of probability based on follow-ups. Consider what can be called 'the universal predictor'. A wise American psychologist, William Kvaraceus,[6] once wrote that 'nothing predicts behaviour like behaviour'. As far as criminal convictions are concerned this certainly seems to be the case. For example, a six-year English follow-up of men aged 21 or older who were convicted of indictable violence (including robbery) in 1972 yielded the following findings:[7]

Number of occasions on which previously convicted of violence	Percentage convicted of violence in follow-up
0	5.0% of 2041
1	19.1% of 376
2	22.3% of 103
3	42.9% of 21
4 or more	84.6% of 13

The table shows that a single variable — previous known violent behaviour — can be used to separate adult men into different probability groups in relation to future violence. Its percentages must not, of course, be taken as accurate estimates of the actual probability that should be assigned to each group, for the following reasons: the follow-up recorded only incidents which led to convictions; the previous records of the offenders probably understated violence, for the same reason; some offenders were in prison during the early part of the follow-up. Almost certainly, the percentages understate the actual probabilities, with the possible exception of the 13 men with four or more

---

[6] In (1966) *Anxious Youth*, Ohio: Columbus.
[7] See Walker, N. (1985) *Sentencing Theory Law and Practice*, London: Butterworths. The follow-up was the work of Philpotts, G. J. O. & Lancucki, L. B., in the Home Office, who supplied these figures.

previous convictions for violence, who were too few to provide a respectable sample.

With these reservations, previous violence is the best predictor of future violence which we are ever likely to have. It may be possible to increase its accuracy a little by adding information about the abuse of intoxicants, the use of weapons, or assessments of personality or mental disorder; but the prediction of violence will never become an exact science.

The Presumption of Harmlessness

The harm someone has caused or attempted to cause, however, is more than a predictor: it is part of the moral justification for subjecting that person to a precautionary measure. We are all at risk of being harmed by members of the free public who have not hitherto harmed anyone, or at least are not known to have done so. This is, in fact, the most frequent example of violence or sexual molestation which comes to official notice. Against this eventuality we can protect ourselves or our nearest and dearest only by taking our own unofficial precautions. It is not simply that society lacks the resources to interfere with possible attackers. Anti-protectionists argue that people who have not yet caused harm to others have a right not to be interfered with. This right is based on the presumption of harmlessness. One may recognise this right, but ask whether, like other rights, it can be renounced or forfeited. Someone who has harmed, or tried to harm, another person, can hardly claim a right to the presumption of harmlessness: he has forfeited that right, and given society the right to interfere in his life. (The presumption of harmlessness should not be confused with the presumption of innocence in criminal trials, which would succumb to the Swedish fallacy.) The right to interfere need not be seen as a duty: as will be argued later, courts should have discretion to decide, in the light of the nature of the apprehended harm and other considerations, whether to exercise that right, and how drastically. The justification is not a duty based on retribution but the offender's forfeiture of an immunity.[8]

A Negligible Contribution?

There are further anti-protectionist arguments to be considered, some of which are more hard-headed than those discussed above. Among these is the undeniable argument that a policy of precautionary detention makes only a small contribution to the protection of the public. Most murders, rapes and other

---

[8] Although expressed in my words this is the argument offered by Ian White, the Cambridge philosopher, to the Floud Committee on *Dangerousness and Criminal Justice* (1981), London: Heinemann, and endorsed by them.

serious crimes against the person are committed by people who have not been detected in previous offending (or, at least, not in anything worse than dishonesties or traffic offences). If those whose crimes inflict grave harm (the argument goes) are simply given the ordinary sentences which are regarded as appropriate to those crimes, any crimes which they commit after their eventual release would make a negligible addition to the volume of really harmful crimes. Much depends, of course, on how their contribution to the total is estimated, and whether the result can be dismissed as negligible. Researchers in the United States, but not, so far, in the United Kingdom, have tried various methods of calculation. One of the difficulties is that while it is easy to identify crimes that could have been prevented by longer detention in cases when those crimes have been traced to their perpetrators, this is far from easy in the case of unsolved crimes, which are numerous. No doubt some were committed by people released from custodial sentences for similar crimes, and some were committed by people who had not: but in what proportions? The most impressive attempt known to me is by Greenwood and Abrahamse.[9] Using self-reports and other information about the careers of robbers (and other types of violent offender) in Californian and Texan penitentiaries, they estimated that something like a 15 per cent reduction in California's robberies could be achieved by identifying 'high-rate' robbers and lengthening their sentences. As they also found, however, it cannot be assumed that a similar reduction could be achieved in every jurisdiction (or for every sort of crime). In Texas, where sentences for robbery are longer, and robbery rates lower, the estimated reduction was smaller — about seven per cent.

The only comparable research in England sought to answer a rather less relevant question: what percentage of men convicted of indictable offences in 1971 would have been prevented from committing their next offence if their convictions had led to detention for one year? The answer was 25 per cent — by no means negligible.[10] But most of their offences were not of a kind from which protection is demanded at the cost of long detention; and when it is we have in mind periods much longer than a year.

Nobody has suggested how we should decide when a percentage of the type estimated by Greenwood and Abrahamse is small enough to be dismissed as negligible, implying that it is not sufficient to justify precautionary sentences. When the subject of discussion is the prevention of murders, rapes and other grave crimes against the person, it requires courage to call any percentage 'negligible'. But, the argument has been used, and therefore must be faced. Its weakness is that it treats the propriety of using precautionary detention as if it

---

[9] See Greenwood, P. W. & Abrahamse, A. (1982) *Selective Incapacitation*, Santa Monica: Rand.
[10] See Brody, S. & Tarling, R. (1974) *Taking Offenders Out of Circulation* (Home Office Research Study 64) London: HMSO.

were merely a question of the best use of a scarce resource. This abandons the moral high ground on which earlier arguments tried to stand, and, indeed, carries the implication that if the relevant percentage were large enough, precautionary detention would be justifiable. What is more, the argument assumes that the scarce resource is better devoted to non-precautionary objectives: deterrence, correction, treatment, and the infliction of desert. If 'better' is used to mean 'more effectively', detention is notoriously ineffective at achieving these objectives. If, instead, it means 'morally better', that could be argued only by the kind of retributivist who regards the infliction of desert as a duty which overrides all other considerations.

Political Fear

We must not overlook one more anti-protectionist argument.[11] Statutory powers to detain, deport or otherwise interfere with a citizen's liberty can be abused, and abuse may be politically motivated. A regime with overwhelming power might use precautionary laws as a convenient means of disposing of awkward opponents with apparent legitimacy. So it might, as the Soviet Union showed. What the argument ignores, however, is the fact that a regime powerful enough to abuse laws in this way could, and probably would, create laws of the kind it needed. A democracy does not protect itself merely by refraining from legislation.

A Compromise?

Anti-protectionists have, however, offered a compromise. Its origin is a little odd. In the introductory chapter of *Taking Rights Seriously*[12] Ronald Dworkin describes the restraint and treatment of the dangerously insane as an insulting infringement of their rights to dignity and liberty, and commented that '... we ought to recognise the compromise with principle that this policy involves; and should treat a man against his will only when the danger he presents is vivid, not whenever we calculate that it would probably reduce crime if we did'. This was stated more or less *obiter*, and without any acknowledgement that the problem involved more than the 'treatment' of the 'insane'. We are not told what is meant by the metaphorical but all-important adjective 'vivid'. The *obiter dictum*, however, was developed by Bottoms and Brownsword into a reasoned attempt at a compromise:[13]

---

[11] See Radzinowicz, L. & Hood, R. G. (1981) 'Dangerousness and Criminal Justice: a few reflections', *Criminal Law Review*, pp. 756–61.
[12] (1977), London: Duckworth.
[13] From 'Dangerousness and Rights' in (1983) *Dangerousness: Problems of Assessment and Prediction* (ed. Hinton, J. W.) London: Allen and Unwin.

The concept of vivid danger needs more analysis than Dworkin gives it. We suggest that it has three main components: *seriousness* (what type and degree of injury is in contemplation?); *temporality*, which breaks down into *frequency* (over a given period, how many injurious acts are expected?) and *immediacy* (how soon is the next injurious act?); and *certainty* (how sure are we that this person will act as predicted?). The certainty element is pivotal. If there is a very low score on the certainty factor, then whatever the danger it is hardly vivid. However, as the score increases on the certainty element, the risk becomes increasingly vivid and we then have to look very carefully at the kind of danger threatened. Clearly, a low score on the seriousness scale is going to militate strongly against the danger being described as vivid.

This is certainly a sound psychological description of the ways in which people's minds seem to work. It can, however, be interpreted in two ways: first, as a mere gloss on Dworkin — a more detailed definition of the circumstances in which a breach of principle is *excusable*; and, secondly (and as Bottoms and Brownsword mean it) as a definition of the circumstances in which it is *justifiable*. If the former interpretation is accepted, there is not much more to be said. If the latter, we are left wondering exactly what combinations of temporality, probability and seriousness amount to a justification. We are not told how to juggle with them: simply that this reasoning has led the authors to the conclusion that only causing or attempting 'very serious violence' is sufficiently 'vivid'.

What Kinds of Harm?

This raises more questions than it answers. What sorts of violence are 'very serious'? Are non-violent sexual offences, of the kind committed by persuasive paedophiles, excluded, or defrauding pensioners of their savings? Bottoms and Brownsword might have said (but did not) that they had in mind the possibility of non-custodial precautions for such offences. (Paedophiles could be blacklisted from teaching or child-care posts, fraudulent traders could be forbidden to hold directorships, reckless drivers could lose their licences, and so on.) It is unlikely, however, that this is what they had in mind: such precautions are notoriously easy to circumvent, and it would have been hypocritical to rely on them. For them — and for us — the all-important question is 'What justifies *detention* for the protection of others?'.

Although every jurisdiction has its short list (or not so short list) of crimes which qualify for precautionary incarceration there have been surprisingly few attempts to state the principle on which the selection is based. Even Feinberg's four volumes on harms[14] do not discuss the problem. Some jurisdictions allow offenders to qualify simply by incurring a sufficient number of convictions, more or less irrespective of their seriousness. California's notorious 'three strikes law' is an example which in 1995, led to a 25-year sentence for a man who robbed some children (without violence) of a slice of pizza. The English preventive detention statutes of 1907 and 1948 were not much more enlightened: Grimwood[15] was sentenced to eight years' imprisonment for stealing a few shillings from a gas-meter.

More enlightened are jurisdictions which insist that the harm caused, attempted or threatened must be of a serious nature. Section 2(2)(b) of the Criminal Justice Act 1991 states merely that the offence must be of a violent or sexual nature (as defined in the statute) and that a longer than normal sentence must, in the opinion of the court, be 'necessary to protect the public from serious harm from the offender' (see chapter 5). Restricted hospital orders (see chapters 4, 5 and 6) are today meant to be used only to protect the public from 'serious harm', but it is left to the Court of Appeal to interpret 'serious harm'. The English list of crimes qualifying for life sentences used to be a long one, but in practice nowadays the sentence is used only for certain homicides and serious offences of sex or violence.

Powers or Duties?

Even if it is clear what kinds of harm should qualify for precautionary custody, legislators still have to decide between making custody discretionary or mandatory. The objection to discretionary custody is that it can result in unfairness: in one court a man with four convictions for armed robbery may simply get the sentence which the judge thinks he deserves, while in another court he might receive a sentence designed to take him out of circulation for a very long time. Consequently, some American penologists[16] have preferred 'categorial incapacitation', a policy which decrees that if the offence falls into a certain category the offender must receive a precautionary sentence. In its crudest form it defines the category by reference only to the legal label of the offence: rape, robbery or whatever. It could be considerably refined, however, so that to qualify, the offender must also have previous convictions of the same nature (as in the Californian 'three strikes law'), and other qualifying conditions could be added.

---

[14] See, for example, Feinberg, J. (1984) *Harm to Others*, Oxford: Oxford University Press.

[15] *Grimwood* (1958) *Criminal Law Review* 403. The sentence was reduced to two years by the Court of Criminal Appeal.

[16] See, for example, von Hirsch, A. (1985) *Past or Future Crimes*, Manchester University Press. He acknowledges his debt to Jacqueline Cohen.

11

English legislators prefer discretion, and rely on the judiciary and the Court of Appeal to keep the inevitable quota of inconsistent sentences within tolerable bounds. Their reasoning is that, however intricate and refined the qualifying conditions, there will always be cases in which the court should be free to refrain from passing a sentence of precautionary length. An extreme example would be a serial rapist who had suffered a stroke. This approach is consistent with the argument, discussed earlier, that certain offences give society the right, but not the duty, to impose precautions. Consequently, s. 2(2)(b) of the Criminal Justice Act 1991 allows, but does not compel, a court to impose a longer than normal prison sentence for a violent or sexual offence. There are exceptions to the discretionary approach. Magistrates used their discretion to disqualify careless or drunken drivers so inconsistently that legislators made disqualification mandatory in certain circumstances. The life sentence, because it replaced the mandatory death sentence, remains mandatory for murder, while discretionary for some other offences. This, however, has been the subject of so much recent criticism that it seems unlikely to survive much longer.

2

Violence and Mental Disorder

Paul Bowden[1]

With the exception of those arrested for a criminal offence, the involuntary detention and treatment of the mentally disordered is one of the few ways in which a state can legitimately deprive an individual of their liberty. Such action is usually taken on the grounds of the interests of the individual, or for the protection of others (United Nations Commission on Human Rights (1991)). While recognising that the mentally ill are usually more a risk to themselves than to others, only their dangerousness will be considered here. This contribution also shows that risk assessments are a central feature of mental health legislation at the stages of admission to, and discharge from, hospital, and, with the closure of psychiatric hospitals, increasingly in treatment in the community. It is shown that professionals, like the public, overestimate risk, which, although real, contributes very little to general levels of violence. Finally, an attempt is made to place what is known about the phenomenology of violence into the context of the motivation of behaviour generally.

Statutory Risk Assessments

Compulsory powers with regard to both family and mental health matters are steeped in assessments of risk. Under the provisions of the Children Act 1989, psychiatrists contribute to family proceedings in situations where there is reasonable cause to suspect that a child is suffering, or is likely to suffer, significant harm, and to assess the needs of the child and the family and the need for protection (Department of Health *et al* (1994)). Risk assessments in these situations may centre on mental health issues and can carry considerable

---

[1] Alec Buchannon made a significant contribution to the ideas contained in this chapter.

weight, often forming the basis for controlling, or completely denying, adults' contact with children in a parental capacity.

The civil sections of the Mental Health Act 1983 (MHA 1983), which provide for compulsory admission to hospital, all contain a clause relating to 'the protection of other persons' (s. 2, admission for assessment; s. 3, admission for treatment; s. 4, admission for assessment in cases of emergency; s. 5, application in respect of a patient already in hospital; s. 7, application for guardianship).

This 'protection of others' clause is also a consideration in renewing sections (s. 20, duration of authority) and discharging patients (s. 72, powers of tribunals). The responsible medical officer (RMO) may also grant leave of absence to any patient detained under the civil sections of the MHA 1983, but 'the protection of other persons' can be a cause of imposing conditions on such leave: e.g., to live at a certain residence, attend for medical examination and treatment, receive visits from a social worker (see Gostin (1986)). Where the nearest relative has powers to discharge a detained patient they cannot do so if the RMO certifies that, if discharged, the patient would be likely to act in a manner dangerous to other persons, or to himself.

That part of the MHA 1983 which refers to patients concerned in criminal proceedings also contains a clause which gives higher courts the power to restrict discharge from hospital (under what is known as a restriction order: s. 41). Among other matters the court must be satisfied, when making a restriction order, that it is necessary to protect the public from 'serious harm'. Prisoners transferred to hospital for urgent treatment under s. 47 (sentenced) and s. 48 (unsentenced) are often subject to s. 49 (restriction on the discharge of prisoners transferred to hospital) which has a similar effect to s. 41, and the same is true of persons charged with murder who are found unfit to plead or legally insane (Criminal Procedure (Insanity and Unfitness to Plead) Act 1991).

When a patient under a restriction order leaves hospital he is as a rule conditionally discharged and the supervision of such patients in the community is carefully monitored:

> The purpose of the formal supervision resulting from conditional discharge is to protect the public from further serious harm in two ways: first, by assisting the patient's successful reintegration into the community after what may have been a long period of detention in hospital under conditions of security; second, by close monitoring of the patient's mental health or of a perceived increase in the risk of danger to the public so that steps can be taken to assist the patient and protect the public. (Home Office and Department of Health and Social Security (1987) p. 3))

The Secretary of State can discharge a patient from a restriction order if he is satisfied that the order is no longer required 'to protect the public from serious harm' (s. 42). Similarly, for tribunals to absolutely discharge patients they have, among other matters, to be satisfied that continued detention in hospital is not necessary 'for the protection of other persons' (s. 73).

When patients who have been detained under s. 3 of the MHA 1983 (admission for treatment) or s. 37 (hospital order on a person involved in criminal proceedings) and ss. 47 and 48 (transfer of a prisoner to hospital for urgent treatment) it is the responsibility of their health authority to provide after-care services (s. 117).

The closure of psychiatric inpatient facilities and a series of scandals following the conviction of mentally ill persons following killings in the community have led to an augmentation of s. 117 of the MHA 1983 by a care programme approach (CPA) which was first proposed in a White Paper, *Caring For People* (Department of Health (1989)). The CPA places the responsibility for both treatment in the community and effective follow-up after discharge from hospital on an appointed key worker who is charged with maintaining a therapeutic relationship with the patient and liaison with other services (Department of Health (1990)).

In April 1994 the Government introduced supervision registers for mentally ill people (National Health Service (NHS) Management Executive (1994)). Health authorities were required to ensure that all units providing health care set up registers which identify and provide information on patients who are, or are liable to be, at risk of committing serious violence or suicide, or of serious self-neglect, whether existing patients or newly accepted by the psychiatric services. The NHS management executive requires supervision registers to identify the nature of the risk:

(a)   category of risk and nature of specific warning indicators;

(b)   evidence of specific episodes of violent or self-destructive behaviour (including relevant criminal convictions) or severe self-neglect.

The purpose of the register is declared as being to identify those patients who require the highest priority of care under the CPA and includes not only the mentally ill but also those with personality (and psychopathic) disorder who are currently receiving treatment from psychiatric services.

In March 1995 the Mental Health (Patients in the Community) Bill was presented to the All Party Mental Health Group. It proposed a new community power, called supervised after-care, for patients detained under s. 3 or s. 37, and it became law in November 1995. The criteria for the proposed new order are: mental disorder; other matters, including a risk of serious harm to the safety

15

of other persons; that being subject to supervised after-care will help to secure the required services.

Dangerousness assessments of the mentally disordered, whether informed or lay, are at the heart of many other restrictive practices: decisions regarding bail and sentencing (see chapter 5); release on licence and parole (see chapter 8); even the death penalty. If the concept of mental disorder is extended to include paraphilias, such as paedophilia, risk may also be a consideration in employment.

Public Attitudes

Many believe that the attitude of the public to the mentally disordered is generally antipathetic (Borenstein (1993)) and distorted by media hype (Williams and Dickenson (1993)). To study issues related to public attitudes Levey and Howells (1995) examined the reactions of 342 persons to a case vignette of a deluded and hallucinating man who neglected himself and displayed grossly inappropriate social behaviour. The participants were members of the general public (119), psychology undergraduates (179), and nursing students (44). The subjects were given a definition of schizophrenia and asked if they agreed or disagreed with a number of statements. Levey and Howells found that those questioned perceived people with schizophrenia to be very different from themselves and highly unpredictable. The percentages who agreed with the following statements are given in brackets: schizophrenics often attack people for no particular reason (41.8%); schizophrenics are likely to commit minor sexual offences (27.2%); schizophrenics are a danger to small children (25.1%); schizophrenics are likely to commit crimes of serious violence (e.g., murder) (15.3%). Presumed differentness from oneself emerged as the central facet of how people with schizophrenia are perceived. Differentness is associated with seeing people as dangerous and unpredictable, a reluctance to associate with them, and reported fear. Fear of the mentally ill was not specifically related to perceived dangerousness or unpredictability but to perceptions of differentness, which Levey and Howells believed to be at the heart of stigmatisation and stereotyping. (Many of the findings bear comparison with those of the British Crime Survey (Home Office, 1983) which looked at public concern about crime in general.)

Pitfalls in Prediction

While Taylor's (1993, p. 83) optimistic hope that 'Most violence by most psychotic people should be predictable, and preventable through treatment, given the resource' has yet to be fulfilled, Webster et al (1994) from the

University of Toronto have summarised research on the prediction of dangerousness among the mentally disordered. Two US cases provided quasi-experiments; in both *Baxstrom* (1966) and *Dixon* (1971) the courts' decisions resulted in the release of large numbers of individuals, previously detained on the grounds of dangerousness. Studies of reconviction rates showed two important findings: low base rates of violence (meaning that it is difficult to predict); and a large number of false positive predictions. In 1984 Monahan extolled the virtue of enriching the predictor variables (which were, in this case, the signs of mental disorder) and strengthening the criterion variable (dangerous behaviour), in the search for a new generation of research. Webster *et al* (1994) calculated the 'positive predictive power' (PPP) (being the number of true positives divided by the sum of true positives and false positives, multiplied by 100) for some of the 1980s research, which focused mainly on short-term predictions. The levels of false positive error remained high (Sepejak *et al* (1983) 56%; Convit *et al* (1988), 74%; Klassen and O'Connor (1988), 59%; Kirk (1989), 59%.

It is common ground that clinical predictions of dangerousness are inaccurate (Cocozza and Steadman (1978)) and tend to overpredict (Steadman and Morrissey (1981)); and, currently, the drive is to move away from both dichotomous 'Yes/No' decisions, and those which have no time-frame, towards dangerousness assessments which are based on specific factors and are couched in the language of probabilities. The words of Webster and Menzies (1993, p. 35) add a note of realism: 'Adding a high-intensity assessment service to a system otherwise deficient in ability to deliver actual treatment and rehabilitation programmes may in fact do more harm than good'.

Are the Mentally Ill Dangerous?

Link *et al* (1992, p. 290) concluded that in comparison with factors such as age, gender, socioeconomic status, drug use and family breakdown, the contribution made by mental patient status was relatively modest: '... a trivial contribution to the overall level of violent/illegal behaviour in American society'.

At a time when the homicide rate was rising inexorably, and the relative contribution which mental disorder makes to that trend was decreasing, the Royal College of Psychiatrists decided to launch an enquiry into serious violence by psychiatric patients (Steering Committee of the Confidential Enquiry into Homicides and Suicides by Mentally Ill People (1994)). Some have seen the enquiry as a political expedient designed to bolster confidence at a time when the establishment of community care is faltering. For others it is a prudent enterprise and explicit recognition that the mentally ill do pose a risk.

Lidz, Mulvey and Gardner (1993) described a study of the accuracy of predictions of violence to others which was undertaken at a large US university-based hospital with responsibility for an urban catchment area. Beginning at an emergency department, clinicians and research psychiatrists assessed potential for violence to others over the ensuing six months. Scores from both groups of raters were summed, generating a score between 0 and 10. A cut-off point of 3 was chosen, subjects were followed up over the six-month period and collateral informants were interviewed. Excluding those whose follow-up was unsatisfactory, 357 patients were matched on sex, race, age, and admission status with a group considered to be non-violent. Violence was determined from reports (the patient or collateral informant), or from official sources, and was defined as a minimum of laying hands on another person with violent intent or threatening someone with a weapon. Of the whole sample, 40% were black American, 60% were men, and the mean age was 28. The following percentages are given in order of those predicted violent and the controls:

previous hospitalisation (52% v 48%);
history of violence (83% v 36%);
violent incident preceded referral (22% v 0.03%);
prior arrest for violent crime (18% v 10%).

The diagnoses were:

schizophrenia (15% v 16.3%);
affective disorder (15.9% v 29.7%);
substance abuse (41% v 31.6%);
personality disorder (13.9% v 6.8%);
other (14.2% v 16.6%).

Actual violence among the predicted and controls were in the proportions of 53 per cent and 36 per cent respectively. There was a significant relationship between predictions and incidents, indicating that clinicians can predict dangerousness at a better than chance level, even when demographic factors are controlled. There was, however, a relatively low sensitivity (the number of true positives) and specificity (the number of true negatives) to the predictions. While the violence of the predicted violent patients was qualitatively more serious than controls, it was the clinicians' prediction about the presence or absence of violence which had some degree of accuracy, rather than their level of concern.

The accuracy of predictions was not influenced by age and race, but gender revealed surprising and important differences. Women were more often violent than men (49% v 42%), and, while the predictions of violence in men were at the above-chance level, there was no evidence that they could successfully predict violence in women (Steadman *et al* (1993) showed that more women than men (32.8% v 22.4%) reported at least one violent incident in the community after their hospitalisations). When a further analysis controlled for the effect which a previous history of violence made to predictions it was shown that in the group as a whole accuracy was better than chance, even when clinicians were not predicting on the basis of history.

Violence by the Mentally Ill

Any search for the common mediators or determinants of violence and mental disorder, such as age, sex, socioeconomic status, and history of substance abuse, is confounded by the fact that in some diagnostic categories violence is part of the diagnostic criteria (e.g., antisocial personality disorder), whereas in others it is an associated feature (e.g., schizophrenia) (Swanson *et al* (1990)).

Relatively late in risk research it was recognised that studies of populations defined by identification with either the criminal justice or health care systems may introduce bias. The subject was addressed most clearly in the Epidemiological Catchment Area (ECA) study reported by Swanson (1994). One of the most important findings of the ECA survey was the relatively large proportion of mentally disordered persons who had neither been admitted to hospital for a mental health problem (84%) nor arrested (87%), although the proportions in individuals with both mental health and substance abuse problems (comorbidity) were notably less (62% and 73%, respectively). Histories of both previous hospitalisation and arrest produced much higher probabilities of violent behaviour, and a combination of the two gave an even greater relative value. Thus, the percentage probability of violent behaviour was 1.63 in those without a psychiatric diagnosis and with no history of arrest or hospitalisation, and 7.31 where histories of arrest or hospitalisation were present. The corresponding figures for combined schizophrenia or major affective disorder were 5.2 and 25.88 respectively, and for comorbidity 14.30 and 49.22. Swanson (1994, p. 129) concluded: 'Therefore, the subgroup of mentally disordered persons who have been identified by both of these systems (criminal justice through arrest and health care through admission to hospital) had been selected, in effect, for violent behaviour, which indicates the severity of their disorder or deviance'.

What, then, of the large number of studies of psychiatric patients where 'threat to others' is one of the criteria for admission to the service (e.g., Petrie

19

et al (1982); Tardiffr and Sweillam (1982); Craig (1982); Myers and Dunner (1984); Krakowski *et al* (1988))? A more recent example of the violence-bias introduced by contact with a health care system is the finding that 20 per cent of schizophrenics admitted to hospital for the first time had behaved recently in a way which threatened the life of others (Johnstone *et al* (1986)). Steadman and Felson's (1984) conclusion that patients reported more violent behaviour and more incidents involving weapons than did subjects in a matched community sample was confirmed by Link *et al* (1992), who compared patients identified by contact with one hospital with never-treated community residents of a defined area of New York. Both interview-elicited and officially recorded criminal behaviour was considered. While offending and violence were more common in patients, repeat-contact status (compared with first-contact and former patients) was particularly significant, suggesting perhaps that the *severity* of disorder is important. Schizophrenia characterised by an *exclusively delusional course* is thought to be more often associated with violence than more mixed forms of the condition (Robertson and Taylor (1993)).

That there is a special relationship between violence and mental disorder has been shown by Swanson (1994) in his report of the National Institute of Mental Health (NIMH) ECA project based in several cities in the United States. Although the survey was designed to determine the prevalence of untreated psychiatric disorder in community populations, it was used to provide the first large-sample estimates of the prevalence of assaultive behaviour among persons with and without mental disorders in the community.

Swanson's survey used the NIMH Diagnostic Interview Schedule (DIS) to create the following DSM III (American Psychiatric Association (1980)) diagnostic categories: schizophrenia and schizophreniform disorder; major affective disorders; anxiety disorders; substance abuse; and antisocial personality disorder. An attempt was made to assess violent acts in general and those which were conditional on marital status, parental role and substance abuse. One year was chosen as the time-frame of recent violence.

Of 10,059 respondents, 3.7 per cent committed at least one of five defined kinds of violent act in the one-year period preceding the interview. Those who assaulted others were two-and-a-half to four times more likely to have psychiatric disorders. However, *substance abuse* made a major contribution to this finding. Those with mental illness alone were twice as prevalent in the violent subgroup, while substance abuse alone or comorbidity in the form of substance abuse with mental illness was five times more prevalent. (Swanson *et al* (1990)) showed that nearly one-third of those with schizophrenia or schizophreniform disorder also met the criteria for alcohol or drug abuse or dependence. In addition, these authors showed an almost linear relationship between the *number of diagnoses* and the rate of violence; the rate tripled as the number of diagnoses increased from one to three or more, suggesting that violence is linked to the gross amount of psychopathology or that people with multiple diagnoses are more likely to have a substance abuse disorder). Those violence measures which included the one-year recency criterion were more likely to include the mentally ill than those defined by adult-lifetime measures. The absolute risk of violence in the presence of mental illness was low, at about seven per cent in the course of one year (although the relative risk was three times more than in the non-ill population), but the proportion was much higher among substance abusers (27%). In 1990, Swanson *et al* suggested that where mental disorder was complicated by substance abuse violence was both qualitatively and quantitatively different, involving more diverse victims, more serious violence, and the use of weapons. Furthermore, female substance abusers were violent as often as their male counterparts. Socioeconomic status (SES), which was assessed on the basis of educational level, occupational status and household income was included in the analysis and the following adjusted chi-square results were found using a logistic regression model of predictors of violent behaviour in the last year:

substance abuse only (chi-square 127.72);
age 18–29 (72.71);
comorbid (61.87);
age 30–34 (23.97);
lower SES (11.22);
affective disorder (10.57);
separated/divorced (5.62);
schizophrenia (5.04);
lower middle SES (3.83).

The chi-square for anxiety disorder was not significant. (In 1990 Swanson *et al* reported that race was not related to violence when SES was controlled).

A study by Link *et al* (1992) confirms much of what Swanson described and took matters further. Samples of community residents and psychiatric patients were examined using a standardised interview. Violent and illegal behaviour was assessed using official records and self-reported behaviour. Four groups were identified: never-treated; former patients (not in treatment in the previous year); repeat-treatment; and first contact. All three patient groups had persistently higher percentages engaging in violent/illegal behaviour — sometimes two or three times higher — than never-treated community residents. These measures were significantly different across all six measures of illegal/violent activity covering both self- and officially-reported behaviour. While sociodemographic variables (age, sex, education, etc.) were significantly related to violent/illegal behaviour, these variables did not fully explain the association between mental patient status and dangerous behaviour. Further analysis showed that much of the difference between mental-patient groups and the never-treated group could be explained by the level of psychotic symptoms with *active symptoms* being associated with recent violent/illegal behaviour independently of any drug or alcohol use.

That mental patients scored higher on both self-admitted and officially recorded violent/illegal behaviour suggested to Link *et al* (1992) that the criminalisation of the mentally ill was not a significant factor. The reverse hypothesis, that deviance is criminalised, also failed to be confirmed since the psychotic-symptom scale was also related to violent/illegal behaviour within the never-treated community group.

Does Phenomenology Help?

Before examining the motivations of violence in the mentally disordered it is important to look at the complexities of the subject with regard to behaviour in general. Answering the question 'Why did it happen?' allows us to attribute causality. Motivation is generally taken as representing what initiates, directs and sustains behaviour (see, for example, Gross (1990)). It is described in terms of the expositor's discipline, which may include philosophy, biology, psychology or the social sciences. (For their part, psychological theories, for example, may encompass analytic, behavioural, humanistic, neurobiological or cognitive approaches). Motivation has an emotional component and emotional experiences may themselves be a result of bodily or behavioural change, with a particular physiological set representing each emotion; alternatively, the label we apply to an emotion may depend on to what we attribute arousal. Linked inextricably with the emotional context of motivation is the concept of stress or harmful emotion.

In their monumental work *Crimes of Violence by Mentally Disordered Offenders*, Hafner and Boker (1973 to 1982) lamented the fact that control groups from the general population were not available to them and they had to rely on hospital in-patients. They compared seriously violent with non-violent schizophrenics. They showed that *delusion(s)* occurred significantly more frequently in the violent group (65% v 53%). 'Moreover in the violent group delusions consisted not so much of delusional mood or unsystematic delusional ideas as of *systematic delusions* associated with *specific themes* such as *jealousy, injury* or *persecution*. This special form of delusion seemed to be accompanied by a delusional experience of *menace* to life and limb ...' (Hafner and Boker (1973 to 1982, p. 157)). What Hafner and Boker suggested was that the seriously violent mentally ill could be distinguished from their non-violent counterparts by first, the presence of *delusions*, secondly, their *systematisation*, thirdly, their *theme*, and fourthly, the *emotional response* of the sufferer.

In 1985, Taylor suggested, from a sample of remand prisoners, that there was an association between delusions and violent offending and, in particular, between violent behaviour and passivity experiences (meaning *a belief that some or all voluntary acts are controlled from outside*). To examine this further Wesseley *et al* (1993) examined a sample of deluded subjects in an attempt to associate phenomenology and action. Action was reported by the subjects themselves and by informants. Half the 59 subjects for whom an informant was available were rated as having either definitely or probably acted on their principal delusion in the previous month and this figure rose to 79 per cent if any delusionally motivated action was included. The previously suggested association between violent behaviour and delusional experiences was not confirmed, but a sense of *threat* appeared relevant. While self-reported action was associated with delusions of catastrophe, informant data suggested that it was persecutory delusions which were the most likely to be acted upon. Buchanan *et al* (1993), in a complementary paper concluded:

When action was described by the subjects themselves, acting was associated with being aware of *evidence* which supported the abnormal belief and with having actively sought out such evidence; a tendency to reduce the *conviction* with which a belief was held when that belief was challenged (having been impelled to test out a belief, to seek confirmation or refutation); and with feeling of *apprehension* (sad, frightened or anxious) as a consequence of the delusion.

Link and Stueve (1994) tried to identify risk factors in psychotic patients. They compared previously hospitalised patients with untreated and, therefore, undiagnosed, community controls. They differentiated between 'threat/control-override symptoms' (thought-insertion and control which are forms of passivity phenomena, paranoid ideas), and other psychotic symptoms. The three threat/control-override symptoms were graded on a four-point scale. Violence was measured in terms of hitting, fighting and weapon-use over specified periods. The authors showed that patients and former patients were significantly more likely to have been violent. Of the 13 measured psychotic symptoms, the three that involved *threat or control-override* predicted rates of relatively recent violent behaviours and accounted for differences between patient groups and community controls. These findings extended Link *et al's* earlier work (1992), which highlighted the significance of the currency of psychotic symptoms and suggested that *emotions* such as fear and anger

23

induced by attempts to coerce the psychotic person may be the determinants of violence rather than the psychotic symptoms themselves.

All these studies suggest, perhaps obviously, that it is the meaning (in the sense of that which is brought to mind and the particular emotions associated with it) attached to abnormal mental experiences which determines the response to them. The findings should be considered alongside the significant body of research evidence which points to the Revised Psychopathy Check List (PCL-R) as being the best predictor of violent recidivism in the mentally ill (Rice and Harris (1992)). In particular, several items from the PCL-R suggest that a *lack of affectual response* is an important characteristic: lack of remorse or guilt; shallow affect; callousness or lack of empathy. Perhaps the apparent discrepancy can be explained on the basis that while the PCL-R measures trait characteristics as a response to others' experiences, the studies mentioned earlier refer to subjective affective states.

While motivational theories (and other 'introspectibles' such as reasons) emphasise how little we know about the meaning of dangerous behaviour in the mentally disordered, Walker (1977) discussed an alternative way of approaching the issue. He suggested that when we posit a 'Why?' question (the one considered here being 'Why do the mentally ill behave dangerously?') the purpose of our question is often not to achieve the far-fetched goals of prediction and prevention but to satisfy the enquirer's curiosity. A dynamic emerges with what we are being asked to explain (i.e., violence in the mentally ill) being redefined continuously depending on our explanations.

It is not a scientific explanation which we seek because, in the context of our question, we are not explaining outcomes which are highly probable; what we are looking for is something which will explain why unexpected behaviour is not as improbable as it seemed. General theories of violence apart, why do the mentally ill behave dangerously? A narrative explanation will tell us that in certain necessary conditions (e.g., certain types of delusions and affective states) violence *can* happen; it will not tell us that it is inevitable (in which case the behaviour would not be unexpected). Repetitiveness can lead from possibility to probability explanation, but it is the introspectibles (meanings and reasons) which help us to see why some actions are highly probable (Walker (1977)).

References

American Psychiatric Association (1980) *Diagnostic and Statistical Manual of Mental Disorders*, 3rd edn (DSM III), Washington DC: American Psychiatric Association.
Borinstein, A. (1993) 'Public Attitudes Towards Persons With Mental Illness', *Health Affairs*, 11, pp. 186–96.

Buchanan, A., Reed, A., Wesseley, S., Garety, P., Taylor, P., Gruben, D. & Dunn, G. (1993) 'Acting on Delusions II: The Phenomenological Correlates of Acting on Delusions', *British Journal of Psychiatry*, 163, pp. 77–81.

Cocozza, J. J. & Steadman, H. J. (1978) 'Prediction in Psychiatry: an Example of Misplaced Confidence in Experts', *Social Problems*, 25, pp. 265–76.

Craig, T. J. (1982) 'An Epidemiological Study of Problems Associated with Violence Among Psychiatric Inpatients', *American Journal of Psychiatry*, 139, pp. 1262–6.

Department of Health (1989) *Caring For People* (CM849), London: HMSO.

Department of Health (1990) *Joint Health/Social Services Circular, Health and Social Services Development 'Caring for People', The Care Programme Approach For People With A Mental Illness Referred to the Specialist Psychiatric Services*, (HC(90)23), London: Department of Health.

Department of Health, British Medical Association, and Conference of Medical Royal Colleges (1994) *Child Protection: Medical Responsibilities*, London: Department of Health.

Gostin, L. (1986) *Mental Health Services — Law and Practice*, London: Shaw and Sons.

Gross, R (1990) *Psychology: The Science of Mind and Behaviour*, London: Hodder and Stoughton.

Hafner, H. & Boker, W. (1973–1982) *Crimes of Violence by Mentally Disordered Offenders* (translation by Marshall, H.), Cambridge: Cambridge University Press.

Home Office and Department of Social Security (1987) *Mental Health Act 1983: Supervision and After-Care of Conditionally Discharged Restricted Patients. Notes For the Guidance of Supervising Psychiatrists*, London: Home Office and DHSS.

Hough, M. & Mayhew, P. (1983) Home Office Research and Planning Unit. *'The British Crime Survey: First Report'*, London: HMSO.

Jacobson, A. (1989) 'Physical and Sexual Assault Histories Among Psychiatric Outpatients', *American Journal of Psychiatry*, 146, pp. 755–8.

Johnstone, E., Crowe, T. J., Johnson, A. L. & MacMillan, J. F. (1986) 'The Northwick Park Study of First Episodes of Schizophrenia', *British Journal of Psychiatry*, 148, pp. 115–20.

Krakowski, M., Jaeger, J. & Volavaka, J. (1988) 'Violence and Psychopathology: a Longitudinal Study', *Comprehensive Psychiatry*, 29, pp. 174–81.

Levey, S. and Howells, K. (1995) 'Dangerousness, unpredictability, and fear of people with schizophrenia', *Journal of Forensic Psychiatry*, 6, pp. 19–40.

Lidz, C., Mulvey, E. & Gardner, W. (1993) 'The Accuracy of Predictions of Violence to Others', *Journal of the American Medical Association*, 269, pp. 1007–11.

Link, B. G., Andrews, H. & Cullen, F. T. (1992) 'The Violent and Illegal Behaviour of Mental Patients Reconsidered', *American Sociological Review*, 57, pp. 275–92.

Monahan, J. (1984) 'The Prediction of Violent Behaviour: Toward a Second Generation of Theory and Policy', *American Journal of Psychiatry*, 141, pp. 10–15.

Monahan, J. & Steadman, H. J. (1994) 'Towards a Rejuvenation of Risk Assessment Research', Ch 1, in Monahan, J. & Steadman, H. J. eds, *Violence and Mental Disorder*, Chicago: University of Chicago Press, pp. 1–17.

Myers, K. M. & Dunner, D. L. (1984) 'Self- and other-directed violence on a closed acute-care ward', *Psychiatric Quarterly*, 56, pp. 178–88.

National Health Service Management Executive (1994) *Introduction of Supervision Registers For Mentally Ill People From 1 April 1994*, HSG(94)5, London: Health Care (Administrative) Division.

Petrie, W. M., Lauson, E. C. & Hollander, M. H. (1982) 'Violence in Geriatric Patients', *Journal of the American Medical Association*, 248, pp. 443–4.

Rice, M. E. & Harris, G. T. (1992) 'A Comparison of Criminal Recidivism Among Schizophrenic and Non-Schizophrenic Offenders', *International Journal of Law and Psychiatry*, 15, pp. 397–408.

Robertson, G. & Taylor, P. (1993) 'Psychosis, Violence and Crime', Ch 8, in Gunn, J. & Taylor, P. *Forensic Psychiatry: Clinical, Ethical, and Legal Issues*, Oxford: Heinemann-Butterworth.

Sapejak, D., Menzies, R., Webster, C. & Jeusth, F., 'Clinical Predictions of Dangerousness: two-year follow-up of 408 pre-trial future costs. Bulletin of the American Academy of Psychiatry and the Law 1983 11:171–81.

Steadman, H. J. & Felson, R. B. (1984) 'Self-reports of violence. Ex-mental patients, ex-offenders, and the general population', *Criminology*, 22, pp. 321–42.

Steadman, H. J., Monahan, J., Robbins, P. C., Appelbaum, P., Grisso, T., Klassen, D., Mulvey, E. P. & Roth, L. (1993) 'From Dangerousness to Risk Assessment: Implications for Appropriate Research Strategies', in Hodgins, S. (ed.), *Mental Disorder and Crime*, Newbury Park, California: Sage.

Steadman, H. J. & Morrissey, J. P. (1981) 'The Statistical Prediction of Violent Behaviour: Measuring the Cost of A Public Protectionist Versus a Civil Libertarian Model', *Human Behaviour*, 5, pp. 263–74.

Steering Committee of the Confidential Enquiry into Homicides and Suicides by Mentally Ill People (1994) *A Preliminary Report on Homicide*, London: Royal College of Psychiatrists.

Swanson, J. (1994) 'Mental Disorder, Substance Abuse, and Community Violence', Ch 5, in Monahan, J. & Steadman, H. J. (eds), *Violence and Mental Disorder*, Chicago: University of Chicago Press, pp. 101–36.

Swanson, J., Holzer, C., Ganju, V. & Jono, R. (1990) 'Violence and Psychiatric Disorder in the Community: Evidence From the Epidemiologic Catchment Area Surveys', *Hospital and Community Psychiatry*, 41, pp. 761–70.

Tardiff, K. & Sweillam, A. (1982) 'Assaultive Behaviour Among Chronic Inpatients', *American Journal of Psychiatry*, 139, pp. 212–5.

Taylor, P. (1993) 'Schizophrenia and Crime: Distinctive Patterns in Association' in Hodgins, S. (ed.), *Mental Disorder and Crime*, Newbury Park, California: Sage.

United Nations Commission on Human Rights (1991) *'Report of the Working Group on the Principles for the Protection of Persons with Mental Illness and For the Improvement of Mental Health Care'*, New York: United Nations.

Walker, N. (1977) *Behaviour and Misbehaviour: Explanations and Non-Explanations*, Oxford: Blackwell.

Webster, C. & Menzies, R. (1995) 'Supervision in the Deinstitutionalised Community', in Hodgins, S. (ed.), *Mental Disorder and Crime*, Newbury Park, California: Sage.

Webster, C., Harris, G., Rice, M., Cormier, C. & Quinsey, V. (1994) *'The Violence Prediction Scheme. Assessing Dangerousness in High Risk Men'*, Toronto: Centre of Criminology.

Wesseley, S., Buchanan, A., Reed, A., Curring, J., Everitt, B., Garety, P. & Taylor, P. (1993) 'Acting on Delusions. I: Prevalence', *British Journal of Psychiatry*, 163, pp. 69–76.

Williams, P. & Dickenson, J. (1993) 'Fear of Crime: Read All About It', *British Journal of Criminology*, 33, pp. 33–56.

3

When Violence is the Norm

Elaine Genders and Shona Morrison

The Quest for Understanding

Violent crime is frequently branded 'mindless', 'senseless', 'insane' — rarely is it portrayed as normal or logical. Criminal behaviour has attracted a great deal of attention from those who wish to 'make sense' of it; violent behaviour even more so. Yet a perusal of recent newspaper headlines is evidence enough that we have gained neither understanding nor control of this most consequential human behaviour.

Modern scientific study of crime and criminals is usually held to have begun during the period of the Enlightenment with the work of the classical thinker Cesare Beccaria (1764) who saw crime as the product of rational thought and free will. However by the end of the nineteenth century this view had been overtaken by a positivist conception of crime as predetermined. Although exceptions exist, the exploration for empirical explanation led most early positivist inquirers to locate the sources of crime and, hence, criminal violence, within the individual. Influenced by social Darwinism, these early positivist theorists looked for clues to criminality in the physical characteristics of individual offenders: they examined the shape, size and physiology of known criminals (see e.g., Hooton (1939); Kretschmer (1921); Lombroso (1876); Sheldon (1942)). Many Victorians, for instance, believed that criminals had a feeble cranial capacity, a heavy and developed jaw, projecting ears, and frequently a crooked or flat nose (Price *et al* (1982)). As scientific knowledge and techniques progressed, attention shifted to less visible biological determinants, and researchers attempted to distinguish offenders according to their biochemical, hormonal, genetic and chromosomal make-up (see e.g., Berman (1938); Crowe (1972); Glueck & Glueck (1950); Goring (1913); Jacobs *et al*

(1965); Lorenz (1966); Maccoby and Jacklin (1980); Mednick *et al* (1984)). Physical correlations for criminal behaviour have always, and continue to be, scientifically seductive (Shoham *et al* (1989); Ware (1993)). However, with repeated failure to identify the physical correlates of most criminality, the focus of the search gradually moved from the body to the mind. Methods of punishment advanced at a similar pace and moved away from physical torture, public humiliation and execution, to strategies of intervention, rehabilitation and social control (Cohen (1985)).

Despite the early promise of the move away from physical explanations for law-breaking, the belief that the 'bad must also be mad' persists, and many of the modern theories that have been developed within the realm of psychology continue to explain the behaviour of criminals in terms of psychopathic, socio-psychopathic and neurotic personalities — all of which are suggestive of character disorders or other clinical abnormalities which could only apply, if at all, to small minorities. Even those such as Eysenck (1964), who seem to have sought 'non-pathic' explanations of criminality, searched in the realm of faulty cognitions or problematic thought patterns: those accredited with such distinctions continue to be tagged with the 'abnormal' label.

Social explanations of crime and criminal violence stand in sharp contrast to explanations which locate the causes of crime within the individual. The twentieth century has witnessed an increasing concern with the social aetiology of crime and the development of a variety of empirically based explanations which attribute the causes of crime to social and cultural forces. Influenced by the ideas of such early social thinkers as Karl Marx and Emile Durkheim, these theories propound the view that criminals are made rather than born; that they are socialised into their environment and taught to behave in ways which may be considered to be rational within their experiences and which conform to the norms of the culture or society from which they come and in which they must live. Thus, in some ways reminiscent of the classical school, both sociologists and social psychologists have recognised that some offenders, at least, may be displaying actions which may even be considered to be rational under certain circumstances (e.g., Hollin (1989); Wolfgang and Ferracuti (1967)). While these kinds of theories emphasise the ordinariness of much crime, acts of violence continue to be portrayed by the media as bizarre, senseless occurrences and their perpetrators depicted as evil, or as socially or psychologically maladjusted individuals.

The various theoretical perspectives developed to explain violent crime provide useful frames of reference and means of conceptualising the phenomenon. However, it has increasingly come to be acknowledged that efforts to locate the source of violence within a single disciplinary framework or set of causes have failed in their endeavour. They are either under-inclusive or over-deterministic; yet the nature of violent crime is neither unitary nor universal. As Rosenberg and Mercy (1991) observed:

> There is a need to develop theoretical perspectives that take into account the multi-dimensional nature of assaultive violence and that clarify those situations and circumstances that can promote or prevent assaultive violence. (p. 15)

McClintock has described how violence may be viewed from the perspective of three different but inter-related levels of reality: the legal, the social and the individual (Council of Europe (1973)). The legal level of reality concerns the legal labelling and legal processing of violent behaviour, whilst the social level refers to the social context of violence and its occurrence. To complete the picture, the individual level of reality is held to encompass both the individual, largely socio-demographic characteristics of those involved in violent encounters and also the meaning which a particular act has for them.

This type of approach focuses attention upon social actions and social institutions, and is essentially descriptive rather than causal. It permits an understanding of the social, ideological and cultural context of violence and, in so doing, provides a framework for the development of a wide range of strategies designed to combat violent crime. Rather than seeking the causes of violent behaviour, it attempts to explore the various factors associated with, and their influence upon, the incidence of violence. It does not explicitly discount the possibility that certain factors may provide a predisposition towards the use of violence in particular contexts and in reaction to particular stimuli, but allows for a consideration of how the interplay between factors such as past experiences, personal attitudes and values, motivations, disinhibitors, emotional arousal, situational opportunity and social response, might influence the occurrence of violence and its definition as a criminal offence. By viewing violence in this way it is possible to produce a picture of violent crime in today's society which is based upon the identification of broad patterns, but also takes account of the disparate reasons, situations and influences which affect different individuals and, ultimately, predispose or incite them to use physical force.

A Study of 'Everyday' Violence

Much of the confusion that surrounds violent crime stems from our ignorance of the circumstances surrounding 'everyday' acts of violence. Popular impressions are formed on the basis of the extreme, sensationalised items deemed to be newsworthy, and by reportage testifying to unprecedented increases in the prevalence of violent offending. However, as all statistical analyses of violent crime have shown, whether they have been based on official records or on the reports of victims, the great majority of violent incidents have no grave consequences for the injured parties (McClintock (1963)). They may be frightening and demeaning, but the degree of injury does not usually require professional medical attention, let alone hospitalisation. Nevertheless, a great deal of concern rightly surrounds those violent acts which do have grave consequences for victims, such as murder, manslaughter, rape, wounding and inflicting or causing grievous bodily harm.

This chapter is based on a study carried out in the West Midlands between 1989 and 1991, which aimed to examine the nature of, and circumstances surrounding, violent crime.[1] Whilst a wide range of violent offences was included in the research, the main concern was with offences of wounding and grievous bodily harm. Two separate offences are included within this broad legal category: the more serious offence of 'wounding or causing grievous bodily harm with intent' (s. 18 of the Offences Against the Person Act 1861) and the less serious offence of 'wounding or inflicting grievous bodily harm' (s. 20). The main distinction between the two offences lies in the requirement

---

[1] The study was commissioned and funded by the Home Office Research and Planning Unit whilst Elaine Genders was a research fellow, and Shona Morrison a research officer, at the University of Oxford Centre for Criminological Research.

The research was conducted in two phases. The first phase was designed to provide a broad overview of the wide variety of contexts in which violence resulting in physical injury might occur. It entailed the collection and analysis of a vast quantity of information from over 2,000 police files relating to violent incidents recorded by the West Midlands police in 1988. These files concerned a wide range of offences, including murder, attempted murder, manslaughter, wounding or causing grievous bodily harm with intent (s. 18 of the Offences Against the Person Act 1861), wounding or inflicting grievous bodily harm (s. 20 of the Offences Against the Person Act 1861), assault occasioning actual bodily harm (s. 47 of the Offences Against the Person Act 1861), rape (s. 1 of the Sexual Offences Act 1956), indecent assault (ss. 14, 15 and 16 of the Sexual Offences Act 1956), robbery (s. 8 of the Theft Act 1968), aggravated burglary in a dwelling (s. 10 of the Theft Act 1968), violent disorder (s. 2 of the Public Order Act 1986), and affray (s. 3 of the Public Order Act 1986). Because of the vast number of cases falling within some of these categories we opted to sample in some instances. In addition, all the cases analysed were scanned to include only those in which physical injury had been caused. However, this chapter is, in the main, restricted to an examination of the two offences of s. 18 wounding or causing grievous bodily harm and s. 20 wounding or inflicting grievous bodily harm. We analysed all cases of s. 18 offences and a one in five sample of all cases of s. 20 offences recorded by the West Midlands police in 1988. The second, more qualitative, phase of the research focused in depth upon these two offences. The aim was to study, through interviews with both the offenders and victims within the same encounter, the various factors influencing, and dynamics of, such incidents. The interview sample was drawn from police files of completed cases which had been recorded in 1990. Ultimately, we managed to interview 79 offenders who had been convicted of either s. 18 or 20 wounding, and 30 of their victims. This yielded a total of 30 'pairs'. In order to try and complete the picture, a limited amount of information about the way most of the remaining victims (who did not respond to requests to be interviewed) had reacted to the incident was gathered from the recorded statements they had made to the police. However, the present chapter is largely concerned with the accounts of offenders.

of proof of intent for the more serious s. 18 offence. During the course of the study we obtained a vast array of quantitative material information from police files which detailed the official processing and situational aspects of violent incidents, as well as the demographic characteristics and official criminal histories of a wide range of violent offenders. In addition, we held detailed discussions with violent offenders convicted on a charge of s. 18 or 20 wounding, about their attitudes to the use of violence, its place in their lives, and the circumstances of the incident which had led to their prosecution and conviction.

In examining the legal, human and social-situational content of violent incidents we hoped to produce a realistic, modern picture of 'normal' violent crime which would take account of the complex interrelationships between these features. However, it must be borne in mind that the picture we present is of 'official violent crime', since all the incidents and individuals studied had been processed through the criminal justice system. Many instances of violence, even of a serious nature, go unreported. Clearly, therefore, our study did not encompass all types and circumstances of serious violence in society.

Inevitably, not all of the findings of the study can be discussed here. In particular, we do not address the many important issues surrounding the legal labelling and legal processing of violent crime. Thus, we do not, in this chapter, consider the relationship between the official labelling and processing of violent incidents and the distribution and aetiology of violent crime. However, the following snapshot, based on interviews with 79 offenders and the analysis of 1,277 police records, is designed to give a flavour of some of the human and social-situational correlates of violent crime: the types of people who engage in violent offending; the circumstances and situations in which they have resorted to such behaviour; and their reasons for so doing. In examining these issues, some consideration is given to the question of how far it might be possible to characterise violent offending as the unintended consequence of what might be regarded as 'normal' aggressive confrontation or as the more pathological actions of persons whose self-image and personal histories indicate a particular propensity to resort to violence — so-called 'violent men' (Toch (1969)).

The Demographic Characteristics of Violent Offenders

In line with common assumptions about the patterns of male and female offending, over nine out of 10 of the assailants reported to the police as having committed a s. 18 or 20 offence were men. They were predominantly young, their mean age being 25; and between two-thirds and three-quarters of them were white.

The Psychiatric and Criminal Histories of Violent Offenders

No study of criminal records alone can fully address the question of how much violent crime may be said to emanate from inherently predispositional factors and, hence, be characterised as the actions of 'violent men'. Nevertheless, an examination of the previous psychiatric and criminal histories of violent offenders may provide a crude basis for further investigation of this issue.

Police files are not the best or most reliable source of information on the psychiatric history of offenders. However, it is noteworthy that only two per cent of those who were reported to have committed an act of violence, and who were detected and charged, were judged by either the police or medical officers to have been psychiatrically disturbed at the time of the incident, or were known to have had any history of psychiatric disturbance.

Not all offenders are caught every time they commit an offence. Hence, criminal records are likely to understate the incidence of previous offending behaviour. Nonetheless, significant differences emerged in the extent to which offenders possessed previous convictions, according to the seriousness of the charge recorded against them. There was a strong indication that offenders charged with the more serious offence of s. 18 wounding were significantly more likely to have a history of prior involvement in the criminal justice system, and to have previous convictions for the more serious offences of violence against the person. Those offenders who possessed a prior criminal history tended to have begun their career of violent offending at an early age. Regardless of their current charge, over one-third of them (37%) received their first conviction before they had reached the age of 16, and a further 44 per cent when they were aged between 17 and 20.

Importantly, however, we were able to identify a particular group of serious offenders who had engaged in a wide variety of violent offending behaviour. When the criminal records of these assailants were examined, we found that the heterogeneity of violent offending was significantly associated with both the extent and severity of previous convictions for violent offences. The more heterogeneous the prior offending, the higher the mean number of court appearances resulting in a conviction and custodial sentence, and the lower the mean age of assailants at the time of their first conviction. Thus, those offenders who had been convicted previously of a wider range of violent offences also tended to have been convicted of a greater number of offences, to have served a greater number of custodial sentences, and to have begun their careers at an earlier age than other offenders. In this way, it is possible to identify what might be referred to as a 'hard core' of offenders who appear to engage in a high degree of violence in a wide range of contexts. These offenders were few in number, comprising just eight per cent of all convicted offenders across the whole range of violent offences studied. Importantly, however, it is not known to what degree the associations identified may be said to represent a pathological behavioural pattern resulting from certain predisposing personal characteristics, and to what extent they reflect a process of deviance amplification as a result of an offender's official involvement in the criminal justice system. Equally, the sort of data available in police records is severely limited in the extent to which it can shed further light on the complexities of the behaviour and motivations of this small group of offenders.

The Human Element

To characterise either violent crime or violent criminals as essentially normal or pathological, is, in most cases, to oversimplify the dimensions and complexities of human behaviour. As Megargee (1991) noted:

> In most situations, the individual can make any one of a number of different responses. People who are threatened can fight, run away, or attempt to make some conciliatory gesture. If they choose to attack, they can do so verbally, or physically, with vigour or with restraint, within certain limits or with no holds barred. Their aggressive behaviour can be directed at those who aroused their ire or can be displaced to other targets. (p. 10) The question we are left with is: how are these choices made?

The decision-making approach, or rational choice model of offending, has recently been developed and discussed by a number of researchers in the context of property crimes (e.g., Feeney (1986); Walsh (1986)). The underlying supposition is that human beings are rational creatures who make choices about crime that are based on a comparison of the costs and benefits of a given action. The format is no different from that employed in the making of other routine choices and it is acknowledged that, as in other everyday decisions, the information which is included in the equation may be faulty or incomplete. However, it has been noted in the case of those under the influence of alcohol or drugs that the ability to make rational judgments may be particularly impaired (Rosenberg and Mercy (1991)). The advantage of this approach is that it allows for individual differences whereby some people may make choices, for a variety of reasons, which are different from what might be socially expected.

While the rational choice model has been liberally applied as an explanation for property crime, it is rarely employed in relation to crimes with less obviously instrumental overtones, such as personal violence. Hollin (1989), lamenting the lack of research in this area, has investigated the value of social decision-making as an explanatory framework for violent action. Social decision-making occurs when individuals, faced with a social problem, weigh up the options available to them, using whatever information is at hand, to reach a conclusion which, at the time, seems to provide the optimal solution (Hollin (1989)).

A decision-making approach based on social cues and perceptions, which are, of course, under some influence from a diversity of cultural, environmental, contextual and dispositional factors, may be the most appropriate framework within which to view the phenomenon of violence — which is, after all, a social phenomenon involving both action and interaction. Thus, violence may be viewed as avoidable rather than inevitable, and the perpetrators as active decision-makers rather than reflexive, conditioned organisms reacting to the stimuli of their environment. However, in order to develop an approach of this nature it is important to document the factors that may impinge on the decision to use violence, such as the values and views of violent offenders: their attitudes towards the use of violence, their perceptions of provocation, and their general outlook upon the social world. The main thrust of this approach is that these factors should be viewed not as 'causes' of violence but as factors influencing a person's decision to use violence. The decision-making process thus acts as a filter between environment and action.

Socio-Cultural Influences

The phenomenon of 'subcultures' is often referred to in discussions of violence and of the men and, less often, the women, who commit violent acts. The origins of subcultural theories of crime and delinquency can be traced back to the classic studies of social enquirers such as Henry Mayhew's observations on the dangerous classes in nineteenth-century London. Whilst the first systematic use of the term occurs in Cohen's (1955) study of juvenile delinquency, its use as a framework to describe and explain violence is most often attributed to Wolfgang and Ferracuti (1967). In their extensive consideration of the meaning of the term subculture, they proposed that

> There are shared values that are learned, adopted and even exhibited by participants in the subculture, and that differ in quantity and quality from those of the dominant culture. Just as man is born into a culture, so he may be born into a subculture . . . There is a culture theme, a sub-ethos, or a cluster of values that is differentiated from those in the total culture . . . The values shared in a subculture are often made evident and can be identified phenomenologically in terms of the conduct that is expected, ranging from the permissible to the required, in certain kinds of life situations . . . There

35

are attached to them, so to speak, norms which define the reaction or response which in a given person is approved or disapproved by the normative group. (pp. 99–101)

This standpoint purports that individuals become criminally violent through a process of socialisation whereby they learn that the use of violence is an acceptable and normal way of dealing with particular problems or situations. Within this context, it is possible to conceive of a subculture as providing a framework of references and values within which certain individuals make decisions.

Notions of masculinity have been central to, and constitute a recurrent theme within, subcultural theories of juvenile delinquency (see e.g., Brake (1985); Cloward and Ohlin (1960); Cohen (1955); Miller (1958); Willis (1977 and 1978)). It is thus hardly surprising to find, within the writings of subcultural and other theorists, reference to masculinity and masculine consciousness as a legitimation of violence. For example, both Toch (1969) and Wolfgang and Ferracuti (1967) attested to the association of physical aggression with the demonstration of 'toughness' or 'manhood', where violence may be seen as an outcome of the impugning of masculinity and honour. Certain kinds of provocation, encapsulated in challenges to the ego, are believed to be strong instigation to the use of violence by 'macho' individuals with a well-defined concept of what it is to be a 'real man' (Wolfgang (1981)). It has been suggested that the functions served by violence include the achievement and verification of masculinity (Thornton and James (1979)) as well as the achievement of other social rewards that would otherwise not be forthcoming (Hollin (1992)). In this way, violent behaviour may be a highly rewarding strategy.

Many of the offenders who were interviewed held strong beliefs about the ways in which men should behave. This was reflected in their attitudes towards the use of violence. They portrayed a 'macho' image, and 'standing up for yourself' was deemed to be important to that image:

'I've got my pride to think of.'
'You have to stick up for your rights.'

Moreover, to behave in this way was considered to be entirely within the realms of 'normal' behaviour. Not only did most of the offenders have a wealth of personal experience of violence but they were accustomed to other people reacting in a similar way to the same types of provocation. Therefore, they did not consider their own reaction to be anything unusual:

'Anybody in my shoes would have done the same in that situation — you can only take so much.'
'In this area you have to show them you can fight back or they come again.'

As Wolfgang (1981) suggested:

The proposition of a subculture of violence suggests that violence is learned behaviour and that if violence is not a way of life it nonetheless is normal, not individual pathological behaviour. (p. 109)

The pro-violence attitude demonstrated by these men towards dealing with those who were 'out of order' often appeared to stem from a code of ethics:

'It was a matter of principles. I always act on them whether it is within the law or not. Justice has now been laid on him.'

These beliefs appeared to go beyond individual male pride or machismo. They seem to stem from an informal justice system that was an intrinsic part of the culture that they belonged to and defended:

'It's just something that's built into you.'
'It was a sense of duty.'

The Black Country, an area within the West Midlands, was widely acclaimed once to have been well known for 'bare-fist fighting'. It would seem that this traditional method of solving conflicts was, by some, still highly regarded. These particular offenders said that they did not carry weapons and most of them claimed that they were opposed, at least in principle, to their use. It appeared that it was not the ethics of using a weapon to harm another that they scorned so much as the unmanliness of not using their fists:

'They're like people who have big dogs. Half wouldn't have the bottle to use them.'

It would appear that although few individuals said that they became involved in very serious violence on a regular basis, violence of a less serious nature was quite common. However, some expressed surprise that what had started as an otherwise 'normal' fight should, on this occasion, have had such serious consequences;

'I never thought I could do something like this.'
'The idea was just to give him a good hiding.'

Most of the offenders were, by their own admissions, provoked into a fight relatively easily, or at least into questioning or threatening the person who they considered had provoked them, by staring at them, saying something to them that they considered to be offensive, or annoying them in some other way. Yet many of them seemed to have been unaware of the potentially dangerous situations they got themselves into through making any response at all to these supposed provocations. They seemed to feel compelled, and to view it as a sign of manliness, to retort to any minor provocation which they interpreted to be a challenge. These men maintained that they had not wanted to enter into a confrontation when they reacted; but they seemed to be unaware of, or to ignore, the likely consequences of their counter-challenge. In addition there was some evidence of a failure to learn from previous experiences. For four out of 10 offenders, the incidents that resulted in their current convictions were similar to previous incidents which they had been involved in and which had usually been initiated in the same way.

The Influence of Dispositional Factors

Mefford *et al* (1981) observed:

Perhaps because of the revulsion that violence generates, we seldom think of it as an expression of inactive, maladaptive non-coping behaviour. (p. 274)

The impact of factors such as subcultural influences on the belief systems of offenders and their translation into values and attitudes provides a useful framework within which to examine and understand the socio-cultural influences on the decision to use violence. However, not all of the men who were interviewed were products of subcultural pockets where violence was viewed as acceptable. This suggests that there must be other factors, perhaps more dispositional ones, which impact upon the decisions of some individuals to use violence. One possibility which has been shown to affect violent behaviour, and which may operate in conjunction with subcultural influences as well as other external factors, is the offender's own social skills and methods of coping with personal problems.

Many of the men who were interviewed appeared to have problems in communicating with others, or with maintaining friendships at more than a superficial level (see Gunn (1973); Rosenberg and Mercy (1991); Storr (1991)).

These offenders did not form a wholly distinct group from those who might be characterised as possessing subcultural traits: it included some of those who demonstrated attitudes and characteristics typically associated with the subcultural perspective, as well as some who did not. Several were noticeably quite inarticulate and others freely expressed that they had difficulties in confiding in other people. These difficulties may have caused a degree of social isolation. There was also some evidence of feelings of social rejection. A number of the men were bitter about old 'friends' who had let them down in their moment of need, let them 'carry the can' for something they were equally responsible for, or, worst of all, had failed to visit them in prison. However, it was also clear that some offenders were aware of the negative influences which emanated from their choice of friends and from their friendship patterns:

'I find if I've got a lot of friends I get in a lot of trouble.'
'They [my friends] tend to fight when in a gang drinking.'

As many as one third of the offenders claimed to have no real friends or to have no friends outside their immediate family. As social skills tend to be learned from interactions with other people (Ellis (1984)), this isolation may have further prevented the learning of these fundamental skills. Whilst lack of social attachments among violent offenders is not a new finding, the potential effects of social isolation upon subsequent violent behaviour require greater investigation. For instance, it is possible that, without alternative means of dealing with the confrontations that arise regularly in a social context, the tendency to resort to violence would be increased.

Possibly the most striking theme to arise from the interviews conducted with offenders was the lack of control which many of them felt they possessed over certain aspects of their lives and their futures. A large number of these men, like the young offenders investigated by Hollin and Wheeler (1982), mentioned their firm belief in the role of luck or fate in their own and other people's lives:

'It's all luck — that's life.'
'Things are meant to happen . . . all done by fate. It's what's happened to me in the past — it just happened.'

Such statements suggest that these individuals may have had an external locus of control (see Rotter (1966)) whereby they perceived their lives and the things that happened to them as being outside their personal control.

Perhaps the most disturbing aspect of the fatalistic attitude was its reflection in the way that involvement in violence was rationalised. Many of the men did not feel that they had made these situations happen, but, instead, that these situations had 'happened' to them. This view was not always used as an excuse for their behaviour. Indeed, many did not appear to feel the need to excuse their behaviour. In fact, they often indicated that, given the circumstances and provocations of the incidents in which they had been involved, it would have been an abnormal reaction to have maintained control. This appears to suggest that some of these offenders, at least, believed that their involvement in violence was not a personal decision but was just part of the 'script' of their lives:

'I didn't look for it — it just seemed to happen.'
'It could happen to anyone.'

In some cases it even seemed as if something or someone had possessed control over them:

'She made me do what I didn't want to do.'
'Him shouting like that was like a red rag to a bull.'

It is, of course, possible to see how recourse to such fatalistic explanations might also serve as a technique of neutralisation to overcome moral scruples thorugh the denial of culpability. Certainly the negative feelings expressed by some offenders about the experience appeared to arise not from their use of violence but from being caught and punished for it. Yet, regardless of their desire to avoid imprisonment in the future, these offenders were resigned to the fact that the choice was out of their hands.

The Influence of Drink and Drugs

According to the information held in police records, four in 10 (41%) of those incidents recorded as a s. 18 wounding and three in 10 (29%) of those recorded as a s. 20 wounding could be termed pub-related, in that they occurred inside or within the vicinity of public houses, discos or night-clubs, or in some other location whilst the injured party was making his or her way home from visiting such an establishment. The association of violence with pubs, clubs and discos clearly suggests some association between violent behaviour and alcohol, and possibly also drug consumption. It is well known that alcohol and drugs may have a disinhibiting effect upon a person's behaviour. It is also widely recognised that some people become aggressive after drinking alcohol or taking certain kinds of drugs, such as amphetamines and barbiturates. However, the nature of the link between intoxication and aggression is still not fully understood and direct causality remains a matter of dispute. Some writers believe that the link is clearly causal (see e.g., Storr (1991)); others (see e.g., Fagan (1990)) argue that such an accusation is unfounded considering the non-violent behaviour of most substance users.

Walmsley (1986) proposed two alternatives to a direct causal link between alcohol consumption and violence. First, he postulated that the relationship might be spurious: for example, it may just be that fights happen in public houses because men gather there or that those who have been drinking heavily are less able to avoid arrest. Secondly, he suggested that the relationship may be indirect and that alcohol is a factor which, when associated with others such as stress or severe communication difficulties, may give rise to violence. Other writers have implicitly acknowledged the important role played by lifestyle or subcultural influences in alcohol-related violence. For example, Lindquist (1991), in a survey of homicides committed by abusers of alcohol and illicit drugs in Sweden, revealed that many of the attacks occurred in settings where drinking was a matter of mutual interest for both the perpetrator and the victim. As McHugh and Thompson (1991) suggested, in such a scenario both parties may be equally handicapped: the social interaction in such situations may best be conceptualised as containing the potential for a downward spiral of misunderstandings. In a similar vein, Lucas (1988), in his study of drink-related violence in Guildford and Woking, noted how violence in both towns was felt by respondents to be inevitable at weekends after the pubs had closed and groups of young men were milling about in the town centre. This was a time when young men gathered in pubs and drank to excess, buying in rounds as a release from the constraints of the working week. Such occasions were characterised by competitiveness, bravado and aggression. In these circumstances, violence could be triggered by seemingly trivial events, such as brushing past someone or even just looking at someone.

Among those interviewed, very few of the assailants in any of the incidents claimed to have been under the influence of drugs at the time the event took place. This is consistent with the findings of other studies which have reported little association between drugs and violence (Hartnoll et al (1986); Mott (1981); Oppenheimer et al (1979)). However, the records revealed that a much higher proportion of both the assailants and complainants had been drinking alcohol. Whilst there is an obvious proven association between drinking and incidents occurring in, around or on the way home from pubs, clubs and discos, alcohol consumption is clearly not restricted to pub-related incidents. Some people drink at home, either alone or in company, or in the street. In other cases, a violent dispute may arise when an individual arrives home from the pub. Indeed, the parties to the offence had been drinking in a greater number of cases than those which could be termed pub-related. This included half of both the assailants (54%) and complainants (52%) in those offences recorded as a s. 18

wounding, and four in 10 of the assailants (40%) and complainants (40%) in those recorded as a s. 20 wounding.

Of the offenders interviewed, some of those who had been drinking prior to the incident said they had still been sober, as opposed to 'merry' or 'drunk'. However, the same number of offenders admitted to having been 'drunk' or 'very drunk'. Yet few of the victims described themselves as drunk when the incident occurred. It was not possible to determine whether these different assessments by victims and offenders reflected different levels of consumption, different degrees of toleration, different perceptions of their states, or, indeed, different ways of justifying their actions and reactions within the incident. It may be significant that over one-quarter of the offenders who admitted that they had been drinking said that they had been in a 'bad mood' for reasons unrelated to the event, for example they had experienced an argument with their partner or were feeling irritated by someone else. This may have influenced their actions, their perceptions of the incident or, indeed, the amount of alcohol they had drunk.

Motivational Forces

It has long been established that much of the everyday violence that occurs is between people who are known to each other (Gunn (1973)). Even in the case of those offences of violence against the person that were reported to the police, records indicated that the assailants and complainants were previously known to each other in six out of 10 (59%) incidents — either as friends or acquaintances (24%); persons who were known to each other vaguely by sight or by name (8%); persons who were related to each other as couples who were or had been married or cohabiting (8%); members of a family related by blood or through marital ties (6%)); or as neighbours, business partners, co-workers, landlords and tenants, co-tenants or dating couples (10%).

Not surprisingly, perhaps, there was a history of prior discord in about half the instances in which the parties were known to one another, and in just under half of these there was some suggestion of previous violence or sustained harassment. According to the offenders who were interviewed, in those incidents where the two parties were known to one another the chances of a confrontation were increased for the simple reason that in most cases they just did not like one another. Where there was a history of actual prior dispute, it seemed that in most cases earlier disagreements had not been settled and were in some way connected to the present incident. Although these earlier disputes had usually occurred weeks, and sometimes months, before the current incident, the parties had not, generally, met in the intervening period, thus precluding any opportunity to resolve the problem.

Regardless of the incidence of previous disagreements and the low opinions the participants held about one another, eight out of 10 of both parties[2] stated that they had never envisaged that anything so serious would erupt between them. Only one-quarter of the offenders admitted to having planned or expected some form of confrontation before meeting with the victim, although they usually asserted that the confrontation was not necessarily intended to be a violent one. Those offenders who had sought a confrontation usually claimed to have done so because of something the victim was alleged to have done to them, or to someone close to them, in the past. For example, several offenders claimed that the victim had previously stolen property from them or that they, a member of their family or a close friend, had been physically harmed or threatened by the victim. In a few cases, the victim had never actually met the offender but was regarded as a threat because he was the present boyfriend, or 'potential' boyfriend, of the offender's partner or ex-partner.

Even where there had been a long-term dispute and therefore an established motive to seek some form of confrontation, the victim was not usually attacked on sight. It was more common for the assault to be preceded by an argument and mutual exchanging of insults, or for the offender to have perceived that the other's behaviour constituted a physical threat or a challenge to fight:

'He put his arm to his side like he was going to take a swing.'
'Why did he pull over if he did not want trouble?'

The problems that arose between those who were not previously acquainted or who had not previously been in dispute and had not anticipated trouble before meeting with the other party frequently arose from insult-trading or arguments over rights, property and women. However, most offenders, and, indeed victims,[3] claimed that they had not started these arguments purely for the purpose of inciting a fight. Some began with comments or 'insults' that the individual may have intended in jest. These interchanges quickly got out of hand, however, with the receiver taking offence and either one or both parties refusing to back down until violence became inevitable. Ultimately, many believed that it had become a 'survival of the fittest' situation.

'It's you or them.'
'I knew I was dealing with a violent bloke and it had to end in violence.'

This type of escalation is reminiscent of Toch's (1969) observation that trivial incidents can sometimes escalate into violent attacks because the

---

[2] Note 1 details the interviewing of victims.
[3] Note 1 details the interviewing of victims.

behaviour of the victim served to aggravate a difficult situation rather than to calm it. However, caution must be exercised in placing too much emphasis on the role played by victim precipitation. The initiation and development of most violent incidents, like those studied here, are influenced not only by the behaviour of the victim but also by the offender's behaviour, the impact that offenders and victims have on one another, and, perhaps most importantly, their perceptions of one another's intentions; in other words, the entire interaction and its dynamics — influenced, of course, by the personal characteristics of the parties involved, their perceptions, and the context in which they find themselves — is more important than any individual aspect of the interchange.

The Violent Encounter

The actual violent encounters varied enormously in intensity, duration, whether and what sorts of weapons were used, and the nature and extent of injuries that were inflicted. Not unexpectedly, police records revealed that weapons were more frequently used in those offences classified as s. 18 wounding (72%) than in those classified as s. 20 wounding (37%). Knives and blades were the most common weapons in s. 18 woundings (23%), although blunt instruments such as hammers, iron bars or items of furniture were also used (20%). Injury in a further one in six cases was caused by broken glass, frequently from bottles or drinking vessels which were readily available in pubs and clubs to be picked up in the heat of the moment. Firearms were rarely in evidence and were used to inflict injury in only a small number of cases (2%). Some of the more unusual weapons that were employed in only a minority of incidents included carbon monoxide gas, battery acid, pit-bull terriers, and motor vehicles.

As might be expected, the severity and extent of injury inflicted upon the complainants varied considerably. The most common types of injury were lacerations or stab wounds, followed by fractures; in both cases injuries were sustained mainly to the face or head. Only one in 10 of the more serious incidents recorded by the police as a s. 18 wounding resulted in severe internal injuries. Nevertheless, one in five of the encounters had left the complainant permanently disfigured or disabled. Such consequences were also suffered by one in 12 of those injured during the course of offences recorded as s. 20 wounding.

In those incidents where a weapon had been used, the injuries tended to have been caused by a single slash, stab or blow. On the other hand, it was more common for attacks where weapons had not been used to involve repeated punching, kicking and head-butting. This pattern appears to be consistent with Luckenbill's (1977) observation that victims of murder were commonly 'dropped' by a single shot or stab when a weapon was used to attack them, but when no weapon was used it took a volley of blows to achieve the same result. It seems to suggest that the aim is to administer a certain degree of injury to achieve a desired or intended result — perhaps simply to put the other person 'out of action' rather than to cause any particular level of harm. In other words, the amount of force used in these incidents may reflect a resort to the time-honoured strategy of making sure the other person stays down and cannot get up to retaliate.

Most of the offenders who were interviewed said that they did not fully realise at the time how much damage they had caused until the police informed them or, in some cases, they read about it in the local newspaper. For the most part, they claimed that they had not intended to injure the victim so seriously and half of them believed that the victim had not deserved the injuries they had received but instead, some lesser injury. It has already been mentioned that a number of the offenders appeared to have a strong traditional code of ethics regarding violence. This arose with regards to weapon-carrying and also appeared to apply to the degree of injury inflicted upon victims. They maintained that their use of violence had been acceptable and justifiable because of the victim's provocative behaviour. However, when more force than necessary had been applied, they claimed to be ashamed of their loss of control and shocked to realise that the damage they had caused could easily have resulted in the death of their opponent.

Failure in self-control leading to impulsive behaviour has been held to be an important and common feature in crime (Glueck and Glueck (1950); Heilbrun and Heilbrun (1977)). It was clear that as the interactions between the two parties progressed, their exchanges became increasingly more aggressive and heated while self-control diminished on the part of the offenders. Some offenders described feelings of 'blanking out' or of instincts taking over when things reached boiling point. It was apparent that many of these individuals, offenders and victims, entered into an exchange while failing to recognise, or ignoring, the danger signals — and by the time they did it was often too late, as the situation was already out of control.

Regardless of the actual threat they faced, a large proportion of offenders claimed that they had no choice in the matter, that they were not in control of their actions when they delivered the injuries in question because so strong was the perceived threat presented by the victim that their actions were ones of instinctive self-preservation. However, an equally large group maintained that they 'had' to use violence to deal with the situation; in other words, there were, potentially, alternative ways to react but the pressures of the situation weighed heavily in favour of the violence option as the best course of action. In addition, they often referred to this in a very resigned way, as if it had been an unpleasant job which they had been forced to deal with:

45

'Violence was the only way of dealing with it.'
'The air had to be cleared — one way or another.'

In their perception of the circumstances, they were providing a most obvious, rational response.

The media stereotype of violent people commonly portrays them as heartless beings with few feelings or emotions, but few of the incidents examined in this study could be described as 'cold-blooded violence'. At all the stages leading up to and emanating from the violent encounter — the anticipation, the initial meeting and development of the confrontation, the violent exchange itself and the aftermath — the majority of offenders experienced negative emotional reactions, such as anger or fear. However, a group of them did claim to have remained calm or indifferent, or to have felt mixed emotions, such as anger mingled with relief, throughout the course of events. Very few said they had actually enjoyed the experience. Nevertheless, only one-quarter of the offenders admitted to having felt any remorse about the injuries they had caused: most claimed that they were still angry with the victim or worried about the consequences of what they had done.

Implications for Control

In seeking an answer to the question of whether serious violence is inevitable, it is imperative to consider both the individual and social dimensions of human behaviour and interpersonal interaction. Certainly when two people find themselves in a hostile confrontation with one another, either as a result of past grievances or a more immediate conflict, violence is not the only option. However, when socio-cultural expectations demand or, at the very least, do not rule out a violent response, when previous similar predicaments have been 'solved' by violent means, when inhibitions have been reduced due to alcohol, and when underdeveloped social skills limit the number of viable alternatives, the violent option becomes increasingly likely — especially when internalised socio-cultural values are at stake. In seeking to understand the escalation of violence and the severity of some of the injuries inflicted, it would seem that it is not uncommon, once the threshold of violent action has been crossed and emotions are charged, for self-control to diminish as the 'red mist' descends.

As to the future, few of the offenders who were interviewed accepted that they were destined to lead a life of violence and even fewer claimed that they had actually chosen this path. Yet while in a thoughtful, rational, unemotional state, over half of them predicted that if they were faced with a similar situation again, they would act in a similar fashion. Undoubtedly it is likely that this figure would greatly increase under the weight of outside pressures, emotional turmoil, and the lack of control experienced during 'the heat of the moment'.

A wide range of strategies may be employed in an attempt to curb the incidence of violent crime, including a variety of situational prevention schemes as well as the targeting of offenders for deterrent or preventive sentences, or for treatment, counselling or other rehabilitative programmes. It is not possible within this chapter to fully document or discuss the implications of our research for the effective targeting of these strategies. However, it is clear that effective intervention must be based not upon political expediency or adherence to an ideological conception of crime and punishment but upon an understanding of the nature and aetiology of violent crime. Our purpose has been to demonstrate the fallacy of searching for monistic causes of violent crime and to underline the value of adopting a multi-disciplinary approach that takes account of the socio-cultural features and social-psychological dispositions of those who engage in violent acts; the structural situational factors which give rise to opportunities for offending; the dynamics of exchange; and the complex, interactive, and sometimes coincidental nature of the relationships between these elements.

References

Beccaria, C. (1764) *Dei Delitti e delle Pene* (On Crimes and Punishments), Milan.

Berman, L. (1921) *The Glands Regulating Personality*, New York: Macmillan.

Berman, L. (1938) *New Creations in Human Beings*, New York: Doubleday Doran.

Brake, M. (1985) *Comparative Youth Culture*, London: Routledge & Kegan Paul.

Cloward, R. A. & Ohlin, L. E. (1960) *Delinquency and Opportunity*, New York: Free Press.

Cohen, A. K. (1955) *Delinquent Boys: The Culture of the Gang*, New York: The Free Press.

Cohen, S. (1985) *Visions of Social Control*, Cambridge: Polity Press.

Council of Europe (1973) *Violence in Society*, Tenth Conference of Directors of Criminological Research Institutes, Strasbourg 28 November to 1 December 1972.

Crowe, R. R. (1972) 'The Adopted Offspring of Women Criminal Offenders', *Archives of General Psychiatry*, 27(5), pp. 600–603.

Ellis, M. J. (1984) 'Play, Novelty and Stimulus Seeking' in Yawkey, T. D. & Pellegrini, A. D. (eds) *Child's Play: Developmental and Applied*, Hillsdale: Erlbaum.

Eysenck, H. J. (1964) *Crime and Personality*, London: Paladin.

Fagan, J. (1990) 'Intoxication and Aggression' in Tonry, M. & Wilson, J. Q. (eds) *Crime and Justice: A Review of Research*, 13, Chicago: University of Chicago Press.

Feeney, F. (1986) 'Robbers as Decision-Makers' in Cornish, D. B. & Clarke, R. V. (eds) *The Reasoning Criminal*, New York: Springer-Verlag.

Glueck, S. & Glueck, E. (1950) *Unravelling Juvenile Delinquency*, New York: Harper and Row.

Goring, C. (1913) *The English Convict: A Statistical Study*, London: HMSO.

Gunn, J. (1973) *Violence in Human Society*, Newton Abbot: David & Charles (Holdings) Limited.

Hartnoll, R. *et al* (1986) 'Evaluation of Heroin Maintenance in Controlled Trials', *Archives of General Psychiatry*, 37, pp. 877–84.

Heilbrun, A. B. & Heilbrun, K. S. (1977) 'The Black Minority Criminal and Violent Crime: The Role of Self-Control', *British Journal of Criminology*, 17, pp. 370–7.

Hollin, C. R. (1989) 'Psychological Approaches to Understanding Serious Crime' in Hollin, C. R. *Psychology and Crime: An Introduction to Criminological Psychology*, London: Routledge.

Hollin, C. R. (1989) *Psychology and Crime: An Introduction to Criminological Psychology*, London: Routledge.

Hollin, C. R. (1992) *Criminal Behaviour: A Psychological Approach to Explanation and Prevention*, London: The Falmer Press.

Hollin, C. R. & Wheeler, H. M. (1982) 'The Violent Young Offender: A Small Group Study of a Borstal Population', *Journal of Adolescence*, 5, pp. 247–57.

Hooton, E. A. (1939) *Crime and the Man*, Cambridge MA: Harvard University Press.

Howard, J. (1784) *The State of the Prisons in England and Wales*, London.

Jacobs, P. A., Brunton, M. & Melville, M. M. (1965) 'Aggressive Behaviour, Mental Subnormality and the XYY Male', *Nature*, 208, pp. 1351–2.

Kretschmer, E. (1921) *Korperbau und Charakter* (Physique and Character), Berlin: Springer-Verlag.

Lindquist, P. (1991) 'Homicides committed by Abusers of Alcohol and Illicit Drugs', *British Journal of Addiction*, 86, pp. 321–6.

Lombroso, C. (1876) *L'uomo delinquente* (The Criminal Man), 4th ed. (1889), Torino: Bocca.

Lorenz, K. (1966) *On Aggression*, London: Methuen.

Lucas, B. (1988) *Project Brahms: A Qualitative Study on Drink Related Violence*, unpublished paper prepared for the Home Office by Questel Ltd.

Luckenbill, D. F. (1977) 'Criminal Homicide as a Situated Transaction', *Social Problems*, 25, pp. 176–86.

Maccoby, E. E. & Jacklin, C. N. (1980) 'Sex Differences in Aggression', *Child Development*, 51, pp. 964–80.

McClintock, F. H. (1963) *Crimes of Violence*, London: MacMillan.

McHugh, M. & Thompson, C. (1991) *The Role of Alcohol in the Commission of Crimes of Violence*, unpublished paper presented to the British Criminology Conference, University of York, July.

Mednick, S. A., Gabrielli, W. F., Jr. & Hutchings, B. (1984) 'Genetic Influences in Criminal Behavior: Evidence from an Adoption Cohort', *Science*, 224, pp. 891–4.

Mefford, R. B., Lennon, J. M. & Dawson, N. E. (1981) 'Violence — An Ultimate Noncoping Behaviour' in Hays, J. R., Roberts, T. K. & Solway, K. S. (eds) *Violence and the Violent Individual*, New York: Spectrum Books.

Megargee, E. I. (1991) 'An Overview of Research on Violence and Aggression' in Home Office's *Prison Service Psychology Conference Proceedings*, London: HMSO.

Miller, W. B. (1958) 'Lower Class Culture as a Generating Milieu of Gang Delinquency', *Journal of Social Issues*, 14, pp. 5–19.

Mott, J. (1981) 'Criminal Involvement and Penal Response' in Edwards, G. & Busch, C. (eds) *Drug Problems in Britain*, London: Academic Press.

Oppenheimer, E. *et al* (1979) 'Seven Year Follow-up of Heroin Addicts: Abstinence and Continued Use Compared' *British Medical Journal*, 2, pp. 627–30.

Price, R. H., Glickstein, M., Horton, D. L. & Bailey, R. H. (1982) *Principles of Psychology*, New York: Holt, Rinehart and Winston.

Rosenberg, M. L. & Mercy, J. A. (1991) 'Assaultive Violence' in Rosenberg, M. L. & Fenley, M. A. (eds) *Violence in America*, New York: Oxford University Press.

Rotter, J. B. (1966) 'Generalised Expectancies for Internal versus External Control of Reinforcement', *Psychological Monographs: General and Applied*, 80, pp. 1–27.

Sheldon (1942) *The Varieties of Temperament: A Psychology of Constitutional Differences*, New York: Harper.

Shoham, S. G., Askenasy, J. J. M., Rahav, G., Chard, F. & Addi, A. (1989) 'Some Biological Predispositions and Multivariate Analysis of the Bio-Psycho-Social Correlates of Violent Prisoners', *Medicine and Law*, 7, pp. 607–28.

Storr, A. (1991) *Human Destructiveness*, New York: Grove Wendenfeld.

Thornton, W. E. & James, J. (1979) 'Masculinity and Delinquency Revisited', *British Journal of Criminology*, 19, pp. 225–41.

Toch, H. (1969) *Violent Men*, Harmondsworth: Penguin.

Walmsley, W. R. (1986) *Personal Violence*, Home Office Research Study No. 89, London: HMSO.

Walsh, D. (1986) 'Victim Selection Procedures Among Economic Criminals: The Rational Choice Perspective' in Cornish D. B. & Clarke, R. V. *The Reasoning Criminal: Rational Choice Perspectives in Offending*, New York: Springer-Verlag.

Ware, J. (1993) 'Wot U Looking At?', *BBC's Horizon*, 24 May 1993.

Willis, P. (1977) *Learning to Labour*, London: Saxon House.

Willis, P. (1978) *Profane Culture*, London: Saxon House.

Wolfgang, M. E. (1958) *Patterns in Criminal Homicide*, Philadelphia: University of Pennsylvania Press.

Wolfgang, M. E. (1981) 'Sociocultural Overview of Criminal Violence' in Hays, J. R. Roberts, T. K. & Solway, K. S. (eds) *Violence and the Violent Individual*, New York: Spectrum.

Wolfgang, M. E. & Ferracuti, F. (1967) *The Subculture of Violence: Towards an Integrated Theory in Criminology*, London: Tavistock.

4

Sexual Molesters

Donald West

What Dangers?

Sex offenders have become modern folk devils. As Sampson (1994) pointed out: 'Public concern about sexual crime has become a panic', and 'Those who perpetrate such crimes are hated and despised more than almost any other offender'. In reality, a small minority of such offenders are a deadly menace, some are fairly innocuous (consenting homosexuals have even been 'de-criminalised'), and most fall somewhere in between.

Some 40 per cent of female homicide victims are killed by a sexual partner (Home Office, 1994) and sexual jealousy is a common motive. Jealous suspicions, considered more or less normal for males in some cultures, can erupt with insane intensity in the delusions of chronic alcoholics and schizophrenics, which account for a significant proportion of mentally ill patients committed to special hospitals after killing their sexual partners (Mowat (1966)). However, since the perpetrators of 'crimes of passion', 'domestic violence' and 'insane jealousy' are not acting to satisfy lust, they are not usually counted as sex offenders.

The exploitation of sex for financial gain, in prostitution, pimping and the pornography trade, can involve vulnerable people resorting to illicit practices and a destructive lifestyle from which it becomes difficult to escape (Høigård and Finstad (1992); West and de Villiers (1992)). Except for attacks by clients, the damage incurred (sexual infections, links with criminality and drug abuse, spoiled sex life, police harassment) is not caused by persons labelled sex offenders.

The harmfulness of violence is self-evident, but only a small minority of sexual attacks involve homicidal violence, significant physical injury, sexual

51

mutilation or even gross brutality. Nevertheless, the effects, both short and long-term, of less physical forms of sexual coercion or aggression can also be severe. The victims, being mostly women and children, have reason to fear what may happen if they resist. The feeling of forced surrender to degrading manipulations or painful penetrations and the risk of lethal infection or unwanted pregnancy are clearly traumatic.

Fear of sullied reputation, anticipation of harrowing interrogations when criminal justice procedures are invoked, feelings of shame, self-blame and fear of revenge attacks or of condemnation by family or sex partner all discourage reporting. Reactions vary, but post-traumatic stress disorders, similar to those experienced by survivors of life-threatening disasters, are frequently reported. Pre-existing psychological instabilities increase the likelihood of such sequelae. The rape trauma syndrome (Burgess and Holstrom (1974)) has achieved sufficient recognition to feature in rape trials (Block (1990)) and compensation claims.

The danger to children from sexual offenders has become a matter of obsessive public concern. Sexually motivated child abductions and murders are extremely rare but receive massive media attention when they occur. In reality young children are far more often killed by their parents or step-parents than by outsiders and are far more at risk of death from traffic accidents than from sexual predators. The almost unique example of serial killings of children by the 'moors murderers' Ian Brady and Myra Hindley still yields news headlines after 30 years. Alleged sexual abuse in satanic rituals, during which babies are reportedly sacrificed and children tortured, revives an ancient witchcraft myth still believed by religious fanatics. Police investigations fail to discover any physical evidence to support these stories, which usually originate in children's vivid imaginations, unwisely encouraged by credulous interviewers (LaFontaine (1994)). Also doubtful are the claims of damage caused by long-forgotten childhood sex abuse based on 'memories' allegedly recovered under hypnosis or drugs during psychotherapy (Richardson *et al* (1991): Yapko (1994)).

Indecent acts with children feature in a high proportion of all criminal prosecutions for sex offences and in child custody hearings. The offending behaviour does not necessarily involve actual penetration or the use of force, or any overt intimidation. Children are used to obeying adult authority and can often be persuaded or bribed into acquiesence or seduced into a collaboration which they later regret. Where the involvement is with a member of the family upon whom the child is physically and emotionally dependent, disclosure can be inhibited by genuine attachment to the perpetrator, fear of breaking up the home or fear of reprisals if disbelieved. Practices experienced as repulsive, frightening or guilt-ridden sometimes continue for years because the child fears the consequences of disclosure.

Depending on the definitions used, surveys have yielded wildly differing statistics of adults' recollections of sexual abuse as children, but even the lowest estimates suggest that at least 10 per cent of the population has been involved in some childhood encounter (Badgley (1984); Baker and Duncan (1985); Nash and West (1985); Russell (1983); West and Woodhouse (1990)). Deleterious consequences, immediate and long-term, are claimed to be both frequent and serious. Every conceivable mental health problem — delinquency, prostitution, drug abuse, anxiety neurosis, depression, sexual inhibitions, eating disorders, multiple personality, schizophrenia — has been linked to a history of sexual abuse in childhood. Particularly worrying is the claim that those molested as children are likely to become sex offenders themselves when they reach adulthood. Much of the evidence for this comes from possibly self-serving claims by detected child molesters, but at least in the case of male heterosexual paedophiles there is probably some genuine connection (Freund and Kuban (1994)).

Given the prevalence of histories of abuse in the normal population, logic implies and research confirms that many children survive without becoming adult casualties (Okami (1991)). Indeed, in some cultures, masturbation of children by parents is not seen as harmful. Many males who have been exposed as young adolescents to gentle heterosexual seduction look back on the experience as pleasant initiation rather than as victimisation. Over-concern about sexual impropriety can deprive children of natural manifestations of affection by parents, comforting gestures by teachers or attempts by passers by to help in circumstances of distress. It is when unwanted molestation is persistent or brutal, takes place in the home where there is no escape and, as is often the case, occurs in the context of multiple emotional deprivations and inadequate child care, that long-term damage is likely (Mullen *et al* (1993)). Given the potential for harm from any form of adult sexual interference with children, even non-violent paedophiles present some danger, but both complacency and over-reaction are potentially damaging to the children concerned.

Ubiquitous and Persistent?

Although sex offences still comprise less than one per cent of all recorded crimes 'known to the police' in England and Wales, there has been a significant increase (from 20,000 in 1983 to 31,000 in 1993), although this is less than the increase in the totality of violent crimes, which have nearly doubled over the same time-span. The number of offenders brought to court and found guilty of indictable sex offences in England and Wales has actually decreased over the same period (6,400 in 1983 to 4,300 in 1993). This suggests that at least part of the change is due to increased reporting and recording of less-serious incidents that do not lead to a conviction, rather than to an escalation of bad behaviour. The sharpest increase has been in recorded rapes, which have more than tripled, from 1,300 to 4,600 (Home Office (1994)), although the number of persons found guilty of rape (always a small fraction of the number of complaints recorded) has increased only moderately, from 330 to 482. Among reported rapes, the greatest proportionate increase has been in offences committed by friends and sexual intimates (Lloyd (1991)). Again, greater readiness of victims to complain and of police to record, even when the prospect of securing a conviction is slight, must be responsible in part.

Sex offenders are more widely distributed throughout the social classes than most other offenders, and many of those apprehended have no previous convictions for either sexual or non-sexual crime. This is consistent with the contention of some feminists that there is nothing unusual about men who rape. Given cultural support for macho ideals of sexual conquest, any man might become an offender. Against this, and notwithstanding the generally low reconviction rate of first offenders, there is a common belief, supported by some professionals, that all sex offenders have an enduring propensity for deviant behaviour. In a recent book on treatment for child sex abusers it is said: 'the goal of treatment is not cure, but the development and maintenance of self-control by the offender on a lifelong basis' (Morrison *et al* (1994), p. xix). Long-term follow-up lends some plausibility to the notion of ineradicable propensity, for although risk of reconviction for rape or aggressive molestation of children is relatively low it continues largely unabated for many years (Soothill and Gibbens (1978); Gibbens *et al* (1981)). Persistent reconviction for serious sex crime is characteristic of a small minority. In a large sample studied by Home Office researchers, the reconviction rate of the totality of sex offenders was low, but men with two previous convictions were 15 times more likely to be reconvicted of a further sex offence than men with only one conviction (Phillpotts and Lancucki (1979)).

Because all but the most serious sexual incidents so often go unreported, especially where secretive behaviour involving children is concerned, conviction records underestimate the extent of offending. In a frequently cited research, Abel *et al* (1987) assessed a large sample of sexual offenders. Given elaborate assurances of confidentiality, many offenders admitted numerous and mostly undetected offences. An average of 23 sex acts with girls and 282 sex acts with boys, a majority directed towards different victims, was admitted by non-incestuous paedophiles. Incestuous paedophiles did not admit as many offences, an average of 81 incidents with girls, 62 with boys, but usually all with the same victim. Exhibitionists had committed an average of 505 such acts, and rapists 7.2. In another US study, the self-reports of rape offenders revealed eight times as many rapes as did their arrest records (Weinrott and Saylor (1991)).

The nature of the misconduct is crucial. Peeping Toms, clothes-line thieves ('knicker-pickers'), obscene telephone callers, and men who expose themselves to women without ever attempting closer contact, may all have multiple convictions, but remain more of a nuisance than a menace; but there are exceptions. The majority of nuisance offenders do not escalate to serious crime, but the minority of very violent offenders frequently have convictions for lesser sexual transgressions in their earlier years.

Indications of Dangerousness

Professionals are often called upon to advise on the risk of future crime by offenders awaiting trial or being considered for parole. Since so much depends on the unforeseeable circumstances to which the offender may be exposed, predictions are necessarily uncertain. As was pointed out in chapter 1, nothing predicts future behaviour as well as past patterns of behaviour. Actuarial predictions, based on objective criteria derived from criminal histories (such as age, marital status, number and type of previous convictions, including convictions for non-sexual offences and violent offences) are generally more efficient than clinical judgments of attitude, personality or mental state. Such features are hard to assess when the offender is desperately trying to create a favourable impression, and clinicians tend to give them too much weight and, consequently, to over-estimate risk. It is relatively easy to group offenders into broad categories of relatively high or low risk, but for unusual individuals who have committed particularly nasty sex crimes the demand for certainty that they will never reoffend in a similar way is almost impossible to meet.

Clinical assessments may not provide blanket predictions, but they are helpful in identifying particular vulnerabilities which serve both as indicators of situations linked with risk and as pointers to the type of supervision, welfare assistance or medico-psychological intervention that might help. Matters such as sex education, masturbatory fantasies, frequency and nature of sexual outlets, victim characteristics, offence precursors, offence behaviours, offence frequency, modes of attack, capacity for empathy and recognition of personal responsibility all require assessment. McGrath (1990) gave a useful account of interview methods for eliciting such information without provoking resistance.

In spite of the emphasis by some researchers on the exceptions (Abel *et al* (1988)), the majority of sex offenders limit themselves, for the most part, to only one kind of deviant behaviour (Marshall and Eccles (1991)). The type of offence is important because it relates both to the nature of the danger to victims and to the likelihood of repetition. The highest recidivism rates are found among untreated exhibitionists. Men found guilty of violent heterosexual assaults have quite low reconviction rates, although in their case even a low statistical risk may be thought socially intolerable. Among child molesters, those who have offended against children in their own household are at lesser risk of reconviction than those who have targeted children outside. Men who have offended exclusively against young girls are reconvicted less often than those who have targeted both boys and girls. Expectation of reconviction among child molesters is highest among men who target boys and who are proactive in seeking contacts outside their household.

Denial of the offence or attempts to justify it by a super-macho stance, for example by believing that the woman was 'asking for it', or arguing that sex is good for children, are attitudes linked with risk. Where motivation to conform is minimal, treatment is impractical. Aggressive sexual predators who harbour irrational grudges against women and use sex to satisfy both lust and anger are particularly dangerous (West et al (1978)).

Admission of aggressive, even homicidal, sexual fantasy and a fascination for sadistic pornography is relevant, but difficult to evaluate, especially if it has not, so far, been acted out or if the very fact of admission indicates a desire for self-control. By using the penile plethysmograph to monitor arousal to depictions of rape scenes, it has been shown that some sex offenders respond readily to representations of uncomplicated copulation, whereas others achieve maximum arousal only if the victim is being subjected to gratuitous violence (Abel et al (1977)). This distinction between sadistic offenders and others is not necessarily important to the victim. Criminals prone to violence in other contexts can be brutal enough in their approaches without being true sadists (Fedora et al (1992)). Moreover, the distinction between violence for erotic satisfaction and violence for more complex motives associated with frustration and misogyny is not easy to establish (Knight et al (1994)). Whatever the motive, violence is an indication both of physical danger and a likelihood of repetition.

Grubin (1994) compared men convicted of murder in the course of a sexual attack, with men imprisoned for rape. Disorganised upbringing, generalised criminality and alcohol abuse were features common to both groups, but the killers were more often social isolates, a feature noted in US studies of serial sex killers. In comparison with non-homicidal rapists the average age of the killers was higher, and that of their victims much higher. The violence they used was often extreme and their mood at the time very angry, provoked by the victim's resistance, by recent insults to self-esteem or by their own sexual incompetence. Previous convictions for rape and reports of sexual deviance were significantly more frequent among the killers. It would appear that among men guilty of serious sexual assault, social isolation, persistent sexual dysfunction and a build-up of hostility towards women are important danger signals.

Among child molesters, reoffending is more likely among those who are sexually aroused strongly and exclusively by the physically immature. An absence of adult relationships and a lifelong fixation on children point to high risk of repetition, whereas offending for the first time by an older man following some personal crisis, such as marital breakdown or widowerhood, may be a one-off event. The results of research using the penile plethysmograph, although somewhat conflicting, suggest that molesters who target children outside their immediate family tend to be more preferentially aroused by under-age subjects, than men who have abused only their own children or step-children. Although useful for demonstrating general trends, the plethysmograph is less reliable in determining the guilt or innocence of individuals. Negative reactions can be faked and the significance of positive responses has to be assessed in the light of the observation that many supposedly normal men who have never offended display atypical arousal patterns (Templeman and Stinett (1991)).

As with all criminals, attitude and personality affect both the risk and the nature of reoffending. Antisocial personality traits such as impulsive aggression, general criminality or indifference to harm done are more frequently detected among rapists and violent offenders than among the generality of child molesters. Hare (1980) showed that high scores on his psychopathy checklist are significantly predictive of recidivism and violence among incarcerated rapists. Many serial sex killers have been found to have psychopathic features, although they also have adequate intelligence and cunning to be able to evade detection for long periods. In contrast, paedophiles often genuinely want to be helpful and loving towards the objects of their desire and may even maintain friendships long after the sexual element has faded (Brongersma (1986)). However, among child molesters any show of violence points to a dangerous antisocial propensity and a lack of concern for the welfare of the children they exploit.

Sex offenders who are substance abusers or problem drinkers often commit offences only when semi-intoxicated. As long as their substance abuse remains uncontrolled the risk of reoffending is high, but maintenance of sobriety does not, in itself, guarantee elimination of an underlying tendency to sexual offending.

Social supports, such as an intact marriage, stable employment and proper accommodation, are particularly important for sex offenders. Men who have been rejected by families and former employers and who endure an isolated lifestyle with no stake in the normal community have correspondingly little to lose by a failure to resist sexual temptations. They may seek companionship and opportunities for deviant activity through identification with others who are similarly placed. Paedophile 'rings' certainly exist, although they rarely fit the popular image of gangs of murderous predators. Sophisticated offenders capable of exploiting the Internet to make computer contact with others with similar inclinations are likely to be well organised and discreet in their search for willing youngsters. It is the emotionally alienated social reject, burning with resentments and with little to lose by taking risks, who presents the greatest danger.

A small minority of sex offenders commit crimes as a result of mental illness. The mentally ill are not generally prone to violence and those who are usually attack persons in close contact with them and not normally in a sexual context. Manic disorders, characterised by states of euphoria and over-confidence, which mimic drunken grandiosity, can lead to disinhibited and offensive sexual behaviour, but not often to serious crime. Schizophrenics with active psychotic delusions about sex are more dangerous. A feeling that sexually tempting women are evil ('Madonna–whore' complex) has deep roots in some religious traditions, which is responsible for acts of seemingly irrational violence to prostitutes, by clients who become angry and vengeful after their sexual needs have been served. The delusions of schizophrenics sometimes carry such ideas to insane extremes. Peter Sutcliffe, the 'Yorkshire Ripper', heard 'voices' that set him on a mission of God to be rid of street prostitutes. He bludgeoned to death numbers of women he thought were prostitutes.

Sexual offending is not characteristic of the generality of the mentally impaired, any more than it is of the generality of the mentally ill, but such people are over-represented among persons arrested for sex offences. Some offend simply because they have failed to learn acceptable courtship rituals, especially if their developing sexuality has been discouraged or punished by misguided carers. Their crude attempts at a sexual approach can be offensive. Their limited adult socialisation skills may cause them to seek the undemanding company of children and lead to inappropriate sexual contacts with children, even though paedophilia is not their primary problem. Serious risk, however, is usually confined to those whose learning disability is combined with antisocial personality traits and a propensity for offending in non-sexual contexts (Day (1994)).

Criminal Justice Responses

The number of persons convicted of sex offences may not have increased, but the use of imprisonment and the length of sentences awarded certainly has. Inmates serving sentences for sex offences in prisons in England and Wales, including those serving life, more than doubled between 1982 and 1992, from

1,394 to 3,156 (Home Office (1994b)). In 1983 only 20 per cent of sentences for indictable sex offences were of immediate custody. In 1993 the figure was 44 per cent for sex offenders, but only 19 per cent for (non-sexual) violence (Home Office (1994, Table 7.2)). These trends reflect public demand, encouraged by the tabloid press (Soothill and Walby (1991)) and by a government policy of tough punishment for unpopular offences.

The increased use of imprisonment has been underpinned by a number of legal changes. The maximum penalty for indecent assaults on males or females was equalised in the Sex Offences Act 1985 by raising the latter from two to 10 years' imprisonment. The same Act upgraded the maximum for attempted rape to life imprisonment. Husbands are no longer protected from charges of raping their wives and the sentencing guidelines issued by Lane LJ for rape and incest emphasise the need for imprisonment. In *Roberts* (1982) 4 Cr App R(S) at 8, he stated that other than 'in wholly exceptional circumstances' a custodial sentence is required for rape. In 1989, in response to an *Attorney General's Reference (No. 1 of 1989)* (1989) 90 Cr App R at 141, he proposed three to five years' imprisonment as appropriate for incest with a girl of 13 to 16 years of age, or six years if the girl is under 13 and there are no special adverse circumstances — such as frequency, persistence, use of violence or the commission of deviant sex acts. The Criminal Justice Act 1991, s. 2(2)(b) provides that 'where the offence is a violent or sexual offence' a custodial sentence will be for such longer term, not exceeding the maximum 'as in the opinion of the court is necessary to protect the public from serious harm from the offender'. 'Harm' in this context includes psychological harm. Section 44 of the Act empowers courts to extend the period of parole supervision for sex offenders from the three-quarter point to the end of their sentence. Section 31 lists the offences included as 'sexual' for the purpose of the Act, which include the non-consensual crimes of rape and indecent assault, offences of incest and incitement of a girl under 16 years of age to commit incest, indecency with or towards a child, and taking or showing indecent photographs of children. It excludes indecent exposure, most offences linked with prostitution (such as living on immoral earnings or keeping a brothel), but includes some homosexual offences, namely soliciting by males (not necessarily for paid sex) and indecency between males where not statutorily decriminalised (i.e., consensual but in a public place or involving anyone under 18 years old.

Severe punishment does not necessarily lessen danger to potential victims. A prosecution case needs to be particularly strong when the consequences of conviction are dire. Charges may be withdrawn when victims become fearful of attacks on their reputation and veracity from offenders desperate to avoid conviction. Plea-bargaining and acquittals allow a proportion of offenders to avoid or reduce legal penalties. As Wright (1984) pointed out, such is the attrition rate that only a small minority of men initially arrested for rape are actually imprisoned and then not necessarily on the original charge. Slight doubts encourage acquittals. A long-term follow-up of men acquitted of rape found that their reconviction-rate for sexual offences was comparable to that of offenders actually convicted of the crime (Soothill *et al* (1976)).

For victims of child sex abuse in the home the effects of criminal justice intervention can be particularly serious. Admission of the offence is the main avenue both to conviction and to making the way for treatment of the offender and reconciliation within the family, but the high probability of imprisonment encourages denial and is used by some abusers to persuade a child to keep silent. The long wait for a Crown Court hearing causes child victims and their families further anguish and may prevent the victim from receiving appropriate counselling while facts remain disputed (Glaser and Spencer (1990)). An eventual acquittal can expose a genuine victim to family recriminations.

Keeping a balance between justice for the offender and protection of the community is peculiarly difficult in the case of sex crimes because of the strength of public feeling. Myra Hindley, a middle-aged woman who has spent longer in prison than many male sex murderers, would hardly present much risk of repeated sex offending were she to be released, but she is paying the price of notoriety and has been included in the Home Secretary's list of persons to be detained until they die.

Recognition that their behaviour may be rooted in disorders for which they need help justifies the provision of treatment for sex offenders within the penal system; but its use interferes with the principle of proportionate punishment. One reason why so few offenders are awarded probation conditional on undergoing some form of treatment may be that the avoidance of imprisonment can be viewed as a reduction of the normal penal tariff. This has not prevented the introduction of treatment regimes for sex offenders in English prisons (Grubin and Thornton (1994)), but the way in which candidates are selected and the conditions in which the treatment is administered hardly amount to a lessening of punishment.

The release date of persons sentenced to life imprisonment is decided by the Home Secretary and the Parole Board (see chapter 8). Lifers, whose crimes, not necessarily overtly sexual, cause suspicion of inappropriate sexual arousal patterns, can be required to undergo testing with the penile plethysmograph and their release delayed if, for example, their responses suggest paedophilia. The media have been quick to point out the possibility of injustice (*Observer*, 28 May 1995).

The Mental Health Act 1983 provides for the committal of mentally ill or psychopathic offenders to hospital in lieu of imprisonment, or the transfer of sentenced prisoners to hospital on similar grounds. Implementation requires recommendations from psychiatrists, who are generally restrictive in their use of the Act, interpreting 'mental illness' as frank psychosis (obvious madness) and 'psychopathy' as personality disorder so severe as to amount to near insanity. The behaviour of some sex offenders is so bizarre and dangerously uncontrolled, or so clearly underpinned by unrealistic attitudes, that a diagnosis of psychopathy is easily justified. However, the application of the label 'psychopath' for the purpose of obtaining a hospital placement for convicted sex offenders depends more on the policies of defending lawyers and the views of the psychiatrists called to see the offender, than on the merits of the individual case (Chiswick (1992)).

The length of detention may be considerably increased as a result of committal to hospital. Most serious offenders and transferred prisoners are placed under Mental Health Act restriction orders (s. 41) which means that doctors cannot allow leave or discharge from hospital without the concurrence of Home Office officials. Appeals to Mental Health Act tribunals can result in release or conditional discharge, but in practice Home Office guidance and recommendations from the responsible medical officer are unlikely to be overruled. The situation of hospitalised psychopaths is especially ambiguous. Although they are not supposed to be committed unless they are amenable to treatment, in practice fundamental change may not occur or may not be demonstrable under the restrictive regimes in special hospitals. Many years may go by without reasons for release from high security emerging. In the case of transfers from prison the normally expected date of release may be long gone before discharge from hospital is thought appropriate. Transfers from prison of sex offenders deemed still to be disturbed and dangerous are, on occasion, engineered on mental health grounds shortly before they would otherwise have been released. This outrages the prisoner and creates problems for the hospital in managing a disgruntled inmate.

The justification for either extending detention or easing punishment to allow for treatment depends crucially on the nature and accessibility of the available treatments and the extent to which they are effective in reducing sexual crime.

Treatments

Treatment for sex offenders takes three broad forms. The cognitive programmes, which might be thought applicable to many other kinds of antisocial behaviour, are essentially educative. The offender is made to confront all the consequences of his actions, to accept responsibility for them, to appreciate the effect on victims and to recognise and learn to avoid situations likely to lead to recidivism. Much can be achieved along these lines by discussion in groups led by an experienced therapist, during which frank, revelatory accounts of past crimes are aired and analysed. The comments of other offenders help to discourage self-serving rationalisations and denials. Given sufficient time and motivation, radical changes of attitude and emotional reorientation can be brought about in even the most serious and persistent of offenders (West *et al* (1978)). Some sexual aggressors lack social skills, and their clumsy approaches and unrealistic expectations in intimate relationships produce misunderstandings and rejection and lead to a dangerous build-up of misogyny. Role-playing in a safe environment can help remedy this and heighten awareness of the feelings and needs of potential sexual partners. Detention in conditions of security is necessary for some offenders, but this should not preclude the setting-up of a closed therapeutic community, where inappropriate behaviours can be constantly monitored and corrected without the damaging reactions that would be provoked if they occurred in the outside community. For offenders with serious personality problems there is a reasonable amount of evidence that this approach can have a significant positive influence (Dolan and Coid (1993)). Learning to relate better to others and to control anger lessens the risk of further outbursts of sexual aggression.

The second form of treatment aims to correct inappropriate sexual arousal (Gunn and Taylor (1993, pp. 560–61)). It is most commonly applied to paedophiles who are sexually excited by immature children, but has been used with men who are maximally aroused by scenes of sexual violence. In orgasmic reconditioning treatment the man is shown varieties of pornographic material and his reactions are monitored by means of the penile plethysmograph, which registers involuntary erectile changes, even when incipient and unnoticed by the subject. Sexual responses to socially appropriate stimuli are promoted and encouraged, whereas arousal to deviant material is punished with electric shocks or discouraged by more subtle means. In the technique of covert sensitisation, subjects can be trained to generate their own punishment for deviant responses by dwelling on the devastating consequences of giving way to their criminal impulse. The treatment is based on the concept that sexual arousal is a reflex conditioned by experience, and is susceptible to modification by consistent reconditioning.

Following conditioning treatment, desirable changes in the sexual arousal pattern, which should enable the offenders to find sexual outlets in socially acceptable ways, do occur and can be measured. The changes can prove temporary and former patterns may return, in which event repeat courses of reconditioning are required.

In former times, vigorous applications of orgasmic reconditioning were used to try to convert confirmed homosexuals into heterosexuals, but this met with scant success, and led to increased impotence and anxiety. Other forms of deviance may be more readily modified, but the technique requires an actively cooperative, well-motivated subject, and is best combined with discussion and counselling. Putting newly-learned appropriate sexual behaviour into successful practice would be a powerful reinforcer, but in closed penal settings this is out of the question. A real test of effectiveness would be a significant reduction in reoffending over a long period of follow-up.

The third form of treatment is suppression of male libido. Surgical castration for this purpose is illegal and considered unethical, but substances can be given which counteract the function of testosterone in maintaining sexual drive. Prolonged administration may cause unpleasant side effects and poor compliance, and therefore authorities tend to recommend temporary usage while other approaches have a chance to take effect (Gunn and Taylor (1993)).

Treatments are best carried out in special units by therapists experienced in using the methods. Orgasmic reconditioning calls for special apparatus and technical training, but such resources are scarce. Each offender has a particular array of problems and particular assets and deficits in his personality and circumstances. The therapeutic enterprise should be eclectic as to method, and directed to individual needs.

Does Treatment Work?

The demands of criminal justice, particularly in relation to serious offenders, severely limit the application of therapeutic ideals. The notion of treatment for sex offenders, unless it is by castration, is unacceptable to many people, since it suggests evasion of just deserts. Yet the consequence of serious sex crimes, for offenders, victims and their respective families, are so devastating that any means to achieve even a modest reduction of risk would seem worthwhile. Unfortunately, realistic programmes call for considerable resources in money, trained personnel and confident, well-motivated leadership, which are all in desperately short supply. Nevertheless, the costs of treatment are a fraction of the costs of investigation, trial and probable imprisonment of a sexual criminal and of support for his victims.

The true potential for treatment approaches cannot be judged by the far from ideal systems operating in England today. A review of US programmes, which deploy more extensive resources, might provide a clearer assessment, but even in that context the efficacy of treatment efforts remains controversial. The uncertainty is due to almost insuperable difficulties in the way of scientific validation of the effect of treatment on recidivism. Sex offenders assessed as dangerous are likely to be detained as long as the risk of reconviction after release is low. Research samples must be extensive and follow-ups carried out over long periods, in order to produce sufficient data. Comparison groups are problematic. Random allocation of subjects to treatment or no treatment, which might provide a proper control, is arguably unethical. A less objectionable control for treated offenders might be to use offenders selected as suitable for treatment, but excluded solely because there was no vacancy.

Methodological perfection in treatment evaluation research is impossible, but reviews of outcome where reasonable controls have been used strongly suggest that treatment does have a significant positive effect (Marshall and Pithers (1994)). Long-term recidivism rates for treated offenders have been reported to be less than half those of untreated offenders. There may be doubts that like is being compared with like, but the figures are encouraging. The outlook for treated paedophiles appears somewhat better than for recidivist aggressors. Some critics, notably Quinsey *et al* (1993) from the Canadian secure hospital at Penetanguishene, argue that the case for effective treatment has not yet been scientifically proved. They point to some extensive programmes that reported no effect on recidivism and note the dubious practice of discounting men who fail to complete a treatment programme. The controversy calls to mind the sorry slogan 'nothing works', which used to be applied to offender rehabilitation generally.

In spite of the difficulties in meeting fool-proof criteria of success, a national treatment system for sex offenders has begun in English prisons (Grubin and Thornton (1994)), but the problem of carrying out effective intervention in a prison setting are formidable. Using a mathematical formula, the system selects the more serious offenders with an estimated high risk of reconviction. Men serving less than four years' imprisonment are not normally included, and those with multiple sex offences on record receive priority. The treatment is based on cognitive techniques and consists of a core programme supplemented by specialised 'modules' (such as anger-management training) allocated according to an assessment of individual needs. Prison officers and other non-specialist staff deliver the treatment with the benefit of guidance from trained psychologists.

The system avoids self-selection, which some prisoners find compromising, but it is, to a degree, coercive, since refusers who do not acknowledge their guilt or their need for treatment are put at a disadvantage in consideration for parole. Inclusion in the programme means transfer to often crowded, vulnerable prisoner units, with limited staff and a consequential reduction in opportunity to participate in the educational and recreational activities normally available to prisoners. Living in a community of sex offenders may reduce, if not eliminate, victimisation, but it may also reinforce deviant interests and prove anti-therapeutic. If a place in a special unit is not available, the men may have to be put into protective isolation in even more deprived conditions under the notorious Rule 43, a system which, in effect, punishes victims instead of controlling bullies. Guarantees of confidentiality which normally operate during therapy do not apply in prison, so that participants may be reluctant to make full disclosures. Since facilities are limited, the less desperate cases, many of whom might benefit from treatment, are excluded, and even those who meet the strict criteria of eligibility do not all find places.

The Criminal Justice Act 1991 puts additional responsibility onto the probation service for the after-care of imprisoned sex offenders, but integrating the work of different services is always problematic, and continuity of treatment between prison and community is difficult to arrange when prisoners are released to far away home areas. The work of the probation service with sex offenders has developed unevenly, often depending on local initiative, without much support from central management. Attendance at group sessions is the usual method of after-care, but resources, access to experts, numbers of offenders, mixture of clients, duration of treatment and treatment goals vary enormously. Arrangements for follow-up are often absent (Barker and Beech (1993)). Workers vary in their ability and willingness to cope with sexual offenders, as do their beliefs about the likelihood of offenders changing their ways. Some areas have set up specialised teams, supported by senior management, who are gaining in experience and training and are establishing coherent policies (Kennington (1994)), but some national coordination and setting of standards is urgently needed.

Given the nature of the prison and probation approaches to the treatment and rehabilitation of sex offenders, the prospect of rigorous scientific validation of outcome is remote. Perhaps the most important element in treatment, although the hardest to assess, is the therapist's ability to form an empathic relationship with these unattractive characters.

Conclusion

Public opinion tends to overestimate the numbers of dangerous sexual offenders, compared with other serious criminals such as armed robbers.

Dangerous sex offenders present two main distinguishing characteristics: an impulsive, aggressive, antisocial personality disorder similar to that seen in some non-sexual offenders, and/or an unusual erotic interest in children or in sexual violence. A combination of personality disorder and antisocial sexual impulses is particularly dangerous.

The best guide to the future dangerousness of untreated sex offenders is their previous behaviour pattern, but this can be supplemented by assessments of attitudes, sexual arousal pattern, mental state and social circumstances. The scope for prediction of risk of future offending is limited by the influence of unforeseeable and uncontrollable life events.

Treatments are available to combat personality disorder, to increase self-control and to change sexual impulses. There is evidence of some effectiveness, but exact scientific measurement is extremely difficult. Treatments are also limited by the uncertain state of scientific knowledge of the causes of deviant sexuality and the complex linkages that can occur between violent and sexual impulses. There is a desperate need for more fundamental research and for experimental treatment centres. In the meantime, humane considerations and the importance of even a small reduction in serious sex crimes favour investment in improved and better-coordinated treatment within prisons, probation services, special hospitals and community health systems, with better-trained personnel and more individualised programmes. The contribution of different elements within treatment packages should be investigated. Legislation designed to increase penal controls on sex offenders should be used constructively to secure treatment rather than to produce more frequent and longer terms of imprisonment for all offenders. While the community must be protected from offenders whose behaviour appears both dangerous and unmodifiable, those offenders who must be securely confined until old age should not be held under unnecessarily punitive regimes.

References

Abel, G. G., Barlow, D. H., Blanchard, E. G. & Guild, D. (1977) 'The components of rapists' sexual arousal', *Archives of General Psychiatry*, 34, pp. 895–903.

Abel, G. G., Becker, J. V., Cunningham-Rathner, J., Mittleman, M. S. & Rouleau, J. L. (1988) 'Multiple paraphilic diagnosis among sex offenders', *Bulletin of the American Academy of Psychiatry and the Law*, 16, pp. 153–68.

Abel, G., Becker, J., Cunningham-Rathner, J., Rouleau, J. & Murphy, W. D. (1987) 'Self-reported sex crimes of nonincarcerated paraphiliacs', *Journal of Interpersonal Violence*, 2, pp. 3–25.

Badgley, R. (1984) *Sexual Offences Against Children*, Ottawa: Canadian Government Publishing Centre.

Baker, A. & Duncan, S. (1985) 'Child sexual abuse: A study of prevalence in Great Britain', *Child Sexual Abuse and Neglect*, 9, pp. 457–67.

Barker, M. & Beech, T. (1993) 'Sex offender treatment programmes: a critical look at the cognitive-behavioural approach', *Issues in Criminological and Legal Psychology*, 19, pp. 37–42.

Block, A. P. (1990) 'Rape trauma syndrome as scientific expert testimony', *Archives of Sexual Behavior*, 19, pp. 309–23.

Brongersma, E. (1986, 1990) *Loving Boys*, 2 vols, Elmhurst, New York: Global Academic.

Burgess, A. & Holmstrom, L. (1974) 'Rape trauma syndrome', *American Journal of Psychiatry*, 131, pp. 980–6.

Chiswick, D. (1992) 'Compulsory treatment of patients with psychopathic disorder: an abnormally aggresive or seriously irresponsible exercise?', *Criminal Behaviour and Mental Health*, 2, pp. 106–13.

Day, K. (1994) 'Male mentally handicapped sex offenders', *British Journal of Psychiatry*, 135, pp. 630–9.

Dolan, B. & Coid, J. (1993) *Psychopathic and Antisocial Personality Disorders: Treatment and Research Issues*, London: Gaskell.

Fedora, O. *et al* (1992) 'Sadism and other paraphilias in normal controls and aggressive and nonaggressive sex offenders', *Archives of Sexual Behavior*, 21, pp. 1–16.

Freund, K. & Kuban, M. (1994) 'The basis of the abused abuser theory of paedophilia: A further elaboration of an earlier study', *Archives of Sexual Behavior*, 23, pp. 553–63.

Gibbens, T. C. N., Soothill, K. M. & Way, C. K. (1981) 'Sex offences against young girls: A long-term record study', *Psychological Medicine*, 11, pp. 351–7.

Glaser, D. & Spencer, J. R. (1990) 'Sentencing, children's evidence and children's trauma', *Criminal Law Review*, June, pp. 371–82.

Grubin, D. (1994) 'Sexual murder', *British Journal of Psychiatry*, 165, pp. 624–29.

Grubin, D. & Thornton, D. (1994) 'A national program for the assessment and treatment of sex offenders in the English prison system', *Criminal Justice and Behavior*, 21, pp. 55–71.

Gunn, J. & Taylor, P. J. (eds) (1993) *Forensic Psychiatry*, Oxford: Butterworth Heinemann, pp. 560–64.

Hare, R. (1980) 'A research scale for the assessment of psychopathy in criminal populations', *Personality and Individual Differences*, 1, pp. 111–19.

Høigård, C. & Finstad, L. (1992) *Backstreets: Prostitution, Money and Love*, Cambridge: Polity Press.

Home Office (1994) *Criminal Statistics England and Wales 1993*, London: HMSO.

Home Office (1994)(b) *Prison Statistics England and Wales 1992*, Cmd 2581, London: HMSO.

Kennington, R. (1994) 'Northumbria's sex offender team', *Probation Journal*, 41, pp. 81–5.

Knight, R. A., Prentky, R. A. & Cerce, D. D. (1994) 'The development, reliability and validity of an inventory for the multidimensional assessment of sexual aggression', *Criminal Justice and Behavior*, 21, pp. 72–94.

LaFontaine, J. S. (1994) *The Extent and Nature of Organised and Ritual Abuse*, London: HMSO.

Lloyd, C. (1991) 'Changes in the pattern and nature of sex offences', *Criminal Behaviour and Mental Health*, 1, pp. 115–22.

Marshall, W. L. & Eccles, A. (1991) 'Issues in clinical practice with sex offenders', *Journal of Interpersonal Violence*, 6, pp. 68–93.

Marshall, W. L. & Pithers, W. D. (1994) 'A reconsideration of treatment outcome with sex offenders', *Criminal Justice and Behavior*, 21, pp. 10–25.

McGrath, R. (1990) 'Assessment of sexual aggressors: Practical clinical interviewing strategies', *Journal of Interpersonal Violence*, 5, pp. 507–19.

Morrison, T., Erooga, M. & Beckett, R. C. (eds) (1994) *Sexual Offending Against Children: Assessment and Treatment of Male Abusers*, London: Routledge.

Mowat, R. (1966) *Morbid Jealousy and Murder*, London: Tavistock.

Mullen, P. E. *et al* (1993) 'Childhood sexual abuse and mental health in adult life', *British Journal of Psychiatry*, 163, pp. 721–32.

Nash, C. L. & West, D. J. (1985) 'Sexual molestation of young girls: A retrospective survey', in West, D. J. (ed.) *Sexual Victimisation*, Aldershot: Gower.

Okami, P. (1991) 'Self-reports of ''positive'' childhood and adolescent sexual contacts with older persons: An exploratory study', *Archives of Sexual Behavior*, 20, pp. 437–57.

Phillpotts, G. J. O. & Lancucki, L. B. (1979) *Previous Convictions, Sentence and Reconvictions*, Home Office Research Study 53, London: HMSO.

Probation Inspectorate (1991) *The Work of the Probation Service with Sex Offenders: Report of a Thematic Inspection,* London: Home Office.

Quinsey, V. L., Harris, G. T., Rice, M. E. & Lalumière, M. L. (1993) 'Assessing treatment efficacy in outcome studies of sex offenders', *Journal of Interpersonal Violence*, 8, pp. 512–13.

Richardson, J., Best, J. & Bromley, D. (eds) (1991) *The Satanism Scare*, New York: Aldine de Gruyter.

Russell, D. (1983) 'The incidence and prevalence of intrafamilial and extrafamilial sexual abuse of female children', *Child Abuse and Neglect*, 7, pp. 133–46.

Sampson, A. (1994) *Act of Abuse: Sex Offenders and the Criminal Justice System*, London: Routledge.

Soothill, K. & Walby, J. (1991) *Sex Crime in the News*, London: Routledge.

Soothill, K. L., Jack, A. & Gibbens, T. C. N. (1976) 'Rape: a 22-year cohort study', *Medicine, Science and the Law*, 16, pp. 62–9.

Soothill, K. L. & Gibbens, T. C. N. (1978) 'Recidivism of sexual offenders: A re-appraisal', *British Journal of Criminology*, 18, pp. 267–76.

Templeman, T. N. & Stinnett, R. D. (1991) 'Patterns of sexual arousal and history in a ''normal'' sample of young men', *Archives of Sexual Behavior*, 20, pp. 137–50

Weinrott, M. R. & Saylor, M. (1991) 'Self-reports of crimes committed by sex offenders', *Journal of Interpersonal Violence*, 6, pp. 286–300.

West, D. J., Roy, C. & Nichols, F. (1978) *Understanding Sexual Attacks*, London: Heinemann Educational.

West, D. J. & Woodhouse, T. P. (1990) 'Sexual encounters between boys and adults', in Li, C. K., West, D. J. & Woodhouse, T. P. *Children's Sexual Encounters with Adults*, London: Duckworth.

West, D. J. & de Villiers, B. (1992) *Male Prostitution*, London: Duckworth.

Wright, R. (1984) 'A note on the attrition of rape cases', *British Journal of Criminology*, 24, pp. 399–400.

Yapko, M. (1994) *Suggestions of Abuse*, New York: Simon Schuster.

5

Bailing and Sentencing the Dangerous

Nicola Padfield

In his introductory chapter, Professor Walker highlights the moral dilemma faced by a humanitarian society which seeks to avoid harm to innocent people, but without drastically interfering with the lives of those who may be deemed 'dangerous'. Nowhere are these conflicting demands more apparent than in the decisions taken by criminal courts. In this chapter, the statutory framework imposed on the people responsible for deciding whether to remand in custody defendants not yet convicted is compared with the framework imposed on those who make sentencing decisions. Given that periods of remand pre-trial are relatively short (average waiting time in 1992 was 11 weeks for defendants committed in custody for trial at the Crown Court: Table 2b; Prison Statistics (1992)), it is hardly surprising that the law permits the detention of offenders who are deemed to be a high risk. More significant have been the attempts of appellate courts to identify the dangerous for the purposes of post-conviction sentencing. However, recent legislative changes have meant that judges are increasingly instructed to look only at 'tariff' sentencing, and to leave questions of risk to the Parole Board and the Home Secretary.

Bail

English law has had a statutory presumption in favour of bail since 1976. This has never meant, of course, that all those charged with criminal offences were automatically released on bail. The average remand prison population in 1994 was 12,400, about 1,700 higher than in 1993 and the highest annual figure ever. What the presumption means in practice is that the police do not have the right to remand someone in custody: a person whom the police have charged with a crime but whom they do not wish to release on bail must be taken before a magistrates' court. Schedule 1, Part 1 to the Bail Act 1976 specifies, in para. 2, the three grounds for rebutting the presumption of bail.

The defendant need not be granted bail if the court is satisfied that there are substantial grounds for believing that the defendant, if released on bail (whether on conditions or not) would

(a)   fail to surrender to custody; or

(b)   commit an offence when on bail; or

(c)   interfere with witnesses or otherwise obstruct the course of justice, whether in relation to himself or any other person.

Thus, a court may remand someone in custody if there are substantial grounds for believing that they will re-offend. The 'substantial grounds' test is, in practice, a loose test which allows many more people than those who would normally wear the label 'dangerous' to be detained in pre-trial custody. In Canada, for example, detention in custody pre-trial is justified only if it is deemed 'necessary', a test which is more strictly interpreted (Trotter (1992); Padfield (1993)). Section 515(10) of the Canadian Criminal Code provides that:

... The detention of an accused in custody is justified only on either of the following grounds:

(a)   on the primary ground that his detention is necessary to ensure his attendance in court in order to be dealt with according to law; and

(b)   on the secondary ground (the applicability of which shall be determined only in the event that and after it is determined that his detention is not justified on the primary ground referred to in paragraph (a)) that his detention is necessary in the public interest or for the protection or safety of the public, having regard to all of the circumstances including any substantial likelihood that the accused will, if he is released from custody, commit a criminal offence or an interference with the administration of justice.

English law, in contrast, does not specify that securing attendance at trial is the primary ground for refusing bail. Nor does it spell out the public interest criteria for protecting the public. In England, the primary concern in recent years appears to have been the number of people committing offences on bail. Whilst the figures reveal that perhaps 10 per cent of offenders commit crimes whilst on bail, the public (and the media) are, understandably, particularly concerned when those on bail for serious offences of violence offend again. This has led to a number of recent statutory reforms.

First, the Bail (Amendment) Act 1993, which came into force in June 1994, gives the prosecution a right of appeal where a court (normally a magistrates' court) has granted bail to someone charged with a serious offence (one, in this context, which carries a maximum sentence of imprisonment of five or more years). As soon as the court receives oral notice of the prosecution's decision to appeal, the person is remanded in custody until after the appeal has been disposed of. The appeal must be heard within 48 hours (excluding weekends and public holidays). Prior to the new Act, there was no such right of appeal available to the prosecution. Figures have not yet been released as to the number of appeals in the first year of operation, nor of the proportion of such appeals which are successful. However, guidance from higher courts is likely to lead, if anything, to a more consistent practice in the magistrates' courts. The Act has not however been without difficulty: the decision of the Divisional Court of Queen's Bench Division of the High Court in *Re Bone* (1995) JP 111 revealed an important gap in the appeal process. The prosecution had appealed against the magistrates' decision to grant bail to a man charged with burglary and attempted burglary. Allowing the appeal, the Crown Court judge had remanded him in custody but had not stipulated the period of the remand, there being nothing in the 1993 Act to require him to fix a date. In the normal case of an application for bail to a Crown Court judge the applicant would be in custody awaiting trial in the Crown Court, so the judge is not obliged to state a date for the termination of the period in custody. The defendant in this case, however, applied successfully for *habeas corpus*, arguing that, whatever the powers of the Crown Court judge, he remained in the jurisdiction of the magistrates' court and that, by virtue of s. 128 and s. 129 of the Magistrates' Courts Act 1980, there is, in general, an eight-day time limit on remands in custody by the magistrates. The court recommended that in future Crown Court judges should always specify the period for which the person should remain in custody, remembering that the period should not exceed eight days from the date of the magistrates' order. When he makes such an order, the judge would not be doing so because the Act requires it, but because such an order was necessary to fill in a lacuna in the Act.

Secondly, two sections of the Criminal Justice and Public Order Act 1994 (CJPOA 1994) limited the presumption of bail. Section 26 inserted a new para. 2A in sch. 1 to the Bail Act 1976, which states:

2A. The defendant need not be granted bail if — (a) the offence is an indictable offence or an offence triable either way; and (b) it appears to the court that he was on bail in criminal proceedings on the date of the offence.

The key words are 'need not', and, here, again the extent to which courts will use para. 2A remains unclear. It would appear to add little or nothing to the existing para. 2: a court will surely have little difficulty in deciding that a defendant who is alleged to have committed a serious offence whilst on bail is likely to commit more offences, and therefore such a defendant would have been unlikely to obtain bail under the previous law.

The other limitation on bail in the CJPOA 1994 was introduced by s. 25, which provides that a defendant charged with or convicted of murder, attempted murder, rape or attempted rape or manslaughter is automatically remanded in custody if he or she has previous convictions for any of these offences. In reality, few such people would have been granted bail even before this enactment. Thus, the legislative tightening of bail may be purely cosmetic. More useful is s. 30 of the Act, which strengthens the courts' powers to reconsider a bail decision in an indictable case at any time if information comes to light which was not available to the police or the court when the original bail decision was taken. After reconsidering the matter the court may rescind or vary the conditions of bail, impose conditions of bail (if no conditions were previously imposed) or withhold bail. Lack of knowledge about the offender may be a major reason why many defendants have been refused bail in the past, and the fact that magistrates will know that they can reconsider their decision may lead to better decision-making.

However, the real problem here is how little knowledge magistrates often have when making their decision. An inter-agency committee, the Bail Issues Steering Group, under Home Office chairmanship, has been working since 1992 to improve the quality of decisions made, by enhancing the quality, accuracy and timeliness of the information available to magistrates. One interesting feature arising out of the Group's initial research was the fact that information on the defendant's criminal record is frequently incomplete and that it is often defence solicitors who are the first to note errors and significant omissions in the record (Burrows *et al* (1994)). This clearly puts the solicitor in a compromising position, especially when he is aware that his client is currently on bail from another court. The official guidance from the Law Society (Law Society (1992)) is that lists of previous convictions should be checked with defendants and that, while advocates are not obliged to make corrections, they should seek their client's consent to make corrections where it might hamper their case. The Law Society advises a policy of 'routinely denying to make any observations', if asked about the accuracy of antecedent reports, thus observing the duty of client confidentiality. If questions about bail are put directly to the defendant, who misleads or deceives the court, and the advocate knows that the answers are misleading or deceitful, then the Law Society's advice is that the solicitor should withdraw from representing the client forthwith.

Bail decisions are usually made swiftly: according to Doherty and East (1985) 87 per cent of bail hearings take less than 10 minutes. Whilst this is partly explained by the paucity of information available to magistrates, it also reflects the haste with which such decisions are taken. Hasty decisions can mean unthinking decisions. Eaton (1987) pointed out in her critical analysis of magistrates' bail decisions that women who are not tied into typical models are much less likely to be granted bail than other more 'typical' women. Brown and Hullin (1993), however, uncovered no significant differences in the treatment of defendants from different ethnic groups in their study of contested bail applications in Leeds in 1989. Regular monitoring of bail decisions, and training of magistrates, must continue in order that the 'right' suspects are remanded in custody.

Section 27 of the CJPOA 1994 gave the police the power, for the first time, to grant conditional bail to those charged. Magistrates have long been able to impose conditions on defendants as a term of their bail (e.g., that they report regularly to a police station or live at a certain address). The court may also feel the need to put an offender under some constraints, such as imposing a one-mile ban from a certain pub. The new power of the police to impose conditions may result either in more people being granted bail by the police than previously, or merely in more people being released on conditions, who would previously have been released unconditionally. This will also need careful monitoring.

Magistrates cannot remand someone in custody indefinitely. Under s. 128 of the Magistrates' Courts Act 1980, a magistrates' court has the power to remand a defendant in custody for up to eight days in the first instance, but thereafter may remand him or her for up to 28 days, provided that the defendant is present in court and has previously been remanded for the same offence. On conviction but pending appeal the offender may again apply for bail (see *Practice Direction: Bail Pending Appeal* [1983] 1 WLR 1292). Whether a person should be kept in custody pending an appeal against conviction, or, indeed, between conviction and the time sentence is passed, raises similar questions to those raised by bail generally.

It is, of course, difficult to assess whether more of those charged with serious offences could safely be left in the community. Two obvious statistics to compare are the rate of offending by those on bail with the acquittal rate of those who have been remanded in custody. Offending on bail is obviously a key factor, yet Morgan (1992) showed the difficulties involved in assessing the rates of offending while on bail. The proportion of defendants convicted of offences committed whilst on bail appears to be in the region of 10–12 per cent, but this varies from offence to offence. The other measure, the acquittal rate of those who have been remanded in custody, is approximately 20 per cent. Another 20 per cent of those remanded in custody ultimately receive community sentences, and a further 20 per cent of men (and a higher percentage of women offenders — over 30%) receive a fine, discharge or other non-custodial sentence. Only 41 per cent of men and 26 per cent of women remand prisoners ultimately receive a custodial sentence (Prison Statistics (1992); for a fuller discussion, see Morgan and Jones (1992)). Thus it can be argued that many of those who are remanded in custody are far from 'dangerous'. This begs a further question: whether pre-trial custody should concentrate on incarcerating the dangerous, or whether it should give priority to remanding in custody those who are thought likely to abscond.

When considering the law on remanding the dangerous in custody pre-trial, the practical and more important question, is whether the courts are capable of assessing those who constitute risks. At a time when much work is being carried out to provide courts with more information concerning those charged with offences (see Lloyd (1992); Stone (1988)), it should be of great concern that the remand population has been rising steadily — by around 200 per month between December 1993 and June 1994, when it attained a peak of 12,700. However, the increase has not been due simply to the number of people being prosecuted (a figure which, if anything, has declined) nor the percentage of defendants remanded in custody: the increase is due more to the fact that fewer defendants are dealt with at their first court appearance, and more are therefore remanded in custody or on bail. It is important that policy-makers should work on ways to reduce the length of time that people spend on remand, as well as on ways to reduce the number of people so held.

Sentencing Dangerous Offenders

For the purposes of this chapter, the sentencing powers of magistrates will be largely ignored. Although over 97 per cent of all criminal cases are decided in magistrates' courts, inevitably 'dangerous' offenders are most likely to find themselves before the Crown Court, which deals with the most serious offences. This chapter also looks only at the sentencing of those who have been deemed mentally fit to stand trial. Every year only a few people are found unfit to plead (see Mackay (1991); Grubin (1993)), although these figures may increase now that the Criminal Procedure (Insanity and Unfitness to Plead) Act 1991 has abolished the mandatory commitment to a psychiatric hospital for those found unfit to plead.

When a defendant pleads not guilty, questions of guilt are decided by the jury, but the judge alone imposes the sentence. The popular image of the judge continues to be that he enjoys a wide freedom in fixing the length of a prison sentence, yet both Parliament and the appellate courts have laid down significant contraints. The recent onslaught of Parliamentary guidance may not have improved, but rather hindered, judicial sentencing performance, in that the courts are less able to develop their own criteria for the imposition of various sentences, without falling foul of the technical details of much recent legislation.

Parliament has provided a statutory maximum penalty for most types of offence. Although normally laid down by statute when the offence was originally created or codified, these maxima are frequently altered in piecemeal ways (Ashworth (1994)). In reality, shifting the maximum is likely to have little effect on sentencing, since the maximum penalty for an offence is rarely imposed (except in the case of life sentences: see below). The Criminal Justice Act 1991 (which was substantially amended by the Criminal Justice Act 1993) went much further than previous acts in attempting to lay down not only maximum sentences, but a detailed and general framework within which sentencers should work. The straightforward message which lay behind the 1991 Act was that the sentence should be in proportion to the seriousness of the offence of which the offender was convicted. At the same time, however, the Act also allowed longer sentences for those from whom society was deemed to need greater protection. The Government made clear (Home Office (1990)) that it was following a twin-track policy, of significant penalties for serious offenders, but lower penalties for less serious crime. At the time it was not clear what effect the Act would have on sentencers: at one level it appeared to reproduce much of what sentencers were already doing, but using terms which were not clearly defined. Given that, in recent years, more effort has been put into the training of both judges and magistrates, and that the Court of Appeal has, at the same time, expanded its function of offering guideline judgments, the Criminal Justice Act 1991 has arguably not helped clarify the law, but, instead, has led to much greater confusion.

Non-custodial Orders of a Precautionary Kind

Although most precautionary sentences are custodial, there are some non-custodial measures which are designed to protect the public from dangerous people. These were unaffected by the framework of the Criminal Justice Act 1991. A court may disqualify a person from holding public office, from acting as a director of a company or from holding a dog licence. A person may be excluded from entering specified licensed public houses (s. 1 of the Licensed Premises (Exclusion of Certain Persons) Act 1980, or from football matches (s. 30 of the Public Order Act 1986; Football Spectators Act 1989). The most obvious example of a non-custodial order of a precautionary kind is disqualification from driving. Most driving offences are endorsable, and may result in the offender having penalty points endorsed on his licence. Once his penalty points have accumulated to 12 or more within a three-year period, he will be disqualified from holding a driving licence for a minimum period of six months.

Although the courts are wary of disqualifying even persistent offenders for long periods, fairly long periods of disqualification are sometimes upheld on appeal. Thus, in *Gibbons* (1987) 9 Cr App R (S) 21 the Court of Appeal dismissed an appeal against a sentence of 12 months' youth custody and a four-year period of disqualification. Peter Pain J said,

> We are told that the prisoner will be released next month, but there will still be three-and-a-half years of the disqualification to run, and that is a serious penalty for a young man who is obviously keen on cars and who has made a living connected with cars. But set against that, one has to consider the safety of the public. It clearly is miraculous that in this case nobody was even hurt in the course of these reckless 18 miles of driving and the fact that there has been an offence of a similar nature not so very long before may show that this young man is particularly excitable when under any form of stress. We share the view that was clearly taken by the learned recorder that it is necessary that he should be disqualified from driving for a sufficiently long period to give him the opportunity to mature to a state where he has got himself under better control and does not yield to the temptation to engage in this disgraceful form of endangering the public.

Another defendant who would clearly be labelled 'dangerous' by most people was *Spence* (1993) 15 Cr App R (S) 653. He pleaded guilty to causing death by careless driving, having consumed alcohol well over the prescribed limit. He had several previous convictions for driving with excess alcohol, was uninsured and had never held a driving licence. The pre-sentence report stated that he still did not regard his intake of alcohol before driving as anything but normal, and considered that it had nothing whatever to do with the offences he committed. It is hardly surprising that the Court of Appeal upheld his sentence of two years' imprisonment and disqualification for four years.

It may be that the penalties for such offences are slowly increasing, after a gentle nudge from Parliament. The Criminal Justice Act 1993 increased the maximum penalty for causing death by dangerous driving to 10 years, and created a new offence of causing death by careless driving while under the influence of alcohol or drugs, with a similar maximum penalty. Following this lead the Court of Appeal recently upheld the disqualification for life of an alcoholic who drove his Mercedes at over 100 mph on a motorway, killing two lorry drivers, and who had more than three times the limit of alcohol in his blood (*Attorney General's Reference (No. 22 of 1993)* (1995) 16 Cr App R (S) 670).

This discussion has already highlighted one major problem: do the courts have any clear idea of who to label 'dangerous'? Bottoms (1977) pointed out that persistent drunken drivers and uncaring factory owners who keep unsafe places of work are not treated as 'dangerous' in the same way as repeat assaultists. Striking modern examples are found in the low penalties imposed on those who cause severe environmental pollution: relatively low levels of fine are the maximum penalty which are imposed even in serious cases of river pollution (Padfield (1995, p. 693)). However, the emphasis in this chapter will be on the law which allows the detention in custody of individual violent offenders who are sentenced to terms of imprisonment. Perhaps the reluctance of the Court of Appeal to encourage greater use by trial judges of their powers to impose longer sentences on dangerous offenders is partly explained by an awareness of the definitional problems, as well as of the difficulties in predicting risk.

Custodial Sentences

There are two main grounds for imposing a custodial sentence: s. 1(2) of the Criminal Justice Act 1991 provides that either the offence, or the combination of the offence and other offences associated with it, was so serious that only such a sentence can be justified for the offence; or, where the offence is a violent or sexual offence, only such a sentence would be adequate to protect the public from serious harm from the offender. These grounds will be referred to in this chapter as 'the seriousness ground' (s. 1(2)(a)) and 'the dangerousness ground' (s. 1(2)(b)). The Act makes clear that the sentencer must specify the ground on which he is relying.

Imposing a Commensurate Sentence: the Seriousness Ground

The first, and most common, ground for imposing a custodial sentence is that the offence was so serious that only such a sentence can be justified. It leaves the judge free to impose a sentence which is 'commensurate' with the seriousness of the offence. In practice, judges seem happy to use this ground for imposing long sentences on dangerous offenders, and do not often use their powers to impose longer than commensurate sentences.

Under s. 2(2)(a) of the Criminal Justice Act 1991, the length of a sentence is 'for such term (not exceeding the permitted maximum) as in the opinion of the court is commensurate with the seriousness of the offence, or the combination of the offence and one or more offences associated with it'. Although the Act did not attempt to define seriousness, the Court of Appeal in two of the first cases decided under the Act, *Baverstock* [1993] 1 WLR 202 and *Cox* [1993] 1 WLR 188, applied Lawton LJ's definition in *Bradbourn* (1985) 7 Cr App R (S) 180, formulated in relation to s. (4) of the Criminal Justice Act 1982:

The kind of offence which when committed by a young person would make all right-thinking members of the public, knowing all the facts, feel that justice had not been done by the passing of any sentence other than a custodial one.

Judges continue to choose a particular sentence by considering the 'tariff' for the offence, laid down in guideline judgments of the Court of Appeal, mostly in appeals against sentence, and by following their own instincts. The Court of Appeal will vary the sentence imposed at trial only where it was 'manifestly excessive or wrong in principle' (s. 11 of the Criminal Appeals Act 1968), and so the judge's discretion is rarely interfered with. In 1993 there were only 1,309 successful appeals (out of 4,848 applications for leave to appeal against sentence) to the Court of Appeal. The remaining 69,500 offenders sentenced in the Crown Court did not appeal.

Whilst the Criminal Justice Act 1991 had provided that a sentencer, in deciding whether a case was adequately serious, could look at only one other associated offence, the Criminal Justice Act 1993 amended this so that now the court may look at 'one or more' associated offences. The philosophy of the original 1991 Act appeared to be 'just deserts', that the offender receive the 'right' penalty for the offence in question. However, many offenders are convicted of offences which, viewed individually, may appear relatively minor, but which in reality form part of a more serious pattern of offending. In *Bexley, Summer and Harrison* [1993] 1 WLR 192, another of the first cases to reach the Court of Appeal under this provision, Lord Taylor, the Lord Chief Justice, explained that the previous offences were still relevant in demolishing false pleas in mitigation. However, his words failed to convince the public, the judiciary, or probably himself. He stated at a press conference in September 1992 that people might find it 'strange' that judges were not allowed to consider other convictions when passing sentence, and in *Bexley* itself he pointed out 'the extraordinary anomaly' caused by s. 29 that a court could take into account as an aggravating feature the commission of an offence on bail, but not the failure to respond to a probation order or suspended sentence.

The original s. 29 compounded this problem by requiring a court to ignore previous convictions unless they demonstrated aggravating features of the offence for which sentence was being passed. This section made little sense, but probably only meant that a bad record should not lead to a disproportionate sentence. However, the Home Secretary feared that the section might be being interpreted as meaning that courts were no longer allowed to take notice of previous convictions. The Criminal Justice Act 1993 amended s. 29, so that:

(1)   In considering the seriousness of any offence, the court may now take into account any previous convictions of the offender or any failure of his to respond to previous sentences.

It also makes it compulsory (in s. 29(2)) for the court to treat offending while on bail as an aggravating feature. Wasik and von Hirsch (1994) argue that the new s. 29 need not be seen as abandoning the conventional theory of 'progresive loss of mitigation', which means that:

> ... while a first offender may present a good case for mitigation in the light of his record, the accumulation of previous convictions results in the progressive loss of that mitigation so that, by the time of the fourth or fifth conviction, all mitigation for a clean record is lost and the offender is sentenced in accordance with the seriousness of the offence (Wasik (1993), p. 69).

Whatever interpretation is put upon it, the amendment reflected a significant change in Government policy.

More problems for sentencers have been created by s. 48 of the CJPOA 1994, which introduces a statutory discount for guilty pleas. For many years, for pragmatic reasons of saving costs and time, courts have given discounts for guilty pleas. In *Claydon* (1994) 15 Cr App R (S) 526 the Court of Appeal went so far as to say that where an offender voluntarily surrenders and confesses, a sentence discount of 50 per cent was appropriate. Now, s. 48 of the CJPOA 1994 requires all courts, when passing sentence, to take account of the timing and other circumstances of a plea of guilty. This creates practical difficulties for sentencers: its application to offenders sentenced to long sentences, especially to those being sentenced under s. 1(2)(b), may cause trial judges something of a headache. Commenting on two cases in which the defendants had sought unsuccessfully to rely on s. 48 to reduce their sentences, even though they had had no possible realistic defence, Thomas stated (at [1995] Crim LR 662) that:

> ... The defendant who is most likely to give an early indication of an intention to plead guilty is precisely the defendant whose case is hopeless, and to continue to deny a discount to such an offender, as these cases indicate is permissible, might be seen to run contrary to the legislative policy of encouraging an early indication of the intention to plead guilty.

One should surely question the justification for discounting a sentence which has been 'justly deserved'. Not only is there a real danger that this statutory discount may lead those who are not guilty to plead guilty (see Sanders and Young (1994), but it makes little sense in desert terms.

Longer Sentences for Dangerous Offenders

The law has long allowed certain offenders to be detained for longer than was justified by their immediate offence. Before 1992, the appropriate sentence in England had been preventive detention (1908–1967), and subsequently the extended sentence, introduced in the Criminal Justice Act 1967. Section 37 of the 1967 Act, entitled 'Punishment of persistent offenders', allowed a court to impose an extended term of imprisonment on a persistent offender who had been convicted on indictment of an offence carrying a maximum prison sentence of at least two years. A persistent offender was one who:

(a)   had committed the most recent offence within three years of a previous conviction for an offence punishable similarly, or within three years of his release from prison for such an offence; and

(b)   had been convicted on indictment for a similar offence on at least three previous occasions since his twenty-first birthday; and

(c)   the total length of imprisonment to which he had been sentenced on earlier occasions was not less than five years (one of which had to have been a term of at least three years, or two sentences for two years or more). The court had to be satisfied 'by reason of his previous conduct and of the likelihood of his committing further offences, that it [was] expedient to protect the public from him for a substantial time'.

Extended sentences have been used, at times, more as a way of punishing a man for his record and not necessarily as a way of protecting the public. The interpretation of s. 37 of the 1967 Act caused much difficulty (see, for example, the House of Lords' decision in *DPP* v *Ottewell* [1970] AC 642), being used sometimes to extend sentences, but also, with the introduction of parole in 1967, simply to ensure compulsory aftercare until the end of a sentence and not simply to the usual two-thirds point. Extended sentences were rarely used, and were imposed more frequently on property offenders than on those who committed crimes of violence against the person. Thomas (1969) was doubtless not alone when he called for the repeal of s. 37 so that the courts could be allowed to evolve their own policies by means of their existing powers.

The new 'longer than commensurate' sentences introduced in the Criminal Justice Act 1991 are limited to a much narrower collection of offences than those which attracted extended sentences, but they are clearly designed for offenders who are perceived to be 'dangerous' and not merely 'recidivist'. Section 2(2)(b) provides that, where the offence is a violent or sexual offence, the length of the sentence should be for such longer term (not exceeding the maximum) as 'in the opinion of the court is necessary to protect the public from the offender'. This is construed as a reference to protecting members of the public from death or serious personal injury, whether physical or psychological, occasioned by further such offences committed by the offender. Where a court passes a custodial sentence for a term longer than is commensurate with the seriousness of the offence, the court must state in open court why it is of the opinion that s. 2(2)(b) applies, and must explain to the offender in open court and in ordinary language why the sentence is for such a term (s. 2(3)). A useful research project would monitor and analyse the reasons given by trial judges. Interestingly, s. 2(4) states that a custodial sentence for an indeterminate period is regarded as a custodial sentence for a term longer than any actual term. This appears to mean that an indeterminate sentence may only be passed where the case falls within the scope of s. 2(2)(b).

The Court of Appeal has made it clear that a sentencer should not impose a longer than normal sentence lightly, especially since even a sentence under s. 2(2)(a) is likely to include an element of public protection. Thus, for example, in *Mumtaz Ali* [1995] Crim LR 260, the Court of Appeal reduced a sentence of three years imposed under s. 2(2)(b) to two years under s. 2(2)(a). In that case, the appellant had driven alongside a young woman walking home shortly after midnight, and had attempted to force her into his car. He was convicted of assault occasioning actual bodily harm. The Court of Appeal held that there was no evidence of dangerous and serious harm in the future. The appellant was a young man of essentially good previous character; there was nothing in his record or in the pre-sentence report that suggested that the offence was anything other than aberration. The offence was serious, and must have had either a sexual motive or one of financial gain, but the court said that a single offence of this kind was not in itself sufficient evidence to allow the statutory test to be satisfied.

In the more serious case of *Christie* (1995) 16 Cr App R (S) 469 the Court of Appeal similarly reduced a sentence of 16 years imposed under s. 2(2)(b) to one of 12 years under s. 2(2)(a). The appellant was involved in a series of robberies of jewellery shops in which firearms or imitation firearms were carried and where property to the value of £17,000 had been stolen. He had 13 previous convictions for various offences, including one for robbery in which guns were used. The Court of Appeal stated that the defedant had plainly demonstrated his willingness to commit offences of the gravest nature, involving, if necessary, the use of a firearm. Noting that the sentences were slightly higher than the starting point suggested by *Turner* (1975) 61 Cr App R 67 for the gravest kind of armed robbery, the court pointed out that when *Turner* was decided there was no statutory provision permitting a court to pass a sentence greater than that which might be considered commensurate with the gravity of the offence. When a court is dealing with offences of great gravity such as armed robbery, the court in *Christie* said that it was incumbent on the court to guard against the danger of effectively imposing an element of the sentence twice over. Where the commensurate sentence for the offence was likely to contain an element which was designed to protect the public, it was wrong in principle to apply s. 2(2)(b) in order to impose a greater length. The message from the Court of Appeal is clear — trial judges should not make use of the powers under s. 2(2)(b) lightly.

Perhaps three main factors explain this reluctance. First, the courts are aware of the human rights/civil liberties concerns that an offender should not be imprisoned except as a punishment for a crime for which he has been convicted — hence, the 'just deserts' rationale of the Criminal Justice Act 1991 generally. Secondly, since there is no precise measure of the appropriate length of even a 'deserved' sentence, it is much more difficult to fix the length of a 'longer than normal' sentence. Thirdly, judges are well aware of the unreliability of predictions of dangerousness, with the danger of significant over-predictions. As Thomas (1994) points out, it is important that the court identifies the evidence on the basis of which the future behaviour of the offender is predicted. Normally this will include previous convictions, the pre-sentence report, psychiatric reports and the facts of the present case. However, in *Crow and Pennington* [1994] Crim LR 958 the court upheld a sentence under s. 2(2)(b) imposed on an offender with no previous convictions on the basis simply of pre-sentence reports. Again, in *Thomas* [1994] Crim LR 174 the Court of Appeal did not accept the submission that there had to be previous violent offending before a violent offender could be made the subject of an order under s. 2(2)(b). The court listed a number of matters which, either in combination or singularly, might lead to such an order. However, in *Thomas* itself, the court reduced a nine-year sentence, passed as a longer than normal sentence under s. 2(2)(b), to one of six years under s. 2(2)(a). The appellant had attacked a woman shop assistant, hitting her on the head with a stone. He pleaded guilty to wounding with intent to cause grievous bodiy harm and attempt robbery. He had previous convictions for theft, but none for violence, except assault on a constable in 1984. These facts, together with divergent psychiatric reports, did not the court held, merit an order under s. 2(2)(b). It seems inappropriate that predictions of dangerousness should ever be made by a court on the basis of one offence only.

Longer sentences under s. 1(2)(b) may be imposed only in the case of 'sexual or violent offences', which are defined in s. 31. 'Sexual offences' are defined by reference to specific statutory provision, which, curiously, omitted reference to attempts. However, the Court of Appeal had no difficulty in *Robinson* (1992)

14 Cr App R (S) 448 in deciding that attempted rape came within the ambit of a sexual offence as defined in s. 31. They upheld a sentence of eight years in a young offender institution imposed on a 16-year-old convicted of burglary and attempted rape, committed on a widow aged 87. A violent offence is one 'which leads or is intended or is likely to lead to a person's death or to physical injury to a person'. This has already led to a number of surprising decisions in the Court of Appeal (see *Richart* [1995] Crim LR 574; *Rogg* [1995] Crim LR 664). As Thomas comments (at [1995] Crim LR 665), 'a man who utters threats to kill, which he may mean to carry out, does not commit a "violent offence" for the purposes of the Act; a burglar who cuts his own hand breaking into a garden shed does (because the offence "leads ... To physical injury to a person")'. The Court of Appeal in *Richart* recommended an amendment to s. 31, but there is no sign that the Government has accepted the need to act.

A 'longer than commensurate' sentence cannot exceed the statutory maximum available for the offence charged. Some offences still have remarkably low maxima: for example, the maximum penalty for the offence of unlawful wounding (contrary to s. 20 of the Offences Against the Person Act 1861) remains at five years' imprisonment. In *Hashi* (1995) Cr App R (S) 121 the Court of Appeal upheld a five-year (i.e., maximum) sentence on a 60-year-old, originally from Somalia, whose jealousy of his ex-wife resulted in the attack in question. The case also raised the issue of whether the risk had to be to the public in general. Judge J had 'no hesitation' in applying precisely the same principle as applied by Mustill LJ in *Birch* (1989) 11 Cr App R (S) 202 (discussed below) in relation to the imposition of retriction orders under the Mental Health Act 1983, that 'the harm in question need not in our view be limited to personal injury or need it relate to the public in general, for it would in our judgment suffice if a category of persons or even a single person were adjudged to be at risk, although the category of person so protected would no doubt exclude the offender himself'.

Until 1988 only the defendant had the right to appeal, but under s. 36 of the Criminal Justice Act 1988 the Attorney General can now refer unduly lenient sentences to the Court of Appeal. There have been several appeals by the prosecution challenging the failure of trial judges to use their powers under s. 2(2)(b). Thus, in *Attorney General's Reference (No. 9 of 1994)* [1994] Crim LR 956, a sentence of six years was increased by the Court of Appeal to nine years. The appellant had run a football club and was convicted of 10 counts of indecent assault, buggery and attempted buggery on young boys. The court commented that if the trial judge had used his powers under s. 2(2)(b) a sentence of 10 years would have been appropriate. As was noted above in relation to the new power of the prosecution to appeal unfavourable bail decisions, the main impact of these Attorney General's references against unduly lenient sentences should be greater consistency amongst sentencers. Henham (1994) suggests that because of the limitations of the present procedure it should either be abolished or replaced by a general prosecution right of appeal.

Discretionary Life Sentences

Another example of the use of the Attorney General's reference procedure is *No. 6 of 1993* (1993) 15 Cr App R (S) 375, in which the court took the opportunity to clarify the procedure for fixing the period which a judge should specify under s. 34 in cases of discretionary life sentences. A life sentence is a possible sentence for a number of offences such as rape, manslaughter and robbery. The criteria to be met before a court should impose a life sentence were set out in *Hodgson* (1967) 52 Cr App R 113. First, the offence must in itself be grave enough to require a very long sentence; secondly, the offender must be a person of mental instability who, if at liberty, will probably re-offend and present a grave danger to the public; and, thirdly, it must appear that the offender will remain unstable and a potential danger for a long or uncertain time. Lord Lane CJ in *Wilkinson* (1983) 5 Cr App R (S) 105 said that:

> ... it seems to us that a sentence of life imprisonment, other than for an offence when the sentence is obligatory, is really appropriate and must only be passed in the most exceptional circumstances. With a few exceptions ... it is reserved, broadly speaking, for offenders who for one reason or another cannot be dealt with under the Mental Health Act, yet who are in a mental state which makes them dangerous to the life or limb of members of the public. It is sometimes impossible to say when that danger will subside, and therefore an indeterminate sentence is required, so that the prisoner's progress may be monitored by those who have him under their supervision.

More recently the Court of Appeal considered the criteria in *Spear* (1995) Cr App R (S) 242 and substituted a sentence of 10 years' imprisonment for the life sentence imposed at trial. Spear had pleaded guilty to wounding with intent to cause grievous bodily harm. He went to the house where his former girlfriend and their child lived, and, in a fight, stabbed his former girlfriend's brother twice with a lock knife. There was evidence that Spear suffered from a severe paranoid personality disorder, with a tendency to react with violence if he felt wronged or slighted, but was not suffering from mental illness. He had several previous convictions for offences involving violence or possessing an offensive weapon, and the offence was committed only one month after he had been released from a sentence of three years' imprisonment for wounding with intent to cause grievous bodily harm. The court was 'concerned about whether in truth the second criterion laid down in *Hodgson* [was] satisfied', and so decided against a life sentence.

When the judge decides to impose a life sentence, s. 34 allows him to specify the part of the sentence which is appropriate 'taking into account the seriousness of the offence, or the combination of the offence and other offences associated with it'. In *Practice Direction (Imposition of Discretionary Life Sentence)* (1993) 1 WLR 223, Lord Taylor explained that the discretionary life sentence should be seen to fall into two parts: (a) the relevant part, which consists of the period of detention imposed for punishment and deterrence, taking into account the seriousness of the offence; and (b) the remaining part of the sentence, during which the prisoner's detention will be governed by considerations of risk to the public. The judge must indicate reasons for reaching his decision as to the length of the relevant part. The role of the judge in these cases is thus limited to deciding the period that the prisoner should serve by way of punishment or deterrence, and the Parole Board then decides whether he still represents a danger to the public. In *Hollies* (1994) 16 Cr App R (S) 463 the Court of Appeal made clear that only in cases of exceptional gravity, where the judge thought that a prisoner should remain a prisoner for the rest of his life, should the judge not specify a period under the Act. Hollies had been sentenced to life imprisonment for six offences of rape, one of wounding with intent to cause grievous bodily harm, and three of soliciting to murder, but the judge did not specify a period for the purposes of s. 34. The Court of Appeal held that the sentencer, although right to consider the appellant to be a danger to young women, should still have specified a period under s. 34. In *Hollies*, the Court of Appeal specified 12 years under s. 34, on the basis that the equivalent determinate sentence would have been a term of 20 years. The period specified should be between one half and two-thirds of what would have been the appropriate determinate sentence. This parallels the parole rules for offenders sentenced to more than four years' imprisonment, who will be released on parole at some point between the one half and two-thirds point in the sentence: early release and parole rules are considered in chapter 8.

Thus, it is now clear that the sentencing judge should normally specify a period under s. 34, and this period itself may be the subject of an appeal. The appropriate procedure has been made clear in a number of cases. In *D* (1994) 16 Cr App R 564, for example, the appellant admitted raping his mother a few months after being released from a sentence of six years for indecently assaulting her. He did not challenge the life sentence, but appealed against the period of 12 years specified for the purposes of s. 34. Lord Taylor CJ had no doubt that a right of appeal existed. The trial judge had specified that if he had imposed a determinate sentence, it would have been 18 years, and on that basis fixed the relevant period as 12 years. The Court of Appeal held that that was too high a figure to take as a starting point. Having regard to *Billam* (1986) 8 Cr App R (S) 48 the appropriate starting point would have been 15 years, and taking two-thirds of that resulted in a period of 10 years. Lord Taylor CJ stressed that 10 years was not necessarily the period that would be sufficient for the appellant's detention: whether he would be fit to be released at that time was a matter which could only be considered then. Another case of pre-meditated rape was *Fox* (1994) Cr App R (S) 370. The appellant, who worked at a mental hospital, committed offences against five mentally deficient women. He would offer the victim a lift in his car, and then have intercourse with her before abandoning her in a remote place. He did not challenge a sentence of life imprisonment, but claimed that the period of 12 years specified under s. 34 was too long. The Court of Appeal considered that the sentencer's starting point of 18 years was too high; the starting point should have been 15 years, and therefore the appropriate period for the relevant part should have been 10 years. That period was therefore substituted for the period fixed by the trial judge, but the life sentence remained. Lord Taylor emphasised that:

> It should be clearly understood by members of the public that the period of 10 years which we have fixed is not a finite sentence at the end of which the appellant will be released. It is only the period before which he should not even be considered for release by the parole Board.

Another example is *Murray* (1995) Cr App R (S) 17, in which the Court of Appeal varied to five years the period of eight years specified as the relevant part of a discretionary life sentence. The appellant, who had stabbed the woman with whom he was living and had driven her body to the police station, pleaded guilty to manslaughter by reason of diminished responsibility. He had been previously convicted of wounding his wife with intent to cause grievous bodily harm, and there was psychiatric evidence that he might transfer his beliefs of sexual infidelity to any subsequent partner. Russell LJ stressed the need to divorce the circumstances of the offence from the future risk to the community.

It is thus becoming increasingly clear that the role of the judge is merely to fix the 'tariff' for punishment: questions of future risk are to be left to the Discretionary Lifer Panel of the Parole Board (see chapter 8).

Mandatory Life Sentences

Since the Murder (Abolition of the Death Penalty) Act 1965, a mandatory life sentence has been imposed on all those convicted of murder (although those aged between 10 and 18 at the time of the offence will be sentenced to detention during Her Majesty's pleasure). While an increasingly vociferous lobby suggests that the time has come to repeal the mandatory sentence, the Government has continued to argue the case that the mandatory sentence marks the fact that murder is an exceptionally heinous crime. The issue has recently been considered by the Home Affairs of the House of Commons, which reported in December 1995, (First Report, Session 1995–6: HC 111) reaching the preliminary conclusion that, even though the mandatory sentence for murder should not be abolished, the responsibility for setting the tariff and for taking decisions on release should be removed from the Home Secretary because it is wrong in principle for the executive (i.e., a politician) to have a role in decisions which determine how long a person spends in prison.

Even in a mandatory life sentence case, it is within the judge's discretion to suggest a minimum period that the prisoner should serve before being considered for release. Normally, however, the judge will say no such thing in open court. He will then be asked to complete a form in which both he and the Lord Chief Justice are consulted as to the period which the prisoner should serve before being considered for reiease. This 'tariff' period for the penal element may be overruled by the Home Secretary. The opinion of the judges is 'no more than a component of the entire body of material' (per Lord Mustill in *Doody* v *Secretary of State for the Home Department* [1993] 3 All ER 92). A prisoner is now entitled to know the Home Secretary's reasons for departing from any judicial recommendation, and to be given information regarding the substance of that advice (*Parole Board, ex parte Wilson* [1992] 2 All ER 576). In *Doody*, Lord Mustill, whilst repeating emphatically that 'Parliament has left the discretion to release with the Home Secretary, and that he has done nothing to yield it up', granted the following declarations:

(1) The Secretary of State is required to afford to a prisoner serving a mandatory life sentence the opportunity to submit in writing representations as to the period he should serve for the purpose of retribution and deterrence before the Secretary of State sets the date of the first review of the prisoner's sentence;

(2) Before giving the prisoner the opportunity to make such representations, the Secretary of State is required to inform him of the period recommended by the judiciary as the period he should serve for the purpose of retribution and deterrence, and of any other opinion expressed by the judiciary which is relevant to the Secretary of State's decision as to the appropriate period to be served for these purposes;

(3) The Secretary of State is obliged to give reasons for departing from the period recommended by the judiciary as the period which he should serve for the purpose of retribution and deterrence.

Rarely does a judge mention in open court a minimum recommended period that a murderer should serve before being considered for release, a power that is granted in s. 1(2) of the Murder (Abolition of Death Penalty) Act 1965. Even when he does, the prisoner may not appeal this recommendation, nor is it subject to judicial review. In *Leaney* [1995] Crim LR 670, the trial judge recommended that a man convicted of murder should serve a minimum period of 20 years. Although the Court of Appeal made it clear that it thought that the recommendation in the case was excessive, it considered itself powerless to do anything about it, and the Lord Chief Justice urged that the matter 'ought to be reconsidered by Parliament as a matter of urgency'. It is an interesting question whether the Court of Appeal was truly powerless. The main authority (relied on in subsequent cases, admittedly) for not allowing an appeal in these circumstances, is *Aitken* (1966) 50 Cr App R 204. So much has changed since 1966, that, arguably, this was a case where the Court of Appeal could have felt free to reconsider its previous decision.

The 'due process' improvements introduced by the courts in recent years have not affected the final discretion of the Home Secretary. In 1994, when all mandatory lifers were told their minimum sentence, approximately 20 were were told that the minimum period was their natural life. The Government argues that to allow judges to decide the sentence for murder would weaken the public's confidence in the criminal justice system. This view was accepted unquestioningly in the European Court of Human Rights in *Wynne* v *UK* (1994) 19 EHRR 333. Wynne sought to rely on the court's earlier ruling in *Thynne* (1991) 13 EHRR 666, that Art. 5(4) of the European Convention of Human Rights, which gives discretionary life sentence prisoners the right to have the continued lawfulness of their detention reviewed, should also apply to offenders sentenced to a mandatory sentence. The court said bluntly that:

> The fact remains that the mandatory sentence belongs to a different category from the discretionary sentence in the sense that it is imposed automatically as the punishment for the offence of murder irrespective of considerations pertaining to the dangerousness of the offender. That mandatory life prisoners do not actually spend the rest of their lives in prison and that a notional tariff period is also established in such cases ... does not alter this essential distinction between the two types of life sentence.

The European Commission, on the other hand, had not accepted the Government's position so readily. It had been split 10–5, the dissenting Opinion challenging the Government's case in a way which was not examined at all by the court, which pointed out that:

While the Government contends that an additional factor, namely, the consideration of the maintenance of public confidence in the criminal justice system, is operative in mandatory cases, we note that in the 1987 policy statement this was relevant to the stage of deciding as to the appropriate length of the tariff and was not stated to be a factor which could require the continued detention of a person who had served his tariff and was no longer considered a risk. We further have doubts as to whether the criterion of maintaining public confidence is not merely a restatement of the risk principle.

These are powerful questions to raise. If the life sentence for murder became discretionary, it would continue to be imposed on those who committed the most dangerous offences. Arguments about the public's perception of the criminal justice system can be applied in many directions.

Mentally Abnormal Offenders

Not all dangerous offenders necessarily find themselves in prison. HO Circular 66/1990 encourages the diversion of mentally disordered people from the criminal justice system. However, 'the arrangements for the care and treatment of mentally disordered offenders remains fragmented, characterised by virtually unfettered discretion at the point of transfer from one institution to the other, and a woeful lack of provision at the least secure end of the psychiatric system' (Fennell (1991)). The Mental Health Act 1983 allows the court, instead of sentencing a prisoner, to make a hospital order. Whenever the court is considering passing a custodial sentence on a person who is, or who appears to the court to be, mentally disordered, the court must first obtain a medical report (s. 4(1) of the Criminal Justice Act 1991). The court may make a hospital order on the evidence of two doctors that the person suffers from a mental disorder needing treatment. However, many offenders who would appear to require better treatment than that available in prison often are not committed to hospital for one of three reasons.

First, the offender must be suffering from one of the categories listed in the Mental Health Act 1983: 'mental illness, psychopathic disorder, severe mental impairment or mental impairment' (s. 1(2)). Secondly, the offender's condition must be 'treatable'. It seems extraordinary that a mentally ill offender whose condition appears to be untreatable is therefore held in prison and not in hospital. Thirdly, there may not be adequate hospital space. A hospital may refuse to accept an offender, either because there is no bed available, or because of concern for the safety of staff. If the judge considers that the offender is a danger to the public and yet he cannot find a secure mental hospital willing to take the offender, the judge may have no option but to pass a prison sentence. Once a hospital order has been made, the offender may be held initially for six months. At the end of that period a medical report will be prepared on him which may authorise the hospital managers to hold him for a further six months. This process may be repeated at yearly intervals. After the first six months, the patient has the right to apply to the hospital's Mental Health Review Tribunal (MHRT) for his case to be considered, and his nearest relative has a similar right.

A Crown Court judge may add a restriction order if he considers it 'necessary to do so to protect the public from serious harm' (s. 41 of the Mental Health Act). This involves the court in predicting dangerousness in a way which should be compared with the procedures discussed above in relation to s. 2(2)(b) of the Criminal Justice Act 1991. Section 41(1) specifies the factors which must be considered before a restriction order is imposed: the court must have 'regard to the nature of the offence, the antecedents of the offender and the risk of his committing further offences if set at large'. In *Courtney* (1987) 9 Cr App R (S) 404, a man suffering from depression pleaded guilty to the manslaughter of his wife by reason of diminished responsibility. The Court of Appeal upheld a hospital order but removed the restriction order which had been imposed, without restriction of time. Watkins LJ held that, 'the question is, did the evidence point to the likely fact that if he is released in the relatively near future, he would constitute a danger to other members of the public?'. However, no further explanation of this question was given.

In *Birch* (1989) 11 Cr App R (S) 202, on the other hand, Mustill LJ (as he then was) explored the difficulties of the statutory definition in some detail. He stressed that a fundamental change is effected if a restriction order is added to a hospital order: the patient's interests are no longer paramount. The judge need not necessarily follow medical advice, and has jurisdiction to impose the restriction order even where doctors are unanimous that the offender is not dangerous. Perhaps most difficult to apply is Mustill LJ's advice that the judge may still send the offender to prison if he considers that, notwithstanding his mental disorder, there was an element of culpability in the offence which merits punishment, for example where there is no connection between the mental disorder and the offence. The effect of a restriction order is that the offender may not be released without the consent of the Secretary of State or an MHRT, but Mustill LJ stated that it is permissible for the judge to take into account the MHRT's powers which 'have an important effect in minimising the starkness of the practical difference between restricted and unrestricted orders'. Despite this, Mustill LJ saw fit to criticise the Mental Health Act in unusually strong terms:

It might have been better if the conflicting social policies reflected in the Act had been expressed in terms which set less stringent conditions for a restriction order, with perhaps a more flexible regime for discharge. As it is, the choice between a disposal which risks being too severe and one which with hindsight may be shown disastrously to have been not severe enough is posed in the terms of s. 41.

How does the court make this choice in practice? If an offender qualifies for a hospital order with restrictions, and a bed is available in a suitable hospital, the general rule is that a hospital order should be made. The Court of Appeal made clear in *Howell* (1985) 7 Cr App R (S) 360 that it is wrong to impose a life sentence in order merely to prevent the patient's possible release by an MHRT.

A person serving a prison sentence may, on the recommendation of two doctors, be transferred to a hospital by direction of the Home Secretary (s. 47 of the Mental Health Act 1983). When making a transfer direction, the Home Secretary may also make a restriction direction. It is clearly a fine line which distinguishes those deemed dangerous who serve their sentence in prison and those who serve it in hospital, and the appellate courts are remarkably resistant to giving trial judges clear advice. Mentally disordered offenders are not an isolated category. Peay (1994) argued convincingly that efforts should be devoted to developing a pluralistic model of the criminal justice system: 'piecemeal tinkering may provide solutions for the problems posed by specific offenders; it is insufficient as a basis for addressing problems across the ordered–disordered offending continuum'. By providing the Mental Health Act route to compulsory detention, Parliament has upheld the stark distinction between normal and abnormal offenders which many find unhelpful. Certainly, psychiatric services are needed in prison as much as they are in hospitals.

Conclusion

Despite Parliament's attempt in the Criminal Justice Act 1991 to impose a framework for judges and magistrates on sentencing, English judges continue to have wide discretionary powers when it comes to imprisoning offenders. However, the release of dangerous offenders may depend less on what the judge says in court than on what the Parole Board and Home Secretary decide in due course. The message from Parliament in recent years has been that, whilst the judge must fix the appropriate tariff period which an offender should serve in prison to meet the demands of punishment and deterrence, it is for the Parole Board and Home Secretary to deal exclusively with questions of risk. In bail decisions, the courts are given much wider powers to remand in custody not only the dangerous but also those who may, for example, abscond or interfere with witnesses, but this is explicable on the basis that remands in pre-trial custody cover only relatively short lengths of time. Time spent in custody on remand will also count towards the eventual sentence imposed after trial.

Any review of sentencing law and individual sentencing cases leads to a consideration of the fundamental question of whether overall sentencing levels in this country are too high or too low (see Ashworth (1994)). Statistics appear to show that offenders are imprisoned more frequently and for longer periods in England and Wales than in other European countries, although less frequently than in the United States. Downes (1988) compared trends in the Netherlands and England to identify forces which have led to a significant lowering of sentence levels in the Netherlands in recent years, whilst at the same time sentence levels in this country have increased. There was some hope that after the enactment of the Criminal Justice Act 1991 the length of custodial sentences in England and Wales would, if anything, decrease. However, with the changes introduced in 1993, the current trend continues upward, but at the same time, the influence of the judge in fixing the precise length of the sentence may be diminishing. As we have seen, if a judge considers a person to be a danger to the public, he may exceptionally impose a longer than normal sentence or even a life sentence, but in those circumstances the judge has only to make clear the period which the offender would have served had he not posed this exceptional risk. After that, the question of release will be considered by the Parole Board. It is therefore increasingly to the Parole Board and not to the trial judge that we have to look for guidance on when those deemed dangerous may be released.

References

Ashworth, A. (1994) 'Sentencing', in the *Oxford Handbook of Criminology*, (eds Maguire, M., Morgan, R. and Reiner, R.) Oxford: Oxford University Press.

Bottoms, A. E. (1977) 'The Renaissance of Dangerousness', *Howard Journal*, 16, pp. 70 *ff*.

Brown, I. & Hullin, R. (1993) 'Contested Bail Applications: the treatment of ethnic minority and white offenders', *Criminal Law Review*, pp. 107 *ff*.

Burrows, J. N., Henderson, P. F. & Morgan, P. M. (1995) *Improving Bail Decisions: the bail process project, phase 1*, Home Office Research and Planning Unit Paper 90: HMSO.

Doherty, M. & East, R. (1985) 'Bail Decisions in Magistrates' Courts, *British Journal of Criminology*, 25, p. 251.

Downes, D. (1988) *Contrasts in Tolerance*, Oxford University Press.

Eaton M. (1987) 'The Question of Bail', in *Gender, Crime and Justice*, Carlen, P. & Worrall, A. (eds), Open University Press.

Fennell, P. (1991) 'Diversion of Mentally Disordered Offenders from Custody', *Criminal Law Review*, pp. 333.

Grubin, D. (1993) 'What constitutes fitness to plead?' *Criminal Law Review*, pp. 748.

Henham, R. (1994) 'Attorney-General's References and Sentencing Policy', *Criminal Law Review*, pp. 499 *ff*.

Home Office (1990) *Crime, Justice and Protecting the Public*, HMSO.

Law Society, (1992) *The Magistrates' Court — a guide to good practice in the preparation of cases*, Law Society.

Lloyd, C. (1992) *Bail Information Schemes: Practice and Effect*, Home Office Research Unit, Paper No. 69, HMSO.

Mackay, R. D. (1991) 'The decline of disability in relation to the trial', *Criminal Law Review*, pp. 87 *ff*.

Morgan, P. M. (1992) *Offending while on bail: A Survey of Recent Studies*, Home Office Research Unit, Paper No. 65, HMSO.

Morgan, R. & Jones, S. (1992) 'Bail or Jail?', in *Criminal Justice under Stress*, Stockdale, E. & Casale, S. (eds), Blackstone Press.

Padfield, N. M. (1993) 'The Right to Bail. A Canadian Perspective', *Criminal Law Review*, pp. 477 *ff*.

Padfield, N. M. (1995) 'Clean Water and Muddy Causation', *Criminal Law Review*, pp. 683 *ff*.

Peay, J. (1993) 'A Criminological Perspective', in Watson, W. & Grounds, A. (eds) *Mentally Disordered Offenders in an Era of Community Care*, Cambridge University Press.

Peay, J. (1994) 'Mentally Disordered Offenders', in the *Oxford Handbook on Criminology*, (eds Maguire, M., Morgan, R., Reiner, R.) Oxford University Press.

Sanders, A. & Young, R. (1994) *Criminal Justice*, Butterworths.

Stone, C. (1988) *Bail Information for the Crown Prosecution Service*, VERA.

Thomas, D. A. (1969) 'Current developments in sentencing — the Criminal Justice Act in practice', *Criminal Law Review*, pp. 235 *ff*.

Thomas, D. A. (1994) *Current Sentencing Practice*, Sweet & Maxwell.

Trotter, G. (1992) *The Law of Bail in Canada*, Carswell.

Wasik, M. (1993) *Emmins on Sentencing*, Blackstone Press.

Wasik, M. & von Hirsch, A. (1994) 'Section 29 Revised: Previous Convictions and Sentencing', *Criminal Law Review*, pp. 409 *ff*.

6

Psychiatric Inpatient Violence

John Crichton

About one in 10 psychiatric patients assault a member of staff in Britain, helping to make hospital workers more likely to suffer occupational injury than industrial workers (Department of Health, Blom-Cooper (Chairman) (1987)). Inpatient violence within psychiatric hospitals has generated a huge amount of interest within the medical and nursing journals, with over 100 publications internationally in the last 10 years (Shah (1993)). The literature concentrates mainly on clinical aspects of violence and the problems of definition, prediction and the relationship between mental disorder and violence. These issues have proved as difficult to study within the hospitalised patient population as they have with patients in the community and, as yet, there are few firm conclusions. A major omission in the literature is the discussion of the legal and moral dilemmas associated with staff response to inpatient violence and these are discussed here.

Psychiatric staff have to work with the difficulty of keeping a safe and therapeutic environment for patients who are probably displaying some type of deviant behaviour upon which their diagnosis will have been based. It is hardly surprising that inpatient violence is common, since dangerousness remains an admission criterion, and violent acts commonly precede a hospital admission (Johnstone *et al* (1986); Lagos *et al* (1977); Tardiff and Sweillam (1980)). The need to control disruptive behaviour goes beyond the simple requirement of order for a ward to function; it is also a treatment objective if the aim of admission is to discharge the patient back to society. Restrictions within hospital go further than simple control, which requires only the use of a containing and controlling force. Restrictions also involve discipline, in the sense that discipline describes the process of *engendering self-control* (Crichton (1995, b, c)). A key case described below is *Pountney* v *Griffiths*

95

[1976] AC 314 where 'control and discipline' were identified as essential ingredients of compulsory detention under mental health legislation, distinct from any therapeutic considerations. There is no guidance as to what would constitute reasonable control and discipline. This is therefore a grey area of both legal and clinical practice.

One solution to these problems is Genevra Richardson's proposed introduction of formal disciplinary proceedings within psychiatric hospitals (Richardson (1993 and 1995)). Professor Richardson argued that such a framework would not be anti-therapeutic and would put much-needed safeguards in place for the use of sanctions within hospital. Her proposal is discussed below. Also discussed are the recording of violent incidents and the role of the police, as these cause specific problems in practice.

The Characteristics of Inpatient Violence

Before considering aspects of the law and ethical questions, it would be helpful to summarise the main findings about psychiatric inpatient violence. Appendix A lists all the main British Studies, and is taken from a review (Crichton (1995, b)) which drew the following conclusions;

(a)   while serious violence is rare, minor assaults are an everyday part of psychiatric hospital life;

(b)   the highest rates of serious violence were found within a maximum security psychiatric hospital (one life-threatening episode a week at Rampton maximum security hospital; Larkin *et al* (1988));

(c)   the highest rates of violence were found at low security intensive care wards where the major admission criterion was patient violence;

(d)   rates of violence seem to be increasing and this is probably a reflection of an increase of violence at large (Walker and Caplan (1993)), an increase in staff awareness of the problem and, hence, increased reporting, and improved research techniques;

(e)   there was no clear relationship between diagnosis and violence; *active* psychotic symptoms however have been associated with higher rates of violence (Noble and Rogers (1989)). This association supports the findings of Link *et al* (1992) and Swanson *et al* (1990), described by Monahan (1993) as the 'missing element' of research into the relationship between mental disorder and violence;

(f)   one study (Noble and Rogers (1989)), using a matched control technique, found that Afro-Caribbean patients were more violent, but there is no consensus on the relationship between race and psychiatric inpatient violence;

(g)   women patients tended, particularly within secure facilities, to cause more violent incidents than men. This is similar to the pattern found in prison, where women prisoners proportionately cause more disruptive incidents;

(h)   a small minority of 'problem patients' caused a disproportionate number of incidents;

(i)   high states of arousal, the imposition of restrictions and provocation by other patients (but not by staff) have been found to be important antecedents of violence (Powell *et al* (1994));

(j)   both staff and other patients were common victims of violence;

(k)   a number of studies have suggested that poor staffing levels, busy staff, temporary staff, under-occupied patients and little ward routine are associated with violence;

(l)   there is general agreement that fear, confusion and disorganisation within institutions breeds violence.

These broad conclusions are also supported by the wide international literature, especially from North America and Australasia. Although studies of inpatient violence are improving in their use of common definitions and research techniques, they are becoming repetitive. Some have attempted to devise scales to predict inpatient violence, but with very limited success (Palmstierna and Wistedt (1988)). There is no indication that actuarial or statistical techniques will prove more successful for inpatients than they have in attempts to predict psychiatric patients' violence in the community. Others argue for safer institutional systems to minimise risk, shifting the focus away from the risk posed by an individual patient to the appropriate use of alarms, observation and training (Stark *et al* (1994)).

The Mental Health Act 1983 and the Code of Practice

The Mental Health Act 1983 (MHA 1983) is the main piece of legislation relating to the mentally disordered. The MHA 1983 was a compromise between organisations such as MIND, which campaigned for comprehensive mechanisms of appeal against detention and aspects of compulsory therapy, and the mental health professions, led by the Royal College of Psychiatrists (RCP) who wished to retain as much as possible of the therapeutic freedom found in the MHA 1959. Instead of creating a set of watertight and rigid statutory rules, as in the Lunacy Act 1890, a Code of Practice (1983)) was intended to give practical guidance to staff when interpreting their duties under the MHA 1983 and could be updated more easily.

The Code of Practice is authorised by statute but it is not directly enforceable. It is influential because breaches of its standards could be relied on to show a breach of the professional's duty of care (Jones (1991, p. 215)). Legal test cases are necessary to interpret the text and make its standards part of common law. Such was the disagreement, however, over the contents of the Code that its publication was delayed until 1990, seven years after the MHA 1983, by which time many professionals had become set in their interpretation of the Act, without the benefit of official guidance.

The Power to Control a Detained Patient

The MHA 1983 focuses on aspects of compulsory hospital admission and discharge. The authority of the Act over admitted patients is only implied by its powers of detention and treatment. In June 1975 the House of Lords considered the case of *Pountney* v *Griffiths* [1976] AC 314. The appellant was a patient at Broadmoor who had brought an action against a nurse alleging common assault. The patient's case was that as he was saying goodbye to his family on a visiting day at the hospital, the nurse had approached him and having said, 'Come along you', punched him on the shoulder. The nurse denied the allegation. The magistrates' court convicted the nurse and gave him a conditional discharge, but the conviction was quashed by the Divisional Court on the ground that the appellant had failed to obtain leave from the High Court before taking his action. For an action to be taken against anyone acting in pursuance of s. 141 of the MHA 1959 (now s. 139 of the MHA 1983) leave must be granted by the High Court, in order to prevent malicious litigation. The patient appealed to the House of Lords, contending that leave in this case was unnecessary as the nurse's actions could not be considered as being specifically pursuant to the Act which, it was argued, did not relate to the day-to-day work of staff. The Law Lords dismissed the appeal, deciding that the nurse's actions were pursuant to the Act, since the patient was compulsorily detained, and that detention necessarily involves 'control and discipline'. It is likely that this case would be decided the same way today and, therefore, still represents the law.

Although the House of Lords acknowledged a need for discipline over detained patients distinct from any purely therapeutic considerations, there is no clear guidance as to what staff action is and is not acceptable by way of control. Gostin (1986) suggests that any discipline should be reasonable and within the spirit of the MHA 1983, i.e., in the interests of the patient or of safety, and should not include punishment or any element of revenge. Hoggett (1990) concludes, after discussing *Pountney* v *Griffiths* that:

> In a hospital such as Broadmoor, where the secure and highly disciplined environment is in itself regarded as a therapy for the patients, the dividing line between what is permitted in the name of treatment and what can only

be justified in the name of detention is particularly difficult to draw. But neither concept could be used to justify any and every regime, however harsh, arbitrary or oppressive.

The decisions leading to the death of Sean Walton described in the Ashworth Inquiry (Blom-Cooper (1992)) illustrate the fine line between what is and what is not justifiable. Twenty-year-old Sean Walton was thought to have attempted a sexual assault on another patient. The charge nurse ordered him to mop up the toilet floor and ordered an unqualified nurse to supervise. Although it was suggested at the Inquiry that this was part of 'over-correction therapy' the Inquiry concluded that it was a punishment. Sean Walton subsequently assaulted the supervising nurse with a brush, who hit Walton on the head in self-defence, and Walton was put into seclusion. The Inquiry concluded that Walton was not psychotic at the time of these incidents, but that the initial decision to seclude was, nevertheless, reasonable. The seclusion was continued the next day with an entry in the nursing notes, 'no remorse for his actions'; but the Inquiry concluded that the continuation of seclusion was unacceptable. Sean Walton died later that day in seclusion, the cause of death being uncertain. What also remains unclear is what staff action would have been reasonable in response to the initial incident.

To help decide the reasonableness of any staff response Hoggett (1990) concluded that staff need to return to the principles found in common law to help guide them. Yet, as will be discussed below, the common law has its grey areas.

The Power to Treat a Detained Patient

Control and discipline are not terms with which psychiatric staff feel comfortable. Even the term 'control and restraint', used to describe the techique whereby staff are trained to safely hold a disturbed patient, has been criticised for including the word 'control'. Instead, the usual response to an incident is described in therapeutic terms. There has arisen a confusion about the role of punishment. If legal experts inform the psychiatric profession that the only control they exert must be devoid of punishment then, perhaps, it is easier not to use the term control at all. 'Treatment' is often perceived by the patient as punishment, but is rarely thought of as such by staff. There is a dichotomy in the minds of staff between treatment, which is acceptable, and control, which is not, largely because the latter is associated with punishment.

Most orders for compulsory detention of patients under the MHA 1983 automatically authorise compulsory treatment (s. 63). In Part IV of the Act there are special safeguards for particularly sensitive treatments such as psychosurgery and electro-convulsive therapy, and pharmacological treatment required for longer than three months against a patient's wishes. In such cases a 'second opinion approved doctor' (SOAD) appointed by the Mental Health Act Commission (MHAC) must review and approve the treatment.

It would be good clinical practice for a patient with a history of violence to have a care plan, which should carefully lay down in advance what response would be appropriate if violence was to recur. It is unclear whether an SOAD can comment on that plan in detail; for instance, not just outlining a maximum dose of medication but prescribing the circumstances in which it is given (e.g., that a high dose of medication given intramuscularly following disturbed behaviour should be followed by close nursing observations and the absence of seclusion). There is currently no provision for a second opinion for psychological or behavioural control treatments, although the Secretary of State for Health has the power to make any treatment subject to the SOAD process.

One common treatment for violent patients is behavioural therapy, which, at its core, reinforces desired behaviour and discourages unwanted behaviour, by reward and punishment. Psychologists argue that punishment in behavioural therapy does not have the same meaning that it has in common parlance and, again, alternative terms have been suggested, such as 'lack of reward'. The Royal College of Psychiatrists (1989) addresses some of the ethical problems of behavioural therapy in a guidance note, yet there remains confusion about the nature of punishment in behavioural therapy, which the following case illustrates.

Case example 1　K was diagnosed as having a borderline personality disorder, a condition often arising from childhood trauma, characterised by impulsivity, intense emotions and swings of mood. She was a successful professional woman but had become suicidal. She would seriously harm herself by cutting her arms, smuggling in razor blades and craft knives. She also colluded in the self-harm of another patient. Most disruptively she would run through fire escape doors, setting off the fire alarm, then she would dawdle at the perimeter of the hospital neither wishing to get too close nor go too far. She made life misery for the nurses, but, at times, this was mutual. In some respects the psychiatric ward re-enacted the abuse of her childhood. When she ran out through the alarmed doors the whole ward was disrupted. All therapeutic activities on the ward were suspended and staff resented chasing her around the grounds. Occasionally, that resentment spilled over acceptable limits and she was sworn at, or manhandled roughly. Finally, it was decided that each time she ran away she was to be put into the seclusion room with her shoes removed: later this was extended to removal of her daytime clothing in exchange for night-clothes. The junior psychiatrist had the task of explaining that this was not punitive but was a behavioural therapy to help foster her subconscious self-control. In some ways her admission was a success; after several months of costly inpatient care she was discharged into the community. She had not committed suicide, nor aided anyone else to do so, and she went back into employment. However, she considered her admission had revealed psychiatry at its worst, and complained bitterly.

Guidance on the Management of Violence in the Code of Practice

Acknowledging the limitations of the Code, this remains the most powerful guide to the management of patients in dangerous situations. Chapter 18 devotes itself to 'patients presenting particular management problems', and includes the following examples:

- refusal to participate in treatment programmes;
- prolonged verbal abuse and threatening behaviour;
- destructive behaviour;
- self-injurious behaviour;
- physical attacks on others.

The Code encourages prevention of such problems by staff recognising the following possible causes: boredom, overcrowding, aggression from others, an unsuitable mix of patients. The Code pays attention to undesirable behaviour and the inability to protect oneself against harm as a result of mental disorder. It stresses that care plans for individual patients should address problem behaviours and that the ward environment should be managed to avoid such situations occurring, giving 12 points of specific advice — such as encouraging energetic activities for young patients and allowing access to a telephone.

For the acute management of a dangerous situation the principles and practice of restraint, emergency medication and seclusion are discussed in detail. The basic principles are that an intervention should reduce the unwanted behaviour and that whatever intervention is used should be regularly reviewed. It is stressed that 'restraining aggressive behaviour by physical means should be done only as a last resort and never as a matter of course', and that any restraint must be 'reasonable in the circumstances'.

The Code concentrates on general preventive measures and the acute management of violence. The task of acute management is straightforward: a dangerous situation must be made safe. What the Code lacks is advice on the medium and long-term management of a situation after it has been made safe.

The Voluntary Patient

A grey area is that of a voluntary patient who wishes to remain in hospital but is violent. Hoggett (1990, p. 217) stated:

> In the case of informal patients who have withdrawn their consent to abide by the hospital's rules, the proper course is not to impose discipline as such, but either to ask them to leave or (where the criteria exist) to impose compulsory powers. Compulsory patients cannot so readily be asked to leave and so cannot be permitted to cause serious disruption to hospital life.

In general psychiatry units, informal patients are commonly discharged because of unacceptable behaviour. In the case of Christopher Clunis, a young Afro-Caribbean man with schizophrenia who went on to kill a member of the public, his early inpatient behaviour was disruptive and, on several occasions, he was abruptly discharged (Ritchie et al (1994, Ch 4)). His behaviour included masturbating openly, entering female dormitories, striking a patient and kicking a patient for no reason (Ritchie et al (1994, Ch 4.3, 4.4)). Although he was a voluntary patient Hoggett would probably argue that Clunis could have been detained under the MHA 1983, since his behaviour was inconsistent with voluntary status and he satisfied the other compulsory admission criteria. In the detention of such patients, staff would have to face the task of imposing acceptable behaviour. There are no systems of appeal for the voluntary patient who wishes to remain in hospital but who faces discharge because of being accused of violence.

Common Law

Common law is 'often invoked in talisman-like fashion by staff in the treatment of patients' (Jelley (1990)); yet there is uncertainty amongst psychiatric professionals about what common law actually is and how it relates to statute law and good practice. There is some confusion, since common law describes several legal concepts; but it is in the sense that it describes the law which is developed through judicial decisions, rather than statute, which is pertinent to psychiatry, and what is meant here. Judicial decisions are hierarchical in nature and help define what the law is through decisions in particular cases: applicable decisions of a court of superior authority must be followed by one of lower standing, the highest court being the House of Lords.

Common law is clearly pertinent to voluntary psychiatric inpatients but is also the justification used in the emergency treatment of detained patients under sections of the MHA 1983 which do not authorise compulsory treatment.

Gostin (1986) suggested that there is an uneasy relationship between common law and statute law and asserted that 'where the statute applies, its provisions override the common law; but where the Act [MHA 1983] does not apply the common law remains in force' Hoggett (1990) concluded that even for patients detained under sections of the Act which allow compulsory treatment 'many matters are still left to the principles of the common law or the discretion of staff and hospital authorities'. The three main areas of common law pertinent to inpatient control are prevention of harm, consent and necessity.

Prevention of Harm

Hoggett (1990, pp. 210–13)) listed four justifications which allow the restraint or treatment of a mentally disordered person whether or not they are detained under the MHA 1983. First, there is statutory provision in the Criminal Law Act 1967 (s. 2) which creates a category of serious offences, called arrestable offences, and any citizen has the power to arrest to prevent such a crime. It is unclear (Gostin (1986)) how far this provision can be used as a justification for restraining the mentally disordered, since a person who is insane within the meaning of the M'Naghten Rules cannot commit a crime. Gostin pointed out, however, that most inpatients requiring restraint would not satisfy the M'Naghten criteria.

Secondly, there are common law powers to prevent a breach of the peace which are preserved in the Criminal Law Act 1967 (s. 2(7)). Where this power is exercised there must be an honest belief, founded on reasonable grounds, that a breach of the peace is imminent (*Howell* [1982] QB 416). At common law it is not only a right for a citizen to act but a duty (*Albert* v *Lavin* [1982] AC 546). Gostin (1986) asserted that this power could be used on a patient, 'whose words or behaviour are such that imminent violence is expected'.

Thirdly, there is the common law right to self-defence. There is debate about whether this justification continues after the provision made in s. 2 of the Criminal Law Act 1967 (Harlow (1974)).

Finally, the common law allows a private person to restrain a 'dangerous lunatic' who seems about to do mischief (*Brookshaw* v *Hopkins* (1790) Lofft 235 at p. 244; *Scott* v *Wakem* (1862) 3 F & F 147; *Symm* v *Fraser* (1863) 3 F & F 859) and this subject is reviewed by Lanhan (1974). Lord Mansfield said in *Brookshaw* v *Hopkins* 'God forbid, too, that a man should be punished for restraining the fury of a lunatic, when that is the case'. In Scotland there has been recent affirmation of this justification: in *Black* v *Forsey* (1988) SLT 572 the House of Lords ruled that 'the common law does indeed confer upon the private individual power lawfully to detain, in a situation of necessity, a person of unsound mind who is a danger to himself and others'. That ruling also made it clear that this justification would not be available to medical staff where the relevant sections of Mental Health Act (Scotland) 1984 could have been invoked.

All four powers were summed up by Hoggett (1990): 'there is the right to restrain a patient who is doing, or about to do, physical harm to himself, to another person, or to property'. All four justifications are likely to be subject to the concept of 'reasonableness'. Force that is used must only be the minimum required and, whatever the response is, it must be in proportion to the threatened harm. In deciding what force would be reasonable it is unlikely that a court would expect a fine judgment: in *Reed* v *Waistie* [1972] Crim LR 221 the court commented that, 'in the circumstances one did not use jeweller's scales to measure reasonable force'.

Hoggett (1990) stated that 'none of these powers permit anything in the nature of retaliation, revenge or punishment'. She suggested that a short time in seclusion might be a reasonable response to a violent patient but a prolonged time could not be justified (e.g., *A* v *United Kingdom* (1980), Application No. 6840/74 Report of the European Commission of Human Rights, 16 July, Strasbourg, Council of Europe). A grey area is the use of intramuscular injections of major tranquillising drugs. In this context, they are more instruments of chemical restraint than therapeutic tools. Most are short-acting, but it is unclear whether those which have an effect over a few days, such as Clopixol Acuphase, could justifiably be used.

Consent

Patients may consent to trespass on their person. Violent patients who are part of behavioural modification regimes may, for example, consent to being put into seclusion. At times in the case example above, 'K' was a voluntary patient and consented to her placement in seclusion. Consent must be voluntarily given and it can be withdrawn at any time (Royal College of Psychiatrists (1989)), as the Code of Practice states (para. 15.12):

'Consent' is the voluntary and continuing permission of the patient to receive a particular treatment, based on an adequate knowledge of the purpose, nature, likely side-effects and risks of treatment including the likelihood of its success and any alternatives to it. Permission given under any unfair or undue pressure is not 'consent'.

In a Quebec case, consent was held to be invalid when a sedative was given to 'help' a patient give permission (*Beausoleil* v *La Communauté des Soeurs de la Charité de la Providence* (1964) 53 DLR (2d.) 65. Coercion would also invalidate consent but it is unclear what would constitute sufficient coercion to do so. Many patients may be refused hospital admission unless they agree in advance to a particular treatment plan, which could include voluntary sanctions. It is unclear whether this alone might be unfair or undue pressure. A US case, *Kaimowitz* v *Michigan* (1973) 42 USLW 2063 acknowledged that coercion would always be present when dealing with detained patients: 'it is impossible for an involuntary detained mental patient to be free from ulterior forms of constraint or coercion when his very release from the institution may depend on his cooperation with the institutional authorities'.

Necessity

The law relating to consent when a patient is incapable of giving true consent is vague, and recent proposals from the Law Commission (1995), if implemented, would help to elucidate this complex area. In 1989 the Law Lords allowed the sterilisation of a woman with serious learning disabilities who was incapable of giving consent (*F* v *West Berkshire Health Authority* [1989] 2 All ER 543). In his judgment Lord Brandon stated:

In my opinion ... A doctor can lawfully operate on, or give treatment to, adult patients who are incapable, for one reason or another, of consenting to his doing so, provided that the operation or other treatment concerned is in the best interests of such patients. The operation or other treatment will be in the best interests if, but only if, it is carried out in order either to save their lives or to ensure improvement or prevent deterioration in their physical or mental health.

Necessity is the justification for various restrictive and controlling measures over patients suffering from severe dementia or severe learning disability. Violence from such patients is very common but is rarely serious and is frequently not reported. Some restrictive ways of dealing with the severely demented have been condemned as unreasonable by the Code of Practice, such as the use of ties or hooks to hold patients to chairs, which was a common way of restricting the aggressive, demented elderly patient.

Recording a Violent Incident

There are few safeguards to ensure that the report of any incident in the clinical notes is accurate or contains the patient's side of the story. This is particularly important since the content of incident reports is often influential in the decisions made by Mental Health Act Review Tribunals (MHRTs) when they are deciding to release a detained patient. The accuracy of violent incident reports was addressed in the Robinson Inquiry, which investigated the killing of a member of staff by a patient known to be violent. An MHRT in 1985 lifted the restriction order (s. 41 of the MHA 1983) placed on Andrew Robinson in 1978 following his conviction for a serious assault on his ex-girlfriend with a shotgun. The tribunal was not made aware of certain episodes of inpatient violence and were criticised by the Inquiry, which gave comprehensive guidance about the recording of violent incidents (Blom-Cooper *et al* (1995, a)). Scott-Moncrieff (1993) gave examples of inaccurate incident reporting to MHRT which exaggerated past incidents. Accurate incident reporting is essential not only if MHRTs are to be properly informed, but if clinicians are to manage future risk of violence effectively. There is no better predictor of future violence than past violence, but this clinical wisdom is undermined if the past history of violence is inaccurate.

Prosecuting Violent Psychiatric Inpatients

There is very little research into the prosecution of psychiatric inpatients following a violent act (Crichton (1995, c)). In the United States, Norko *et al* (1992) reviewed the different arguments for and against prosecution. In Britain, James and Collings (1989) reported a survey of psychiatrists who had initiated prosecutions. Only three per cent of 284 nurses shown a fictional incident where a nurse was punched by an inpatient felt that police involvement would be helpful; 87 per cent felt that it would be unhelpful (Crichton (1995, d). Staff rarely inform police of minor assaults and even serious acts of violence causing injury are seldom reported. The following case example illustrates some of the problems.

Case example 2 A man with paranoid schizophrenia who was actively psychotic, believing he was being tormented and controlled by aliens via his testicles, attended a hospital Christmas party. There, he grabbed the groin of a child at the party and the child's parent insisted on his prosecution for a sexual assault. Some time later, believing that the duty psychiatrist's car was involved in his torment, he attacked the car, badly denting its roof. The staff involved believed that the damage was done because he was labouring under delusions and hallucinations and there was no police involvement. The hospital authorities paid for the damage.

In effect, staff in psychiatric hospitals decide for themselves many of the questions normally left to the criminal justice system — criminal responsibility, desirability of prosecution etc. In addition, the criminal justice system often hands back the problems of justice to the hospitals, when violent patients in the community have criminal charges dropped because they are hospitalised. Following an assault, staff usually appraise whether police involvement would really achieve anything and usually decide that it would not. In many cases it would seem absurd to involve the police: an example is a punch from a patient with severe dementia which causes no damage. But it is in the grey areas of seemingly intentional violence, with partially insightful patients and with reasonably serious consequences, that dilemmas occur.

A similar problem exists within prison concerning the involvement of criminal prosecution (Richardson (1995)). The Woolf Report (1991) drew a distinction between the maintenance of internal order and violence outside the institution. A common conclusion in both hospitals and prisons is that when an assault is sufficiently serious, irrespective of the circumstances, then police involvement is desirable.

The problem remains with regard to who should decide whether an assault is serious or not. If seriousness is judged purely on outcome, i.e., by the nature of the injury, then this does not take account of the role of chance in an assault: an angry push may result in a fall and serious injury, a thrown knife may miss altogether. If it is left to the victim of an assault to decide about police involvement then a number of difficulties arise. Staff may be put under subtle pressure not to give their unit bad publicity. Patients may not have the capacity to decide. A number of authors (Norko *et al* (1992); Appelbaum and Appelbaum (1991)) in the US context suggested that each hospital should have a policy for police involvement after violence. There is currently confusion about when to involve the police and there is a need for guidelines and agreements between managers, professional organisations and the police.

A Disciplinary Code for Patients?

Genevra Richardson (1993 and 1995) put forward the suggestion that formal disciplinary procedures should be available within psychiatric hospitals over detained patients. She started with the assumption that sanctions are commonly used in response to serious disruptive behaviour but are at present not regulated, nor do they have legal safeguards or systems of appeal. She argued that 'patients should be fully aware of what is expected of them and should know, as precisely as possible, what is prohibited and what the consequence of non-compliance will be' and that a disciplinary code 'would be facilitative to the treatment objective, not obstructive of it', that involvement of an independent adjudicator would encourage accuracy and that 'by empowering patients to participate, the whole approach would be designed to restore them some element of responsibiity for the decisions made'.

Richardson suggested, drawing on *Pountney* v *Griffiths* [1976] AC 314, that the introduction of a disciplinary code would be legal, but, unlike Gostin (1986), was clear that disciplinary sanctions would be punitive. She suggested, however, that by giving the code statutory authority there would be the opportunity for public debate of the issues and 'democratic legitimation of the scheme'.

Following Richardson's suggestion, psychiatric patients would be clearly informed about what behaviour would be expected of them. If a patient were accused of a violent incident then a senior member of staff, independent of the clinical team looking after the incident, would investigate the allegation. The investigator would come to a finding about the facts of the case. If the allegations were found proved beyond reasonable doubt then either a disciplinary sanction, such as the loss of a specific privilege, would be awarded or, if the patient's mental state makes a sanction inappropriate, the clinical team would be invited to propose a therapeutic response. The patient would have the right to question witnesses, be represented by a friend or lay advocate and appeal against either the finding of the fact or the response. Richardson stressed the need for clear and comprehensive documentation at every stage.

Richardson acknowledged that there would be problems in deciding what local hospital rules should consist of, what kind of incident would be subject to the disciplinary proceedings and what kind of sanctions would be appropriate, but she suggested that these would not be insuperable problems, especially if all parties, including patients, were involved in their solution. She realised that this proposal is controversial and cogently defended herself against criticisms of proposing a cumbersome system, stale with legalism. Her proposals may be misinterpreted as undermining patients' rights, but as Blom-Cooper *et al* (1995, b) commented, 'at the heart of her proposals there is the aim of furthering patient rights, while placing the problem of discipline in the real world'. My main anxiety (Crichton (1995, e)) about Richardson's proposals, which I shall return to in the discussion (below) concerns the distinction she made between a disciplinary and treatment response (at p. 108):

Where a disciplinary sanction is imposed it must be of determinate length. It is punitive and its duration should not be dependent on an improvement in the patient's condition. Where a therapeutic response is authorised great care must be taken to explain everything to the patient, and to ensure that the response is not in effect a covert punishment and is not regarded as such by the patient.

Discussion and Conclusions

Psychiatric inpatient violence cannot simply be considered as a clinical phenomenon. There are tricky issues of law and ethics which need to be addressed. A summary of the legal position would be that staff can exercise reasonable control over patients, not only immediately following an incident but, for detained patients, in the medium and long term. There is then the problem of ensuring reasonableness of response and, largely, that is what Richardson's proposed disciplinary code corrects. I would predict, however, that professional organisations would be wary of her proposals, not because of their content but because they confront psychiatric professionals with a part of their role with which they feel uneasy: that of agents of social control.

A common observation is that staff feel more comfortable dealing with violence when there is a clear link with psychotic symptoms. In a study of nearly 600 responses from nurses to a fictional incident of disturbed patient behaviour (Crichton (1995, d)), it was found that when psychotic symptoms influenced the behaviour there was a clear preferred response involving the use of medication. When, however, the patient was perceived to be non-psychotic and in some control of his actions, staff were unsure about their response, sanctions were overall felt to be unhelpful, but the clinical reward and punishment of behavioural therapy was preferred for this patient group. A familiar notion is that there can be a division between a deviant act caused by badness and one caused by madness, and it would appear that psychiatric staff find it more difficult to respond to violence when badness is seen as an important factor. The mad/bad dichotomy is false because each concept comes from a distinct domain of discourse: the moral and the clinical. Less clearly, the treat/punish dichotomy is also false for the same reason.

Patients are likely to behave in a disruptive way following a complex interaction of factors, some influenced by mental disorder and some over which they have choice and self-control. This raises the problem of assessing responsibility and all the problems of definition and meaning associated with that term. When staff refer to a patient's responsibility it is often unclear whether they are discussing a legal term, criminal responsibility, a moral notion of responsibility or the intentionality of the act. Realistically, the patient's criminal responsibility for a violent act will never be clear-cut and will have arisen from a mixture of factors, although the law may wish to draw a dividing line if a case comes to court, and it *is in this situation that the false dichotomies of madness and badness, treatment and punishment, seem to be confirmed.* Similarly a patient in hospital may experience his treatment as highly punitive even if its therapeutic nature is stressed. Both 'madness' and 'badness' coexist in some degree to influence a violent act and, similarly, 'treatment' and 'punishment' coexist in the institutional response to violence. Richardson was clear that punitive sanctions can be therapeutic, to which could be added that a therapeutic response can also be punitive. There is a danger that her proposals could be misinterpreted as meaning that her disciplinary code makes too stark a distinction between what is punished and what is treated.

It is easy to be critical of psychiatric services. Both the control of patients and the freedom of patients alarm the public. The task of responding to inpatient violence and other misdemeanours is very much at the sharp edge of state control. There is the need for reasonable balance of control, avoiding the extremes of over- and under-restriction, but, in searching for that balance, the area of moral judgment seems unavoidable in three key areas: first, the moral judgment which dictates what exactly constitutes acceptable patient behaviour; second, the assessment of a patient's personal responsibility for actions: and, thirdly, the judgment of what response, almost certainly perceived by the patient as a punishment, should follow to engender self-control. What is needed is a system that is aware that moral judgments are required if we are to compulsorily treat psychiatric patients at all. To help make moral judgments in psychiatry reasonable the following elements seem essential; multidisciplinary team-working; training; staff supervision; and comprehensive systems of appeal for the patient. It is dangerous to assume that punishment and treatment are mutually exclusive.

Acknowledgements

I would like to gratefully acknowledge the help and advice of Adina Halpern, Nightingale Fellow Commoner, Professor Genevra Richardson and Dr Adrian Grounds in the preparation of this chapter.

References

Aiken, G. J. M. (1984) 'Assaults on staff on a locked ward: prediction and consequences; *Medicine, Science and the Law*, 24, pp. 199–207.

Appelbaum, K. L. & Appelbaum, P. S. (1991) 'A model hospital policy for prosecuting patients for presumptively criminal acts', *Hospital and Community Psychiatry*, 42, pp. 1233–7.

Armond, A. D. (1982) 'Violence in the semi-secure ward of a psychiatric hospital', *Medicine, Science and the Law*, 22, pp. 203–9.

Ashworth, A. & Gostin L. (1984) 'Mentally Disordered Offenders and the Sentencing Process', *Criminal Law Review*, pp. 195–212.

Blom-Cooper, L. (1994) *Report of the Review into the Mental Health Services of South Devon Healthcare Trust*, Torquay: South Devon Healthcare Trust, pp. 56–7.

Blom-Cooper, L. (Chairman) (1992) *Report of the Committee of Inquiry into Complaints about Ashworth Hospital*, Cm 2028–I, London HMSO.

Blom-Cooper, L., Murphy, E. & Halley H. (1995)(a) *The Falling Shadow; one patient's mental health care 1978–1993*, London: Duckworth.

Blom-Cooper, L., Murphy, E. & Halley H. (1995)(b) 'Introduction', Ch 1 in Crichton, J. H. M. (ed.), *Psychiatric Patient Violence Risk and Response*, London: Duckworth.

Coldwell, J. B. & Naismith, L. J. (1989) 'Violent incidents on a Special Care Ward of a Special Hospital'; *Medicine, Science and the Law*, 29, pp. 116–123.

Crichton, J. H. M. (1995)(a) 'A review of psychiatric inpatient violence', Ch 2 in Crichton, J. H. M. (ed.), *Psychiatric Patient Violence Risk and Response*, London: Duckworth.

Crichton, J. H. M. (1995)(b) 'The response to psychiatric inpatient violence', Ch 6 in Crichton, J. H. M. (ed.), *Psychiatric Patient Violence Risk and Response*, London: Duckworth.

Crichton, J. H. M. (1995)(c) 'Psychiatric in-patient violence: issues of English law and discipline within hospitals', *Medicine, Science and the Law*, 35, pp. 53–6.

Crichton, J. H. M. (1995)(d) 'Staff Response to Psychiatric Inpatient Violence', *XXI Annual Congress on Law and Mental Health, June 23–27*, Tromso: Norway.

Crichton, J. H. M. (1995)(e) 'Is it time for a formal disciplinary code for psychiatric in-patients in England and Wales?', *Medicine, Science and the Law*, in press.

Department of Health (1993) *The Mental Health Act 1983 Code of Practice*, 2nd edn, London: HMSO.

Department of Health (Health and Safety Committee) (1987) *Violence to staff in the health service*, London: HMSO.

Fottrell, E., Bewley, T. & Squizzoni, M. A. (1978) 'A Study of Aggressive and Violent Behaviour among a group of Psychiatric Inpatients', *Medicine, Science and the Law*, 18, pp. 66–9.

Fottrell, E. (1980) 'A study of violent behaviour among patients in psychiatric hospitals', *British Journal of Psychiatry*, 136, pp. 216–21.

Gostin, L. (1986) *Mental Health Services — law and practice*, London: Shaw & Shaw Ltd.

Harlow, C. (1974) 'Self-defence: Public Right or Private Privilege', *Criminal Law Review*, pp. 528–38.

Hodgkinson, P. E., McIvor, L. & Philips, M. (1985) 'Patient assaults on staff in a psychiatric hospital: a two-year retrospective study', *Medicine, Science and the Law*, 25, pp. 288–94.

Hoggett, B. (1990) *Mental Health Law*, 3rd ed., London: Sweet & Maxwell.

James, D. V. & Collings, S. (1989) 'Prosecuting psychiatric in-patients for violent acts: a survey of principles and practice', *Abstracts annual meeting London 4–6 July 1989 Supplement 2 Psychiatric Bulletin*, supp. 2, p. 60.

Jelley, M. (1990) 'Common Law and the Code of Practice — A Commentary', *Psychiatric Bulletin*, 14, pp. 449–51.

Johnstone, E. C., Crow, T. J., Johnson, A. L. & MacMillan J. F. (1986) 'The Northwick Park study of first episodes of schizophrenia. 1. Presentation of the illness and procedure relating to admission', *British Journal of Psychiatry*, 148, pp. 115–20.

Jones, R. (1991) *Mental Health Act Manual*, 3rd edn, London: Sweet & Maxwell.

Kennedy, J., Harrison, J., Hillis, T. & Bluglass, R. (1995) 'Analysis of Violent Incidents in a Regional Secure Unit', *Medicine, Science and the Law*, 35, pp. 255–60.

Lagos, J. M., Perlmutter, K. & Saexinger, H. (1977) 'Fear of the mentally ill: empirical support for the common man's response', *American Journal of Psychiatry*, 134, pp. 1134–7.

Lanham, D. (1974) 'Arresting the Insane', *Criminal Law Review*, pp. 516–28.

Larkin, E., Murtagh, S. & Jones, S. (1988) 'A preliminary study of violent incidents in a Special Hospital (Rampton)', *British Journal of Psychiatry*, 153, pp. 226–31.

Law Commission (1995) *Mental Incapacity*, Item 9 of the Fourth Programme of Law Reform: Mentally Incapacitated Adults, Law Com. No. 231, London: HMSO.

Link, B., Andrews, H. & Cullen, F. (1992) 'The violent and illegal behavior of mental patients reconsidered', *American Sociological Review*, 57, pp. 275–92.

Monahan, J. (1993) 'Mental Disorder and Violence: Another Look', in Hodgins, S. (ed.) *Mental Disorder and Crime*, Newbury Park, California: SAGE Publications, pp. 294–5.

Noble, P. & Rogers, S. (1989) 'Violence by psychiatric inpatients', *British Journal of Psychiatry*, 155, pp. 384–90.

Norko, M. A., Zonan, H. V. & Philips, R. T. M. (1992) 'Prosecuting Assaultive Psychiatric Patients', *Journal of Forensic Science*, 3, pp. 923–31.

Palmstierna, T. & Wistedt, B. (1988) 'Prevalence of risk factors for aggressive behaviour and characteristics of an involuntary admitted population', *Acta Psychiatrica Scandinavica*, 78, pp. 227–9.

Pearson, M., Wilmot, E. & Padi, M. (1986) 'A study of violent behaviour among in-patients in a psychiatric hospital', *British Journal of Psychiatry*, 149, pp. 232–5.

Powell, G., Caan, W. & Crowe, O. (1994) 'What events precede violent incidents in psychiatric hospitals?', *British Journal of Psychiatry*, 165, pp. 107–12.

Richardson, G. (1993) *Law, process and custody: prisoners and patients*, London: Butterworths.

Richardson, G. (1995) 'Openness, order and regulation in a therapeutic setting', Ch 8 in Crichton, J. H. M. (ed.), *Psychiatric Patient Violence Risk and Response*, London: Duckworth.

Ritchie, J. H. (Chairman), Dick, D. & Lingham, R (1994) *The Report of the Inquiry into the Care and Treatment of Christopher Clunis*, London: HMSO.

Royal College of Psychiatrists (1989) *Guidelines to Good Practice in the Use of Behavioural Treatments. Council Report CR9*, London.

Scott-Moncrieff L. (1993) 'Injustice in Forensic Psychiatry', *Journal of Forensic Psychiatry*, 4, pp. 97–108.

Shah, A. K. (1993) 'An increase in violence among psychiatric inpatients: real or apparent?', *Medicine, Science and the Law*, 33, pp. 227–30.

Stark, C., Farrar, H. and Kidd, B. (1994) 'Violence in psychiatric units' *British Journal of Psychiatry, 165*, 554ff.

Swanson, J., Holzer, C., Ganju, V. & Jono, R. (1990) 'Violence and psychiatric disorder in the community: Evidence from the Epidemiologic Catchment Area surveys', *Hospital and Community Psychiatry*, 41, pp. 761–70.

Tardiff, K. & Sweillam, A. (1980) 'Assault, suicide and mental illness', *Archives of General Psychiatry*, 37, pp. 164–9.

Torpy, D. & Hall, M. (1993) 'Violent incidents in a secure unit', *Journal of Forensic Psychiatry*, 4, pp. 517–44.

Walker, W. D. & Caplan, R. P. (1993) 'Assaultive Behaviour in Acute Psychiatric Wards and Its Relationship to Violence in the Community: a comparison of two health districts', *Medicine, Science and the Law*, 33, pp. 300–4.

Walker, Z. & Seifert, R (1994) 'Violent incidents in a psychiatric intensive care unit', *British Journal of Psychiatry*, 164, pp. 826–8.

Woolf (1991) *Prison Disturbances April 1990*, Cmnd 1456, London: HMSO.

Appendix A

STUDIES INTO BRITISH PSYCHIATRIC INPATIENT VIOLENCE

Authors	Location	Method	Definition of violence	Numbers of incidents	Crude rate of violent incidents per patient per year	'Problem patients'	Other comments
Fottrell et al 1978	Large general psychiatric hospital over 39 weeks	Prospective reporting Standard forms	Physical violence	69	0.07	14 patients cause 50.3% of incidents	
Fottrell (1980)	Hospital A: Large general psychiatric hospital over 52 weeks. Hospital B: Large general psychiatric hospital over 16 weeks. Hospital C: General psychiatric unit as part of a General Hospital over 52 weeks.	Prospective reporting special forms Spot checking etc. interviews with assailants and victims	1* 2* 3* * 1* 2* 3* * 1* 2* 3*	338 13 2 54 — — 32 1 1	0.32 0.15 0.61	3% of patients caused 70% incidents. 4% of patients caused 59% of incidents. 1% of patients caused 41% of incidents.	Violent patients were more likely to have history of violence. The only 3* incidents were suicide. Incidents happened more frequently on acute wards.
Armond (1982)	4 semi-secure wards in a general psychiatric hospital over between 6.5 to 39 weeks.	Prospective reporting Standard Forms Informal interview.	Actual physical injury and deliberate property damage	40	2.0	3 patients caused 50% of incidents	More incidents took place after changes to ward routine.
Aiken (1984)	17 bed secure ward in acute general psychiatric hospital over 26 weeks	Prospective reporting Special forms	Assault against staff causing actual harm	* 1* 14 2* 21 3* 6	7.8	4 patients caused 56.1% of incidents	Violent patients had a significant history of violence.
Hodgkinson et al (1985)	Large general psychiatric hospital over 104 weeks	Retrospective reporting Standard forms	Assaults on staff	Year 1 274 Year 2 348	Unable to calculate from data in the paper.	5% of violent patients caused 26% of incidents.	77% of violent patients only involved in 1 or 2 incidents.
Pearson et al (1986)	Large general psychiatric hospital over 52 weeks	Retrospective reporting Standard forms	Damage to property or injury to another person	* 1* 197 2* 82 3* 4	0.65	1 patient responsible for 12% of incidents	
Larkin et al (1988)	Maximum security hospital over 26 weeks	Prospective Special forms with checking	Behaviour which could cause damage to the patient, others or property.	1144 (31 life threatening)	3.9	4% of patients caused 60% of incidents.	Male crude rate 1.4; female 12.0. Females comprising 25% of population; responsible for 75% of incidents

114

Appendix A

STUDIES INTO BRITISH PSYCHIATRIC INPATIENT VIOLENCE

Authors	Location	Method	Definition of violence	Numbers of incidents	Crude rate of violent incidents per patient per year	'Problem patients'	Other comments
Coldwell & Naismith (1989)	20 bedded high dependency ward of a maximum security hospital over 52 weeks	Retrospect reporting of standard incident forms, study of ward reports and medical notes	Violent action to people and property excluding verbal aggression	116	5.8 +	19.3 patients caused 62.1% of incidents.	Marked seasonal variation with more incidents in winter
Torpy & Hall (1993)	30 bedded medium secure unit over 156 weeks.	Prospective reporting Standard forms	Physical violence	563 (2 life threatening)	7.9*	1 patient caused 8% of incidents	Virtually no violence in areas designed for occupation or therapy
Walker & Seifert (1994)	6 bedded psychiatric intensive care unit over 26 weeks.	Prospective reporting Special and standard forms.	Physical assaults to another person	* 1° 6 2° 28 3° 3	12.3 +		More assaults from those with a history of drug abuse or a criminal record.
Kennedy et al (1995)	77 bedded medium secure unit over 203 weeks	Retrospective reporting Standard forms	An attack on property or assault involving physical contact	* 1° 342 2° 280 3° 66	4.9	1 patient responsible for 6.4% of incidents	Seclusion found unnecessary in management of violence.

+ The authors employ a version of Fottrell's 1980 classification of violence severity 1. No physical injury; 2. Minor injury, e.g., bruises; 3. Major injury, e.g., large lacerations, fractures etc.
* Crude rate of violent incidents per *bed* per year I would like to thank Dr Torpy for supplying additional data so that this rate could be calculated.

115

7

The Management and Discharge of Violent Patients*

John Gunn

'Dangerousness is an important topic for psychiatry. Whether they like it or not, psychiatrists are expected by the population at large to select mentally disordered people who are dangerous to themselves or to others, and to treat them. Psychiatrists are even given special powers to treat such people compulsorily, usually in a hospital, if patients object to the treatment that is offered. This seems to be true in every country of the world ... it is an inescapable part of everyday psychiatry to make judgments about dangers and risks which the patient poses to himself or to other people. Much of the mystique of psychiatry comes from the public awareness of this role. Indeed some of the public hostility to psychiatry is also related to this role, which is sometimes construed as the psychiatrist relinquishing his medical function for a police one!' (Gunn and Monahan (1993)).

Given its impeccable source, the quotation above must be valid! Indeed, in Britain recently we have been dragooned into setting up 'supervision registers', on which psychiatrists are supposed to put the names of patients who are dangerous to themselves or to others and who require special supervision. Yet this has been a highly contentious development. Psychiatrists are also increasingly being asked to undertake 'risk assessments'. Are these reasonable, rational tasks? This chapter will be concerned with the ways in which individuals who are both psychotic and violent are assessed in England and Wales, in the hope that this question can be approached.

---

* A shortened version of this paper, with a different emphasis, under the title 'Let's get Serious about Dangerousness', was read at a retirement conference held in Birmingham (29 September 1995) in honour of Professor Robert Bluglass. That version appears in the proceedings of the conference, Criminal Behaviour and Mental Health 1996, p. 6.

Psychosis and Violence

It is now considered axiomatic, in Britain at least, that psychosis is associated with violence. Approximately 10 years ago matters were different:

> Virtually all the work from the first half of this century showed that mental hospital patients were less likely to commit violent acts than the general population (e.g., Ashley (1992); Pollock (1938); Cohen and Freeman (1945); Brill and Malzberg (1962); Brennan (1964). Later studies showed that the rates for violent crimes among mental hospital patients appear higher (e.g., Rappeport and Lasson (1965); Giovannoni and Gurel (1967); Zitern *et al* (1976); Grunberg *et al* (1977 and 1978)). Steadman *et al* (1978), however, suggested that the real increase in arrest rates among mental patients lies within a recidivist group. Comparing their sample of 1975 with their own sample of 1968, and the sample of Brill and Malzberg (1962), collected in 1947, they showed that among ex-mental hospital patients, without prior arrests, the proportion subsequently arrested had remained remarkably constant over this 30-year period. By contrast, the arrest rate of those with at least one prior arrest has been escalating over the years. What seems to have been happening is that offender patients have become increasingly trapped in a cycle of re-offending and are disproportionately represented in the reduced inpatient population of mental hospitals. (Taylor *et al* (1993))

A remand study conducted in Brixton prison at a time when it received most of the men charged with serious offences in London and the surrounding areas (Taylor and Gunn (1984)) indicated a much closer association between serious violence and psychosis. This showed that of all the men charged with homicide and admitted over a 12-month period, some 11 per cent suffered from schizophrenia. Extrapolated this means that we can expect in England and Wales approximately 50 people to be killed each year by people suffering from psychosis. Thus throughout the world many hundreds of people are killed by psychotic patients each year. In other words, the age-old fear that patients who have gone mad might turn violent is probably based on an understanding of the potential horror of psychosis.

The important thing is to keep this in perspective. Saying that 11 per cent of men charged with homicide suffer from schizophrenia is a very long way from saying that a high proportion of patients with schizophrenia commit violence. Schizophrenia afflicts approximately one per cent of the population and many general psychiatrists will not encounter a seriously violent schizophrenic patient in the course of their ordinary practice.

The important Epidemiologic Catchment Area (ECA) Survey from the United States (Swanson *et al* (1990)) has shown that individuals in the community with psychiatric disorders are more likely to engage in assaultive behaviour, by their own report, than those who are free of mental illness and substance abuse. The community base rate for such reports was two per cent, but eight per cent of patients with schizophrenia reported violence in the one year of study. The risk of violence increased considerably for those people with schizophrenia who also abused alcohol or drugs. Some 30 per cent of patients with the double problem reported violence.

Prediction and Risk Management

In the 1970s there was a concerted search for ways of predicting violence. At approximately the same time weather forecasters appeared on television to give a long-term forecast. This was an estimate of the forthcoming four weeks of weather, based on an elaborate and minute statistical analysis of the weather patterns which had appeared in previous years. The Meteorological Office in London has a massive data bank including many climatic variables over many years. The meterorologists searched, with the aid of computers, for weather patterns that were similar to the ones currently being experienced, and then extrapolated a future model on the basis of previous experience. It must have been a serious embarrassment for the staff who had to undertake this task to realise that they were continually able to make accurate helpful forecasts for the following 24 hours, but the speculations for the following 28 days, based on a comparison of previous weather patterns, turned out to be no better than chance or guesswork. Eventually, they gave it up and improved their public image.

Some of the problems with the predictive approach have recently been summarised by Fenn (1990):

Cardiologists do not often predict a myocardial infarction, nor do gastroen-terologists predict colon cancer. Rather, they cite factors that increase a patient's vulnerability, and everyone understands that the discussion involves probabilities rather than absolutes. The difference is not simply semantic. Viewing the assessment of violence as a prediction suggests that the assessment is all right or all wrong. Since the consequences of being wrong are so grave — either death or injury of an innocent person or unwarranted detention of a patient — many clinicians have opted out of the process by embracing research showing that it is impossible to predict violence. They have taken the position that the courts should decide. This nihilistic attitude contributes to an absence of systematic efforts to provide feedback to clinicians about decisions involving dangerousness. But whether or not an individual will be dangerous is an artificial dichotomy posed by the courts; answering it obscures clinically rich questions about which factors may influence the patient's future behavior.

This approach is in contrast to that expressed by the cliché 'nothing predicts violence like previous violence'. Where does this notion come from? It is a misunderstanding of statistics. There are a number of studies which have shown that if a large population of recidivists, whether or not they are considered to be mentally abnormal, is divided into those who have committed previous acts of violence and those who have not, the group with the previous history of violence will generate more of the future violence than the other group. For example, in Norway, Blomhoff *et al* (1990) retrospectively compared 25 patients who were violent with 34 who were not violent after admission to a psychiatric emergency ward in Oslo. There were no differences between the two groups in terms of age, sex, economic status, or living conditions. There were, however, three important differences. The patients in the violent group had experienced more violence in the family of origin, had more often used non-alcoholic psychoactive substances, and more often had a history of violence than the other patients. The strongest association was the last one. The authors concluded that 'in several previous studies violence has proved to be the best predictor of violence. This finding is replicated in our study'. This is wrong because they did not *predict* anything. What they showed was that their violent patients were more likely to have come from violent homes, to use illegal drugs, and to have been violent before. Useful, unsurprising information, but not a prediction.

Therefore, the myth that previous violence *predicts* violence is constantly reinforced by retrospective statistical data. The problem is that whilst statistics which are mathematical extrapolations from group activity can be extremely powerful in describing and, perhaps, predicting group activity (although that needs to be tested prospectively, not retrospectively), they cannot tell us which members of which group will do what.

Actuarial assessors using vital statistics can predict with remarkable accuracy how many children will be born in Britain next year. They can also predict with remarkable accuracy how many people will die, and at what ages. However, it is not possible to say with anything like the same accuracy *who* will bear the babies and *who* will die. Therefore, the actuarial accuracy is not of much value if the question concerns a particular individual. 'Will my daughter become pregnant?' is not a question that most people would want to answer by turning to a statistical table. Nor would it be appropriate if the doctor attending an elderly patient simply referred to statistics when a prognosis for his life-expectancy was sought. In these *individual* situations, we have much richer data, and the power to determine something of what is going on in someone's head, by conversation.

A second myth about prediction is that psychiatrists are no good at predicting dangerousness. This is partly derived from the overworked Baxstrom case, described by Nigel Walker in Chapter 1. The follow-ups of this and other samples were taken to show that psychiatrists lock people up unnecessarily. Yet if psychiatrists are asked to make predictions about behaviour over long periods of time, they are bound to be wrong quite often, and are bound, given their responsibilities, to be cautious about the predictions they make and over-predict rather than under-predict. Like the weather forecasters, however, whilst they often get the long-range prediction wrong, they are fairly accurate at the short term, and tend, in ordinary practice, to stick with predictions or assessments between one interview and the next.

The psychiatrist is in a much better position than the meteorologist. The weatherman cannot influence the weather, but the psychiatrist can influence the dangerousness of his patient by the measures he takes. In psychiatry it would be helpful to forget about predictions and concentrate on management. Psychiatrists can and usually do manage dangerous patients quite successfully. They do not always get it right, but within the body of psychiatry there is knowledge and expertise about the management of dangerousness that the layman discerns and wants used more effectively. It is the psychiatrists' responsibility to acknowledge these skills, to refine them, and to disseminate them (see Gunn (1996)).

How is it possible to assess whether a patient will be violent in the next week or two? The technique is medically straightforward. A wealth of information is collected about the patient. Efforts are made to understand the way in which his violence potential increases. Interviewers try to learn how he thinks. Does the patient have important ideas, maybe delusional ideas, which are associated with violence? If he is deluded, how distressed is he about this, is he looking for evidence? Is his life frustrating, or is he relatively content with his social circumstances? Is there another person in his world with whom he is at odds? Does he have the basic essentials of life, such as money and housing? Assessment of this kind naturally merges into management. Changes in the environment (admission to hospital if necessary), medication, home visits, help with finance and accommodation, useful occupation etc. may all be varied according to need. A more detailed account of how risks can be managed was given by Gunn and Monahan (1993).

Disasters

The biggest problem faced by psychiatrists is that risk management techniques, however good, sometimes go wrong, and, of course, some psychiatrists do things badly. If things go wrong, disaster may strike, perhaps in the form of a homicide followed by media outcry, political reaction — and scapegoats are sought. In Britain we have had a series of highly publicised psychotic homicides (see Gunn (1996)). Let us examine one.

Christopher Clunis killed Jonathan Zito in 1992. Mrs Zito demanded action and continues to demand action, having formed her own pressure group and her own charity. An enquiry was held and the Ritchie Report was issued in 1994 (Ritchie *et al*).

An abbreviated history of Christopher Clunis is shown in Table 1, and a potted psychiatric history is shown in Table 2.

Table 1

CHRISTOPHER CLUNIS	
Violence	
1986	attempted to hit sister
1.1.88	hit fellow patient
May 88	found with knife — threatened violence
22 May 89	? attempted strangulation
7.6.89	lunged at police with knife
2.7.89	threatened to stab patient
6.7.89	threatened to stab patient
29.9.89	punched patient, grabbed a knife
Feb 90	tried to gouge patient's eye out
July 90	physical abuse to fellow employees
14.8.90	struck resident with walking stick
12.3.91	chased residents with carving knife
24.7.91	fight with another patient
2.8.91	punched nurse, broke glass, attacked patient
14.8.91	kicked and burnt another patient
27.8.91	inflicted severe facial lacerations to resident
23.10.91	punched resident in face
3.5.92	set fire to Bible, attacked resident with knife
7.5.92	hit duty solicitor
7.10.92	tried to hit GP
9.12.92	hit stranger in face, chased boys with screwdriver
17.12.92	KILLED JONATHAN ZITO WITH KNIFE

Table 2

CHRISTOPHER CLUNIS		
Lengths of stays		
1986	Bellevue Hospital, Jamaica	Not known
1987	Chase Farm Hospital	25 days, 4 days
1988	Chase Farm Hospital	3 days, 4 days
	Kings College Hospital	7 days
	Dulwich North Hospital	9 days
	Brixton prison	21 days
	Dulwich North Hospital	16 days
1989	St Charles Hospital	110 days
1991	St Thomas's Hospital	21 days
1992	Belmarsh Prison	24 days
	Kneesworth House Hospital	80 days
	Guy's Hospital	34 days

Tables 3 and 4 illustrate the brevity of inpatient attention that Christopher Clunis received, and also something of the social factors in his life. If moving house and changing close relationships are both major life events which may precipitate mental disorder, then this brief summary of life changes between 1986 and 1992 gives some indication of the pressure that Christopher Clunis was under.

Table 3

CHRISTOPHER CLUNIS	
Diagnoses	
1986	paranoid schizophrenia
29.6.87	schizophrenia with negative features
2.7.87	schizophrenia or drug-induced psychosis
24.7.87	depression
1.1.88	drug-induced psychosis, or manipulation for a bed
29.3.88	psychotic or schizoaffective illness
3.5.88	schizophrenia, drug-induced psychosis or organic illness
7.6.89	paranoid schizophrenia
23.7.91	schizophrenia
5.5.92	paranoid psychosis
14.8.92	paranoid schizophrenia
26.8.92	(diabetes)
10.9.92	normal mental state, abnormal personality

Table 4

CHRISTOPHER CLUNIS
Accommodation 1986–92
8 hospitals (13 admissions) 4 hostels 4 bed and breakfasts 1 flat 2 prisons
(35 professionals)

The case shows a number of important features, including a persistent reluctance to admit to hospital, probably owing to a shortage of beds. Admissions, when they occurred, were brief.

The Ritchie Report made a long list of recommendations, most of which, apart from the supervision register, have been ignored or rejected by the Government. Table 5 gives a sample.

Table 5

RITCHIE REPORT (Clunis Case)
Recommendations
1. Better communication
2. Involve patient's family and GP
3. Obtain accurate history and verify
4. Consider and assess past violence
5. Plan, provide, and monitor aftercare
6. Identify particular needs of homeless patients
7. More medium secure beds
8. More general psychiatric beds
9. A range of health service accommodation
10. More approved doctors (psychiatrists)
11. More social workers
12. Do not overlook or minimise violence
13. Provide long-term care
14. Do not allow geographical boundaries to interfere with care
15. Do not postpone decisions when patient is threatening and intimidating

It is clear from the Ritchie Report that an inquiry of this kind can be heuristic. Numerous reports in the same vein identify similar problems and come to the same conclusions (see Gunn (1996)). After a series of significant reports of this kind, the value of yet more new reports diminishes. Further public inquiries would be helpful if all the recommendations from previous inquiries were implemented and disasters continued to occur. In Britain, at present a paradoxical situation exists where recommendations from reports like the Ritchie Report are largely not implemented, but a lot of time and energy is spent on further inquiries. At the time of writing, there are approximately 24 such reports in the pipeline and, unless the figures ascertained from the Brixton remand study fall sharply, there will be potentially 50 cases per annum in which an inquiry could be held. Not only do such inquiries divert attention from the recommendations of the previous inquiries, but they also take up a lot of resources and considerably reduce the morale of stretched clinical teams. Indeed, on occasions medical staff (the shortage of whom is part of the problem) who have done their best in difficult circumstances have left the NHS entirely, either because of ill-health induced by the inquiry, or because they have felt driven out by criticisms.

Powers of Psychiatrists

Most legal systems give psychiatrists, restrained in a variety of ways, some legal powers to enable them to more effectively manage difficult and dangerous patients. The British system is often regarded as an international model. In Britain there are three separate sets of arrangements, within the three different jurisdictions of England and Wales, Scotland, and Northern Ireland. The law for England and Wales will be discussed here. Details of other British law can be found in Gunn et al (1993, a), and a comparative survey of seven other systems has been given by Harding et al (1993).

British mental health legislation has been developing and changing throughout the twentieth century. At the beginning of the century the emphasis was on hospitalisation and containment, so that it was difficult for patients to get out of large institutions which, by then, had been established for the mentally disordered once they had been detained. At the end of the century, the emphasis is reversed. Now it is difficult for a patient who could benefit from, and indeed might welcome, hospitalisation, to get into hospital at all. If they are admitted, such patients are likely to be discharged within a few days or weeks, as was shown above in the Clunis case.

Within this changing context the compulsory powers available to psychiatrists have also changed their emphasis. Legislation for England and Wales (the Mental Health Act 1983) deals with four categories of mentally disordered persons: those with mental illness (undefined); those with severe mental impairment; those with mental impairment; and those with psychopathic disorder. Psychiatrists are, on the whole, more comfortable with the use of the mental illness category, which they tend to equate with psychosis. Psychosis affects one to two per cent of the population, and is a readily recognisable and, to the psychiatrist, straightforward disorder. As indicated above, it is associated with violence in some cases, and the few remaining inpatient services, after the dissolution of the mental hospitals, are largely geared to admitting this category of patient, even though they are only geared to brief admissions.

The 1983 Act includes not only the four categories listed above (and in three cases legally defined), but also 'any other disorder or disability of mind', which implies that every kind of mental disease is covered by the Act, apart from the specific exceptions which are mentioned in s. 1, indicating that a person may not be dealt with under the Act as mentally disordered 'by reason only of promiscuity or other immoral conduct, sexual deviancy, or dependence on alcohol or drugs'.

The powers to detain under treatment and hospital orders are further limited in relation to mental impairment and psychopathic disorder by requiring that 'treatment in hospital is likely to alleviate or prevent deterioration of the condition'. This treatability clause gives enormous scope for rejecting patients and, being without objective tests, is highly controversial.

The other matter which is made explicit within the Act (s. 131) is that the emphasis on treatment should be on informality rather than compulsion.

The majority of patients detained under the Act are civil cases, admitted for assessment or treatment without any question of criminal behaviour being involved. Under the most widely used sections of the Act (ss. 2 and 3) patients may be detained either for the safety of others, or for their own safety, or for the sake of their own health. It is certainly not necessary for a patient to be a danger to others before detention can be effected (Weleminsky and Birley (1990)).

Patients charged with or convicted of criminal offences are usually dealt with under Part III of the Act, under which hospital orders are available to both the Crown Court and magistrates' courts (including youth courts) for individuals who have been convicted of an offence for which they could suffer imprisonment, provided that two doctors are prepared to sign a form stating that the offender suffers from mental disorder (any one of the four categories) and the managers of a hospital agree to have the patient. This gives very wide powers to admit offenders to hospital, and the practical effect is to hand the offender over to medical care in much the same way as people are dealt with under the civil provisions of the Act.

The problems encountered in operating these aspects of the Act are largely concerned with resources. The finding of a bed is critical and is usually the determining factor as to whether or not a patient can be dealt with within the NHS.

For patients who are considered, by the court, to be dangerous there is a special provision within the Act for restricting their discharge. The effect of such a restriction order is to give the powers of leave, transfer, and discharge, which are normally held by the responsible medical officer, to the Home Secretary. Such restriction orders are imposed after a hospital order has been made under s. 37 of the Act. They are not available for non-offender cases admitted under other parts of the Act, and are only available when 'it appears to the court, having regard to the nature of the offence, the antecedents of the offender, and the risk of his committing further offences if set at large, that it is necessary for the protection of the public from serious harm' (s. 41). One of the reporting (form-filling) doctors in respect of the hospital order has to give oral evidence in court before the order can be made. The order can only be made in the Crown Court. The legislation does allow a time-limit to be put on a restriction order, although, in practice, this almost never happens and most such orders are made 'without limit of time'.

Sentenced prisoners may also be mentally disordered. Either their mental disorder was not recognised at the time of their trial, or no hospital was available to them at the time of sentencing, or they have become ill in prison. In any of these circumstances the Home Secretary may sanction transfer to hospital under s. 47 of the Act, in which case restrictions are usually added under s. 49 and are much the same as those added by a court under s. 41.

A useful addition to the powers of the Mental Health Act 1983 is available to psychiatrists in England and Wales under the Powers of Criminal Courts Act 1973. A probation order can be made, for periods up to a maximum of three years, which includes a condition of psychiatric treatment. This is to be 'under the direction of a duly qualified medical practitioner ... with a view to the improvement of the offender's mental condition'. Like other probation orders it is a voluntary arrangement, which means that the offender, the probation service and the named doctor must all agree before it can be awarded by the court. Once it is established, however, serious challenges to the authority of the medical and probation supervisors may be dealt with as a breach of probation and could lead the offender back to court for a different type of sentence. Leaving hospital against medical advice, or failing to attend an outpatient clinic, are examples of matters which can be regarded as a breach of probation.

Only one 'duly qualified' medical practitioner is required to testify to the mental condition of the offender. The mental condition is defined as that which requires and may be susceptible to treatment, but does not warrant detention under the Mental Health Act 1983. The treatment to be offered must be specified and can be residential treatment, outpatient treatment and/or treatment under the direction of the named psychiatrist. More detailed specification is not required and the specifications can be changed, as the order proceeds, by agreement between the doctor, the probationer and the probation officer. Such probation orders may be given for a wide variety of offences, ranging from serious offences such as manslaughter or wounding, to more trivial offences. Such arrangements may be especially suitable for drug addicts and alcoholics, but they are used for a wide variety of psychiatric conditions.

Mental Health Review Tribunals

Mental health review tribunals have been available in England and Wales since the implementation of the Mental Health Act 1959. The tribunal is appointed by the Lord Chancellor and consists of legal, medical and lay members. The chairman is always a legal member, and when the tribunal is to hear the case of a restricted patient the legal member is drawn from a panel of specially appointed lawyers. Most patients detained for more than 72 hours under the Mental Health Act 1983, can apply to a mental health review tribunal (MHRT) within certain periods of eligibility. Only one application may be made in each eligibility period. If a patient does not make use of his opportunity to apply, after a time his case should automatically be referred to the tribunal by the hospital managers, or, if he is a restricted patient, by the Home Secretary.

Tribunals have a range of options open to them. For example, the tribunal must discharge an unrestricted patient who, in its opinion, does not meet the criteria for detention which would have been used on admission, or whose condition no longer makes detention in hospital necessary in the interests of his health or safety, or for the protection of others. In the case of a patient on a transfer direction, who still has part of his prison sentence to serve, the discharge is back to prison. Restricted patients are dealt with by the special type of tribunal chaired by a judge, or a recorder who is a QC from the Lord Chancellor's special list. The tribunal has powers to order either an unconditional discharge of a patient or, more usually, a conditional discharge, in appropriate circumstances. Both of these types of discharge will necessarily be against the advice of the Home Office. A patient who is conditionally discharged, however, must abide by the conditions set (e.g., attending a particular clinic, living in a particular place) and can be recalled to hospital by the Home Secretary if he breaks the conditions, deteriorates or reoffends (see Barker and Gunn (1993); Bluglass (1984), for further details).

Secure Hospitals

Physical security is a management device which is essential to provide safety from and for a small proportion of dangerous patients. Many countries use imprisonment as their main secure containment strategy. Whilst, to some extent, this is true in Britain, there is also a strong tradition for hospitals to be the main focus of secure containment for the mentally disordered dangerous patient. Throughout the nineteenth century moderately secure local hospitals (the county asylums) developed throughout the United Kingdom. These are now disappearing and are largely being replaced by community care. Such hospitals provided security for very large numbers of people, most of whom did not require it. In addition, nineteenth-century Britain developed maximum security hospitals, such as Broadmoor which was opened in 1863. Two further maximum security hospitals have been developed in this century — Ashworth Hospital in Liverpool, and Rampton Hospital in Nottinghamshire.

As the large mental hospitals began to close, increasing pressure was put on maximum security hospitals, which became grossly overcrowded as a result. This overcrowding was one of the stimuli which caused the Government to set up the Butler Committee in the early 1970s to examine secure hospitals in England and Wales and the whole question of forensic psychiatry. An interim report in 1974 (Home Office, DHSS (1974)) recommended the urgent development of medium security hospitals throughout the NHS. Very slowly money has been allocated to this purpose, and now almost 1,000 beds are available for medium secure provision for mentally disordered offenders. The total provision of maximum and medium security beds within England and Wales is still inadequate, however, and patients requiring this type of management, at least for a period, are not always admitted, and may be dealt with within the prison system or moved into the private health care sector at considerable cost to the public services. Secure institutions are dealt with in more detail in Gunn *et al* (1993, b).

Discharge from Hospital

In an ideal world there would be an adequate range of residential arrangements for patients with chronic disorders, such as schizophrenia, ranging from a few expensive specialised beds in maximum security hospitals, to a large number of medium security beds, and an even larger number of open beds, with the majority of patients living in a variety of community arrangements, such as hostels, sheltered homes, with relatives and in other private accommodation. Placement at the different levels of security and supervision would depend upon clinical need and would not be determined by resource priorities. Unfortunately, this is not the case and there are some extraordinary anomalies within the current British system. For example, there are more maximum-security beds within the NHS than there are medium-security beds. A further anomaly is that those who manage the medium security beds available are reluctant, because of the pressures on them, to take patients for more than medium-term periods, so that there is currently no facility within the NHS for longer-term care within medium security, even although it is inevitable that some patients will require this type of management. Open, but specialised, wards which cater primarily for mentally disordered offenders are almost non-existent. An open ward operates at the Bethlem Royal Hospital (part of The Maudsley Hospital), but it is in jeopardy because of funding problems. Equally rare are specialised hostel and other arrangements within the community for mentally disordered offenders. The Maudsley Hospital also has such a service within the Brixton area of London, but it is often difficult to find arrangements that are willing to take mentally disordered offenders in community settings.

Many psychiatrists are trying to provide a comprehensive service with a small number of rapid-turnover beds in an acute setting, often a district general hospital. However, this is unsatisfactory for the management of patients with long-term disorders who need slow, stable management. One of the obvious lessons that emerges from the Clunis case is that the doctors and social workers managing him had nowhere satisfactory to place him. This may partly explain why the doctors were driven to trying to demedicalise his case on a number of occasions. It is certainly part of the explanation for the Ritchie recommendations for an increase in hospital places for mentally disordered offenders.

Under s. 117 of the Mental Health Act 1983 there are duties placed on local authorities and the Secretary of State in respect of patients being discharged from hospital, who have been detained in hospital. The Act specifies that it is the duty of the health authority and the local social services to provide, in cooperation with relevant voluntary agencies, after-care services for the departing patient. For many years this was not an effective duty because it was not spelled out in any detail, and the stimulus of the Ritchie Report was required to jolt the Government and others into clearer requirements under s. 117. In recent years, the policy has been refined into what is generally known as the care programme approach, which now formally requires a thorough assessment of both health and social care needs for anyone leaving hospital, and the development of a written care plan which is agreed by the relevant agencies who will assist with the patient's care. A key worker is appointed to coordinate that care and regular reviews take place on approximately a half-yearly basis. These reviews are the meeting ground for the responsible medical officer, social workers, nurses, other medical staff, and other people involved in the patient's care. Decisions are agreed and written down.

This strategy is now widely understood, generally welcomed and uncontroversial. Staff find the strategy difficult to implement because of a shortage of resources, so that a patient's placement and care may be something of a compromise with what would be regarded as ideal. Nevertheless, in a good multi-disciplinary team the system ensures that patients are not overlooked and their needs are reviewed regularly.

In 1994, a new dimension was added to the care programme approach in the form of a supervision register. This arose directly from a proposal in the Ritchie Report and was one suggestion taken up with alacrity by the Department of Health. It means that in addition to the documentation kept under the CPA further documentation should be kept for groups of patients who are regarded as at special risk. To quote the NHS Management Executive (1995) guidelines:

> Patients with longer-term, more severe disabilities, and particularly those known to have a potential for dangerous or risk-taking behaviour, need special consideration, both at the time of discharge and during follow-up in the community. No decision to discharge should be agreed unless those taking the clinical decisions are satisfied that the behaviour can be controlled without serious risk to the patient or to other people.

The document goes on to say that:

> ... patients who have a history of aggressive and risk-taking behaviour present special problems and require very careful assessment. They pose particular challenges to clinicians who have to try to predict their future behaviour and the risks of further violence. It is widely agreed that assessing the risk of a patient acting in a aggressive or violent way at some time in the future is, at best, a inexact science. But there are some ways in which uncertainty may be reduced.

An earlier document (NHS Management Executive (1994)) suggested three categories of patients: (a) those at significant risk of suicide; (b) those at significant risk of violence to others; and (c) those at significant risk of severe self-neglect. The later document then suggests four measures: first, making sure that all relevant information is available; secondly, conducting a full assessment of risk, including 'prediction indicators derived from research'; thirdly, defining situations and circumstances known to present increased risk; and, fourthly, seeking expert help, which is interpreted within the guidelines as consulting a forensic psychiatrist. The patient should be told that his name has been placed on the register and that the information is confidential to the clinical team. However, if the patient moves to a new area, the data should accompany him, the patient's GP should be informed and disclosure can be made to criminal justice agencies either where the patient consents or if disclosure 'can be justified in the public interest'. Provider units (hospitals etc.) are obliged to keep statistics about the supervision register.

The supervision register has proved highly controversial and is not supported by the Royal College of Psychiatrists, for several reasons. First, such a register seems unnecessary, given the detailed care programme approach which is already available. If the care programme approach is working properly, then it is difficult to see what the supervision register can add. Many professionals fear that confidentiality will not hold. It is difficult to see why such a register should be developed, in addition to the confidential care programme approach documents, if it is not to have a different level of confidentiality. Perhaps the most worrying aspect of the supervision register, however, is that it tends to impose full responsibility for matters which may go wrong in a patient's management on the key worker, who may be (and usually is) only a nurse or social worker. This is a heavy burden for any professional to bear if a disaster has occurred, and could be seen as a device for preventing blame from rising up the hierarchy to politicians. One commissioning agency has decided to restrict the register to patients who are dangerous to others. This has fuelled further fears about the real nature of the register.

The supervision register will largely be made redundant by a new piece of legislation which will operate from April 1996. Under the Mental Health (Patients in the Community) Act 1995, a new system of supervised discharge will be brought into operation for those who are thought to be at risk to themselves or others. The responsible medical officer will be able to make application in respect of patients deemed to be at *substantial* risk of harm to themselves or others if they did not receive after-care. As with the supervision register, the supervision will be the personal responsibility of a nominated supervisor, who will have powers to require the patient to live at a specified place, attend for medical treatment, occupation, education, or training, and will have powers to convey a patient to the appropriate places, including back to hospital. The period of leave of absence from compulsory hospital care will be extended to 12 months. As with most mental health legislation, this Act will be introduced without new resources.

The Home Secretary and his Advisory Board

In England and Wales the Home Office has some of the functions which are performed in other countries by the Department of Justice. Within the criminal policy department of the Home Office, one division, C3, exercises control over the mentally abnormal offenders who have been convicted and are sent to hospitals by courts under a restriction order, sentenced prisoners who have been transferred to psychiatric hospitals, those who are unfit to plead, and those who have been found not guilty by reason of insanity. Patients under restriction orders may be sent to any psychiatric hospital, but about half are sent to special or maximum security hospitals (Ashworth, Broadmoor, Rampton).

Discharge decisions for restricted patients are almost never initiated by Home Office officials. The procedure is that the responsible medical officer (a consultant) requests permission for leave or discharge of his patient from C3 Division. The civil servants endeavour to collect as much information about that patient as possible and informal contacts take place, perhaps including a visit by the civil servant to a ward round. Questions which the civil servants are most interested in include the motivation for the index offence, the evidence for persisting and/or preoccupying fantasies about violence, the response to medication (if any) and the patient's ability and/or willingness to cooperate with medication, impulsive or explosive behaviour, frustration tolerance, insight into the disorder, and the role of alcohol and drugs in the patient's life and/or offending.

When all the appropriate information has been gathered, the key civil servant will put a recommendation to the minister concerned. If the minister agrees, the leave or discharge is authorised. If the minister disagrees, he may give an indication to the local team about the kinds of steps which would make the case more persuasive. The patient is entitled, under the Mental Health Act 1983, to appeal against Home Office refusal for discharge when that patient is next eligible for a Mental Health Review Tribunal hearing.

When a patient under a restricted hospital order is conditionally discharged from hospital, whether by the Home Office or by a tribunal, he will be subject to a combination of social work and medical supervision. If either the social supervisor or the responsible medical officer wants to change the conditions of the conditional discharge, proposals can be put to the Home Office or to the discharging tribunal. In the case of deterioration and a proposal for readmission this goes directly to the Home Office in all cases, and is usually acted on very promptly. The patient can be back in hospital within a few hours of such a request by a member of the clinical team.

Advisory Board on Restricted Patients

Since 1973 the Home Secretary has had an advisory board to inform him about particularly difficult cases within the restricted patient group. The Board is chaired by a lawyer and includes a second lawyer, as well as two forensic psychiatrists, two social workers, and two 'lay' members with particular experience in the criminal justice system. Cases are referred to the Board by the key civil servant responsible for a particular case, who identifies that case to be especially worrying, or by the minister himself, perhaps during a decision-making phase. Exceptionally either the responsible medical officer or the local hospital managers will refer the case if they are worried about their patient.

The Board meets once a month to discuss a number of patients. Before each meeting every member is provided with a copy of the Home Office dossier on a patient, and one member is delegated to visit that patient in hospital and to present a report from that visit to the forthcoming Board meeting. The purpose of the visit is to discuss the case with the responsible medical officer, to check that all the relevant information from the patient's file is also in the Home Office file, to meet the patient to get his perspective on the situation, and to explain the procedures and make the whole process less impersonal. The visitor is not expected to provide a specialist report, so that the reports from the different kinds of visitors should be roughly comparable one with another. After presentation to the Board and a collective discussion, the chairman writes an advisory note for the minister on the case concerned. This advisory note is in no way binding on the minister.

Conclusion

Psychiatrists are inevitably involved in the assessment and management of dangerous patients. In spite of the universal human inability to predict behaviour on a long-term basis, psychiatrists can contribute to the safe management of mentally disordered offenders by using standard, straightforward, psychiatric techniques. The essence of this strategy is to collect large amounts of clinical and social data about an individual patient, to monitor that data on a frequent basis in some detail, and to intervene to reduce symptoms and stressors when necessary. The psychiatrist has available to him not only the skills of psychiatry, which in many ways are the most important of the resources, but also facilities which have been provided, including residential facilities of various kinds, from secure hospitalisation to hostels (in the best areas), and legal powers to restrict the freedom of action of patients who are not in a position to manage themselves responsibly. The legal restraints available to psychiatrists are limited by statute and are curtailed by the judicial processes of a mental health review tribunal. In particularly serious cases the legal powers and therefore the control of the patient's care is shared with the Home Office, and the Home Secretary has the last word, except that the Home Secretary is also subject to the curtailments, on occasion, of a mental health review tribunal.

Does all this mean that it is reasonable to ask psychiatrists to undertake risk assessments? Given the approach outlined in this chapter, the answer has to be 'Yes'. When undertaking a risk assessment a psychiatrist is actually on familiar territory, making a clinical judgment about a patient's mental condition, his behaviour disturbances, and the prognosis of those disturbances. A psychiatrist, however, does not do this in a vacuum; he is concerned to alter adverse aspects of a patient's condition, and to try to give advice about placement and management which will optimise health and thus reduce aggressive and other aberrant behaviour. In a difficult case psychiatrists will make sure that the patient is either under continuous scrutiny, or is in frequent contact with local health and social work services. This is more appropriately labelled risk management than risk assessment. It has very little to do with criminological prediction, which concerns the behaviour of groups (and is analogous to vital statistics).

The limiting factor in this system is obvious. It is resources. Detailed assessments take time, a multi-disciplinary approach means plenty of staff, and, above all, adequate and *appropriate* residential accommodation is essential. Risks cannot be safely managed without such resources. Political decisions may be taken that resources are not to be provided because money should be spent elsewhere, but the risk in doing that should also be assessed and understood. It is unreasonable to insist on responsibilities (e.g., of nominated supervisors) that are not matched by appropriate resources. A serious debate about this matter would be worth all the other debates about risk assessment put together!

The main purpose of this chapter has been to indicate that the recurring criminological nightmare of poor, long-term prediction is largely irrelevant to the practical management of violent and potentially violent patients. On waking from the nightmare the practical problems of a dynamic and management strategy may seem even more difficult. However, as this chapter has tried to point out, such problems are not insurmountable and many of the nuts and bolts required to make a good risk management system work are already available.

References

Ashley, M. C. (1922) 'Outcome of 1,000 cases paroled from the State Hospital', *New York State Hospital Quarterly*, 8, pp. 64–70.

Barker, A. & Gunn, J. (1993) 'The courts and bodies overseeing and administering the laws in the United Kingdom (and Ireland)', in *Forensic Psychiatry, Clinical, Legal and Ethical Issues*, Gunn, J. & Taylor, P. (eds) Oxford: Butterworth-Heinemann.

Blomhoff, S., Seim, S. & Friis, S. (1990) 'Can prediction of violence among psychiatric patients be improved?', *Hospital and Community Psychiatry*, 41, pp. 771–5.

Bluglass, R. (1984) *A Guide to the Mental Health Act 1983*, Edinburgh: Churchill-Livingstone.

Brennan, J. J. (1964) 'Mentally ill aggressiveness, popular delusions as reality', *American Journal of Psychiatry*, 120, pp. 1181–4.

Brill, H. & Malzberg, B. (1962) 'Statistical report based on the arrest records of 5,354 male ex-patients released from New York state mental hospitals during the period 1946–1948', *Mental Hospital Service Supplement* 153, Washington DC: American Psychiatric Association.

Cohen, L. H. & Freeman, H. (1945) 'How dangerous to the community are State Hospital patients?', *Connecticut State Medical Journal*, 9, pp. 697–700.

Fenn, H. H. (1990) 'Violence: probability versus prediction', *Hospital and Community Psychiatry*, 41, p. 117.

Fregier, H. A. (1840) *Les Classes Dangereuses dans les grandes villes*, Geneva: Slatkine-Megariotis Reprints 1977, quoted in (1985) 'Dangerousness, mental disorder, and politics', in *Dangerousness*, Webster, C. D., Ben-Aron, M. H., Hucker, S. J., Cambridge: Cambridge University Press.

Giovannoni, J. M. & Gurel, L. (1967) 'Socially disruptive behaviour of ex-mental patients', *Archives of General Psychiatry*, 7, pp. 146–53.

Grunberg, F., Klinger, B. I. & Grumet, B. (1977) 'Homicide and de-institutionalisation of the mentally ill', *American Journal of Psychiatry*, 134, 685–7.

Grunberg, F., Klinger, B. I. & Grumet, B. (1977) 'Homicide and community-based psychiatry', *Journal of Nervous and Mental Disease*, 166, pp. 868–74.

Gunn, J. (1996) 'Let's Get Serious About Dangerousness', *Criminal Behaviour and Mental Health* (forthcoming).

Gunn, J., Briscoe, O., Carson, D., d'Orbán, P., Grubin, D., Mullen, P., Stanley, S. & Taylor, P. J. (1993)(a) 'The law, adult mental disorder and the psychiatrist in England and Wales', in *Forensic Psychiatry, Clinical, Legal and Ethical Issues*, Oxford: Butterworth-Heinemann.

Gunn, J., Grounds, A., Mullen, P. & Taylor, P. J. (1993)(b) 'Secure institutions: their characteristics and problems', *Forensic Psychiatry, Clinical, Legal and Ethical Issues*, Oxford: Butterworth-Heinemann.

Gunn, J., & Monahan, J. (1993) 'Dangerousness', in *Forensic Psychiatry, Clinical, Legal and Ethical Issues*, Oxford: Butterworth-Heinemann.

Harding, T. W. & Montandon, C. (1982) 'Does dangerousness travel well?', in *Dangerousness: Psychiatric Assessment and Management*, Hamilton, J. R. & Freeman, H., London: Gaskell.

Harding, T., Adserballe, H., Berner, W., Dontschev, P., Hucker, S., Jablensky, A., Westmore, B. & Wettstein, R. M. (1993) 'A comparative survey of medico-legal systems', in *Forensic Psychiatry, Clinical, Legal and Ethical Issues*, Oxford: Butterworth-Heinemann.

Home Office, Department of Health and Social Security (1974) *Interim Report of the Committee on Mentally Abnormal Offenders*, Cmnd 5698, London: HMSO.

Lidz, C. W., Mulvey, E. P. & Gardner, W. (1993) 'The accuracy of prediction of violence to others', *Journal of the American Medical Association*, 269, pp. 1007–11.

NHS Management Executive (1994) HSG(94)5, London: Department of Health.

NHS Management Executive (1995) HSG(95)27, London: Department of Health.

Pollock, H. M. (1938) 'Is the paroled patient a menace to the community?', *Psychiatric Quarterly*, 12, pp. 236–44.

Rappeport, J. R. & Lasson, G. (1965) 'Dangerousness — arrest rate comparisons of discharged mental patients and the general population', *American Journal of Psychiatry*, 121, pp. 776–83.

Ritchie, J. H., Dick, D. & Lingham, R. (1994) *The Report of the Inquiry into the Care and Treatment of Christopher Clunis*, London: HMSO.

Steadman, H. & Cocozza, J. (1974) *Careers of the Criminally Insane*, Lexington: Lexington Books.

Steadman, H. & Keveles, G. (1972) 'The community adjustment and criminal activity of the Baxstrom patients 1966–70', *American Journal of Psychiatry*, 129, 3, pp. 304–310.

Steadman, H. J., Cocozza, J. J. & Melick, M. E. (1978) 'Explaining the increased arrest rate among mental patients: the changing clientele of State hospitals', *American Journal of Psychiatry*, 135, pp. 816–20.

Steadman, H. J., Monahan, J., Robbins, P. C., Appelbaum, P., Grino, T., Klassen, D., Mulvey, E. P. & Roth, L. (1993) 'From dangerousness to risk assessment: implications for appropriate research strategies', in *Mental Disorder and Crime*, Hodgins, S. (ed.) Newbury Park: Sage.

Swanson, J. W., Holzer, C. E., Ganju, V. K. & Jono, R. T. (1990) 'Violence and psychiatric disorder in the community: evidence from the Epidemiologic Catchment Area surveys', *Hospital and Community Psychiatry*, 41, pp. 761–70.

Taylor, P. J. & Gunn, J. C. (1984) 'Violence and psychosis, *British Medical Journal*, 288, pp. 1945–9, and 289, pp. 9–12.

Taylor, P. J., Mullen, P. & Wessely, S. (1993) 'Psychosis, violence and crime', in *Forensic Psychiatry, Clinical, Legal and Ethical Issues*, Oxford: Butterworth-Heinemann.

Weleminsky, J. & Birley, J. (1990) 'Mental Health Act 1983' (Correspondence between the President and the Director of the National Schizophrenic Fellowship), *Psychiatric Bulletin*, 14, pp. 235–6.

Zitren, H., Hardesty, A. S. & Burdock, E. G. (1976) 'Crime and violence among mental patients', *American Journal of Psychiatry*, 133, pp. 142–9.

8

Parole and the Dangerous Offender

David Hirschmann

Prisons are primarily places of punishment, and when a prisoner reaches the end of a custodial sentence, which is usually shorter than the nominal sentence awarded, he must be released. For a number of reasons it may be thought desirable to release someone on either a temporary or parole licence before that point, and a lifer, for whom there is no definite end of sentence, will be expected to be tested out on temporary licences before being released on a life licence. Temporary releases, which include, for example, one-day unescorted visits to a funeral or prospective employer, regular daily releases to work outside a prison, weekend or longer home leaves, are granted by the Prison Service or Home Office; parole and life licences are recommended or granted by the Parole Board. The rules and criteria differ, but the common factor is the need to assess the degree of risk to others. Although this chapter focuses on parole, many of the issues concerning the identification of dangerous or high-risk offenders arise when deciding on temporary releases.

Parole is based on two beliefs which are difficult to test, but are also difficult to abandon. The first, 'rehabilitative belief',[1] is that early release under probation supervision of a prisoner can significantly reduce the chances of his committing more crimes in the future. However, the laudable aim not to keep

---

[1] The expression comes from Lacey *et al*, who make a much stronger claim that '... parole has its roots in a rehabilitative belief that choosing the right moment for release would increase chances of reform, and its reality in pragmatic concerns with costs and prison overcrowding'. (Lacey, N., Wells, C. & Meure, C. D. (1990) *Reconstructing Criminal Law*, London: Weidenfeld and Nicholson, pp. 22–3. See also, *The Parole System in England and Wales: Report of the Review Committee* (1988), (The Carlisle Report), London: HMSO for the history of parole in Britain since 1967.

a person in prison longer than necessary has always been tempered by what may be called the 'preventive belief', that some offenders are too dangerous to be returned to the community and should be kept in prison as long as justice permits. There are important jurisprudential issues concerning the legitimacy of various forms of preventive detention, some of which are discussed in chapter 1. There is also one matter of principle which has direct bearing on a parole system based on a balance between rehabilitation and prevention. Ideally, if the system is just, it must be possible to identify those who will be less likely to re-offend if they are supervised by a probation officer on leaving prison early, and those who are, in some sense, too dangerous to release early. Even if we can achieve the ideal, there will still be a considerable number of prisoners who belong to neither category. How these offenders are treated will depend upon whether the parole system places more emphasis on prevention or rehabilitation. This chapter describes the way in which the new arrangements for parole and life licences, introduced in the Criminal Justice Act 1991 (CJA 1991) have changed parole procedures so that, in principle, prevention takes precedence over rehabilitation.

The chapter is in five parts. The first part describes the new sentence structure and who is entitled to be considered for parole or life licence. The second part summarises the new directions or criteria for the Parole Board's decisions and the training guidance given by the Home Secretary and the Board to its members. The third part describes some of the material on which the decisions are based and the fourth part contains comments on some practical and theoretical issues. The final part comments briefly on prisoners' rights.

Since the subject of this book is the dangerous person, it should be noted at the outset that the term 'dangerous' and its cognates rarely appear in any of the formal documents relating to parole and life licences. Instead, assessments and decisions are concerned with the risk of offending while on licence, the risk of committing a serious or violent offence, or whether it is necessary for the protection of the public to keep a person in prison. Further, not every prisoner denied parole is held to be dangerous. However, the term is convenient and will be used where it will not mislead.

The Structure of a Prison Sentence

The Parole Board advises the Secretary of State as to whether someone should be released on parole, and in some cases has the power to direct release. The Board considers three kinds of prisoner, those serving *determinate sentences*, those who receive *mandatory life sentences* and those who receive *discretion-*

ary life sentences.[2] The CJA 1991 introduced radical changes to the structure of determinate sentences, so that the time served in prison for a given sentence was increased, those with shorter sentences were released on licence whatever the risks, and decisions about parole licences were limited to those who had shown themselves, by the sentences they had received, to be capable of serious offending.

Determinate Sentence Prisoners

When parole was introduced in April 1968 determinate sentence prisoners were already entitled to one-third remission. Those who showed promise or determination to reform were able to earn a further reduction in the time they spent in prison once they had served one-third of the sentence. The minimum length of sentence which gave an entitlement to parole was reduced over the years in order to ease overcrowding, but the formal structure, one-third remission, up to one-third early release on licence, remained unchanged.[3] Those who were thought able to benefit from early release on licence were supervised: all the others eventually went back into the community with, at best, voluntary probation support, whatever the risks of reoffending. Following the Carlisle Report (1988), the CJA 1991 introduced a new structure; remission has been abolished and, except for adults sentenced to less than one year, all prisoners serve part of their sentence in the community. Those serving less than four years are *automatically released* at the halfway stage, unless they have received 'added days' for prison disciplinary offences. Those sentenced to less than one year are released *unconditionally*, whereas those serving at least one year and under four years are *conditionally released*, remaining at risk of recall to serve the remainder of their sentence in prison if they re-offend. All young offenders and adults sentenced to at least one year and under four years are also on licence to the three-quarter point of their sentence. The licence periods for an adult can thus be from as little as three months to just under one year.

There are definite advantages to the new arrangements for 'short sentence' prisoners. Apart from the administrative advantages of reducing the number of cases to be considered for parole by about 14,000, every automatic conditional release offender will be supervised by, and therefore be in contact with, a probation officer for one-quarter of his sentence.[4] In theory, there is a loss. This

---

[2] There are three, not two, types of lifer: mandatory, discretionary (as defined by s. 34 of the CJA 1991), and a nameless category — those sentenced to non-mandatory life for whom the judge forgot or chose not to specify a minimum period under s. 34(2). Their position is like that of mandatory lifers: only the Home Office can decide when their cases come to the Board, and the Board can only recommend, not direct, their release.

[3] See Carlisle Report (*supra*, n. 1), Section 20.

[4] See chapter 9.

group will contain some offenders who will go on to commit serious offences during the period when, under the old scheme, they would still have been in prison. Others who would benefit from parole with additional licence conditions (see below) will now be released with a standard licence, and an opportunity for focused work on reoffending will be lost. It will be important, although difficult, to learn whether the new system has an influence on reoffending rates in the next few years.

Those offenders sentenced to four years or more are eligible for parole, or discretionary conditional release (DCR) on a parole licence, at the halfway point of the sentence. If they are not released then their cases are reviewed annually thereafter until the two-thirds point, when they are automatically released to be supervised in the community until the three-quarters point. Sex offenders, unlike other categories of violent offender, can be required to be supervised to the end of sentence if, and only if, the judge so decides at the time of sentence (see chapter 5). Therefore, every prisoner with a determinate sentence has some supervision on release from prison, and for long-term prisoners this can be for a significant part of the sentence. A prisoner serving 12 years who is not paroled will still be supervised for one year.

The new system applies to all those sentenced since October 1992 and the Board will continue to have to consider cases under the old sentence system, whereby parole can be granted after the one-third point and before the two-thirds stage, for some years to come. Apart from the earliest date when they can be paroled, all old determinate sentence cases coming to the Board are now treated in the same way and according to the same criteria. However, some offenders can still return to the community without any supervision, whatever the risks.

Most of these changes are broadly in line with the recommendations in the Carlisle Report. One difference is that the Report had argued for automatic conditional release for those serving four years or less, but, in the Government's subsequent (1990) White Paper, *Crime, Justice and Protecting the Public*,[5] the upper bound is set at less than four years because many offenders given sentences of exactly four years have been convicted of serious sexual and violent crimes and 'the Government believes that careful and individual consideration is needed before such prisoners can be released early from custody'. DCR is to act as a filter, releasing only those who are not liable to commit serious offences on licence and keeping others away from the public for longer. The use of length of sentence to distinguish automatic discretionary release from conditional discretionary release is convenient, but appears arbitrary. Even if it is true that many prisoners serving exactly four years have

---

[5] (1990) *Crime, Justice, and Protecting the Public*, London: HMSO.

been convicted of violent or sexual offences, there will also be many who are as dangerous and receive less than four years. Risk of violent or serious sexual reoffending, like dangerousness, is an estimate of future behaviour and sentence length is not known to be correlated with such future risk. The offender's criminal record is the best single available predictor of future criminality,[6] but that is not closely correlated with sentence length.

Life Sentences

The structure of a life sentence, whether mandatory or discretionary, has not changed. It still contains, essentially, two components, the 'tariff' to satisfy the needs of retribution and general deterrence, and a preventive element. A discretionary lifer is given an indefinite sentence only because of the gravity of the offence and the likelihood of continued serious risk for the foreseeable future, so that once the tariff has expired he is kept in prison solely for preventive reasons. When the punitive part of the sentence has been served he is entitled to a hearing before the Board, who must direct his release if it is satisfied that it is no longer necessary to keep him in prison to protect the public. All discretionary lifers, whenever sentenced, are entitled to such hearings. A mandatory lifer is not so entitled and, as explained later, he may be detained for reasons other than punishment or risk.

The Directions for Release on Licence

The Parole Board, whose members include judges, psychiatrists, probation officers and criminologists, as well as a large number of 'independents' (many of whom have worked in a professional or voluntary capacity in some part of the criminal justice system), advises the Home Secretary on release on licence, on recall and on any other matters referred to it. The Home Secretary cannot act against the advice if the Board recommends that a prisoner should not be released, although he can override a positive recommendation for DCR or the release of a mandatory lifer. The Home Secretary, however, has delegated to the Board the power to release those offenders serving from four years to less than seven years. For those serving longer sentences, power to release has not been delegated, although Carlisle had argued that the Board should be given the power to release in all determinate sentence cases. The Board hopes that, in time, sufficient trust in the new system will be gained to allow the seven years' threshold to be raised or abolished.[7]

---

[6] von Hirsch, A. (1895) *Past or Future Crimes*, Manchester: Manchester University Press, p. 131.
[7] (1994) *Report of the Parole Board for 1993*, London: HMSO, p. 2.

The Home Secretary's willingness to delegate some executive responsibility to the Board was coupled with another important change introduced by the CJA 1991. Before this Act the Board had made use of criteria for refusing parole. and for recalling offenders on licence. These were given by the Secretary of State and formed part of the Board's training of its new members. The status of these criteria was not always clear.[8] In particular it was not made explicit whether the Board had to be satisfied that someone should be or satisfied that he should *not be* released on licence. In place of the old criteria,[9] the Home Secretary has now given directions and training guidance to the Board. These are published as an Appendix to each annual Report of the Board since 1992 and remove any doubt about what the Board must decide.

Directions for Determinate Sentence Prisoners

For DCR cases, the decision of the Board should focus primarily on the risk to the public of a further offence being committed when the offender would otherwise be in prison, and this should be balanced against the benefit to the prisoner and the public of early release under supervision which might help rehabilitation and so lessen the risk of reoffending in the future. Further, each case should be considered on its individual merits, without discrimination on any grounds. These directions do not differ greatly from the old system's. It is the addition of three conditions which have changed the emphasis of parole decisions. The new conditions or criteria about which the Board should be satisfied before recommending parole are:

(a)   the longer period of supervision which parole would provide must be likely to reduce the risk of further imprisonable offences being committed. In assessing the risk to the community a small risk of violent offending is to be treated as more serious than a larger risk of non-violent offending;

(b)   the offender must have shown by his attitude and behaviour in custody that he is willing to address his offending and has made positive efforts and progress in doing so;

(c)   the resettlement plan must help to secure the offender's rehabilitation.

---

[8] See Hood, R. & Shute, S. (1995) *Paroling with the new Criteria. Evaluating the Impact and Effects of Changes in the Parole System: Phase Two*, Occasional Paper 16 of the Oxford University Centre for Criminological Research. The report on the first phase was published in 1993 and sets out a baseline from which to assess changing practices through the observation of a number of panels in the months before the new Act's provisions came into force.

[9] These can be found in Appendix 1 of the *Report of the Parole Board for 1991* (1992) London: HMSO, and earlier reports.

The Board must always take into account the supervising officer's recommendations as to suitability for release.

All three conditions should be fulfilled if the Board is to be satisfied. The first condition requires the Board to be satisfied not just that the prisoner will keep to the licence conditions but that supervision for the longer period is *likely to reduce* the chances of further reoffending. In some cases one can be confident that the prisoner will not offend during the licence period, but much less confident that supervision will reduce the chances of his offending at a later date. Such an offender should not get parole. The wording of the first condition is unfortunate. Some members of the Board have pointed out that if the Board was satisfied that it was extremely improbable that a prisoner would offend again, the sentence itself, for example, having had an impressive effect, he should not be released because supervision would not lower the risk further. The Home Office has allowed that, notwithstanding the literal reading, the Board could be satisfied that the first condition was fulfilled.

For the Board to be satisfied that the second condition is fulfilled it is not enough that the prisoner has tried to learn how to avoid offending in the future; there must be sufficient evidence for the Board to be satisfied of *actual* progress. It will be difficult for the Board to be satisfied as to the third condition, if only because many plans can do little to counteract the effects of economic conditions. In current circumstances most offenders on release will not be employed. Hood and Shute (1995) found evidence that the new criteria led to more of those considered a high risk being refused parole than was the case under the old system.[10]

The Directions are followed by Training Guidance, a list of 12 factors which the Board should take into account in reaching its decision, although 'the weight and relevance may vary according to the circumstances of the case', thus allowing considerable discretion in their use. The 12 factors can be put into three groups: first, evidence from the past, concerned with the offender's background, previous convictions, previous responses to supervision, the nature and circumstances of the offence, probation and medical reports presented to the court and the sentencing judge's comments when available (which is rare); secondly, evidence about the present, including prison behaviour, current attitude to other inmates, contribution to prison life, remorse, insight into offending behaviour, attitude to the victim, and steps, given available resources, to achieve training objectives or treatment as set out in the sentence plan (see below); and thirdly, evidence about the future, including the realism of the release plan and resettlement prospects, likely

---

[10] 'Prisoners not released early in their sentences are less likely than formerly to be released at subsequent reviews' (Hood, R. & Shute, S. (*supra*, n. 8) at p. 56.) This was so even if they were old system cases and would be released at the two-thirds point without any supervision.

response to supervision, relationship with the probation officer, and whether there are risks to the victim or others, or risk of retaliation by the victim, family or local community. The Board should also take account of any statistical indicators which are available and any other risk indicators, including the prisoner's representations.

Directions for Life Sentence Prisoners

In the case of mandatory lifers, the Board's role is to make a recommendation to the Home Secretary who must accept a recommendation not to release on licence, but can reject a positive recommendation. The Board is concerned solely with risk and is directed to consider whether 'having regard to the degree of risk involved of the lifer committing further imprisonable offences after release, it remains necessary for the protection of the public for the lifer to be confined'.[11] The Home Secretary's decision may go beyond risk because he is concerned with the wider political implications which a release may have. This is one reason why it was noted above that not every prisoner denied parole is held to be dangerous.

As in the DCR directions, the Board must consider each case on its individual merits, although curiously the words 'without discrimination on any grounds' are omitted. There are only two conditions or criteria which the Board must consider. These are: (a) whether the lifer has shown by his performance in prison that he has made positive efforts to address his attitudes and behavioural problems, and the extent to which progress has been made so that the risk that he will commit a further imprisonable offence is *minimal* (my italics); and (b) whether the lifer is likely to comply with supervision. The training guidance on the factors to be taken into account is similar to the list for DCR cases, but includes 'the possible need of any special licence conditions to cover concerns which might otherwise militate against release'. The Board, I believe, also takes that factor into account in determinate cases when it considers that it is better to release an offender under a more stringent than normal licence rather than keep him in prison for longer. Some members of the Board find talk of addressing behaviour inappropriately moralistic. The use of 'behavioural problems' in (a) (above) suggests that there is a general assumption which underlies the Home Office's risk assessments for lifers. The implication is that anyone sentenced to life imprisonment will have behavioural problems which caused his offence. It is a very bold assumption to make about the relation between abnormal psychology and legally defined criminality.

---

[11] The directions are in Appendix B of the *Report of the Parole Board for 1993* (1994).

A lifer's progress through the prison system is carefully assessed at each stage and the move from closed to open conditions is seen as involving new, potentially graver, risks.[12] However, it is also an essential testing-out stage which nearly every lifer must pass through if he is to be released. The Board has been given specific directions on the move to an open prison, and in considering whether a lifer should be transferred it should balance the risks against the benefits of such a move. Specifically, it should consider (a) whether the risk of absconding or of committing further offences is minimal, (b) whether he has made positive efforts to address his attitudes and behavioural problems and whether he has made significant progress, and (c) whether he will benefit from being able to continue to address areas of concern in an open prison and to be tested in a more realistic environment.

The Release of Discretionary Lifers

A discretionary life sentence is only given, or should only be given, when it appears probable at the time of sentence that the offender will remain, because of his mental condition, a potential danger for a long time.[13] Once he has served the punitive part of the sentence, he should be kept in prison, assuming no other offence has been committed, only because he is considered to continue to be liable to commit grave offences, i.e., is detained for purely preventive reasons. Once reviewed and considered in the same way as mandatory lifers, the discretionary lifer is now considered under the Parole Board Rules 1992 by a discretionary lifer panel, which consists of three members of the Board. The chairman is a judicial member, the second member is usually a psychiatrist and the third member is a probation officer, criminologist or 'independent' member. The lifer can have legal representation, but the proceedings are kept as informal as possible and are not adversarial. The Home Secretary's position is usually presented by a 'life governor' and both parties have access to all the documents prepared for the hearing and can apply to the chairman of the panel for witnesses to attend. The panel must consider whether it is satisfied that 'it is no longer necessary for the protection of the public that the prisoner should be confined' and, if it is satisfied, it *must* direct release. That decision is entirely a matter for the Board. If the panel is not satisfied it can recommend to the Home Secretary that the lifer should be moved to a lower category of prison and also recommend when the case should be heard again (the case will normally be heard every two years).

---

[12] See Mitchell, B. (1992) 'Preparing Life Sentence Prisoners for Release', *Howard Journal*, 31, pp. 224–39.
[13] Chapter 5. Members of the Board were referred to *Picker* (1970) 54 Cr App R 330.

Giving Reasons

The reason for all recommendations concerning DCR and lifer cases referred to the Board must be given to the prisoner. The reasons should refer to the directions for that category of prisoner, and relate evidence to the particular criterion not satisfied if release is refused or is not recommended. If release is recommended, the evidence should show that all parts of the criteria are satisfied. 'Evidence' is not used in the legal sense; it refers to what the Board has learned from reports presented or what is said at hearings. Initially, giving reasons in DCR cases presented problems. Members had been used to recording reasons against release by referring to the letter or heading of the appropriate criterion; the nature of the offence, the release plan, and so on. They had no experience of recording reasons for release. Some of the difficulties were observed and discussed by Hood and Shute.[14] When the new parole system came into force and reasons had to be given, members were constantly reminded to give 'reasons for reasons'.

The Evidence on which the Decision is Made

Decisions on DCR cases are made by a panel of three members solely on the basis of the papers presented in the applicant's parole dossier. Usually a psychiatrist or psychologist will be on a panel dealing with sex offenders and, if they can be identified beforehand, those offenders who present serious mental problems. Otherwise, the Board does not appear to operate a policy about which discipline is represented on which panel.[15] The dossier brings together whatever evidence exists which bears on the factors in the training guidance. It should contain a list of previous convictions, a police report on the current offence, a copy of the pre-sentence report, the prisoner's sentence plan and annual reviews, a parole assessment from the prison and an assessment by the probation officer who will supervise the parolee on release. The report of an interview by a Board member, the prisoner's representations and the rate of reconviction (ROR) score (the new statistical risk indicator) must be attached. Reports assessing his performance on any courses which are designed to reduce risk, such as anger management, sexual offending, alcohol or drug abuse courses, will be included if they are available. The Board must rely on prisons to produce most of this material, which has caused difficulties in many cases.

---

[14] Hood and Shute, (*supra*, n. 8), pp. 54–5.
[15] The CJA 1991 reduced the size of panels from four members to three, although the Board argued strongly against the move. Hood and Shute note the loss of multi-disciplinary panels. Similar points can also be made about cutting the membership of lifer panels where the loss of expertise will be at least as noticeable.

Prisons also have problems with outside agencies and it is not uncommon for cases to be delayed or referred to another panel because there is no police report of the index offence.

When the new parole system was introduced, applicants were given the right to read their dossiers before the panel met and to be given reasons for the decision afterwards. Reports therefore needed to be directed to the questions considered by the panel and also be sufficient to provide the grounds for the reasons for the decision reached. So the opportunity was taken to make some fundamental changes to the dossier. A more subtle means of presenting statistical estimates of risk was included in every DCR dossier for male prisoners. The forms completed by prison officers focus on risk and rehabilitative work in prison, and documents about sentence planning and achievement which have a direct bearing on the new criteria are included. The Parole Board interview with the prisoner, which replaces the old local review committee interview, is a major innovation.

Sentence Planning

Every prisoner sentenced since October 1992, when the relevant provisions of the CJA 1991 came into force, can expect to be interviewed early in his sentence in order to identify targets to be met in the coming year. These agreed targets have some bearing on the chance of reducing re-offending and can include completing an anger management course, setting literacy goals, completing a further stage of vocational training, and achieving a new level of physical fitness. Progress should be reviewed annually when new targets can be set. The panel will use the information in the reports to assess the extent to which the offender has managed to understand why he offends and how to avoid doing so again.

Sentence planning may seem ambitious, given the numbers of offenders involved and the difficulty of ensuring that prisoners remain for long enough in an establishment to see a programme through to the end. Custody and control will too often have to take precedence over rehabilitation. Provision of suitable courses to help prisoners meet targets is uneven. Nevertheless, the scheme is seen by the Board as a response to the need to enable prisoners to work in a constructive way towards their release. The difficulty for the Board is that too often a target is set which cannot be attained during the period because the prison lacks the needed resource or because the prisoner is moved to another prison.[16] The panel will use the information in the reports to assess the extent to which the offender has managed to understand why he offends and how to

---

[16] See Hood and Shute (*supra*, n. 8), p. 52.

avoid doing so again. If a prisoner fails, for example, to complete a course designed to help him to understand and overcome his problem, the panel may give this as a reason for being dissatisfied with that prisoner's progress. The prisoner will have a valid grievance if he was moved from the prison before the course ended.

Prison reports also contain information about prison behaviour, but the usefulness of such information illustrates a general problem in trying to assess the risk of someone offending outside prison on the basis of information about his behaviour inside. Bad behaviour, particularly in the period leading up to the parole date, will often be taken as an indication of risk (e.g., an unwillingness to co-operate with authority or a failure or inability to contain anger in a stressful situation which could lead to a violent offence). Although there may be disagreement in specific cases, in general people agree about the significance of information concerning bad behaviour. However, there appears to be less agreement about the significance of good behaviour. To some, good prison behaviour is, in itself, an indication of a willingness to accept authority and accept supervision, whilst others of a more sceptical nature want to know *why* the prisoner is behaving well.

These judgments concerning the relevance of behaviour to risk seem to be part of commonsense or folk criminology, an area where there is much unresolved disagreement. In many cases expert evidence does not exist to help settle the issue. Agreed generalisations about the effectiveness of programmes for sex offenders inside and outside prisons are relatively rare (see chapter 4).

When statistical studies are made of the factors which are correlated with re-offending, most of the information before a panel is, from a statistical point of view, of little significance. For a number of years the Parole Unit, that part of the Home Office responsible for administering the parole system within the prison service, produced a reconviction prediction score, which gave an estimate of the probability of reconviction of the offender within a fixed period after release, regardless of the length of time he might have on licence. This estimate was not used as part of the grounds for a parole decision, nor was it calculated for each applicant. It was agreed that the new directions would require the use of a statistical risk indicator, and the Home Office Research and Planning Unit designed a more sensitive prediction score.[17] Instead of giving a single estimate, the new method estimates the probability of re-offending for each month after the parole date, up to 24 months. It has been said that if a parolee avoids re-offending in the early part of the licence he is more likely to complete his parole successfully. The new score, known as the risk of

---

[17] Copas, J., Ditchfield, J. & Marshall, P. 'Development of a new reconviction prediction score', *Home Office Research Bulletin No. 36*, London: Home Office.

reconviction score (ROR) confirms that belief, but is more subtle. The study examined the records of 1,500 men sentenced to four years or more after they were released in 1987 and discovered that five factors, which were known at the time of sentence, gave the best estimate of the likelihood of re-offending. These were: age at conviction; the type of offence; the number of previous custodial sentences while under 21 years old; the number of adult prison sentences; and the number of convictions. Interestingly, including other factors did not improve the accuracy of the ROR as a predictor. The ROR shows that although the risk of re-offending increases with the length of time on parole, the rate of re-offending is highest in the first few months; and for all groups the risk at two years is not very different from the risk at 12 months. Someone who would be a low risk on a one-year licence probably remains a low risk on a two-year licence. Similarly, someone who is a high risk for one year on parole remains a high risk for two years. Using only the five variables, the study was able to calculate a score for the likelihood of committing any offence (apart from most summary ones), and also of committing an offence which led to a prison sentence (a 'serious offence'). Since the new directions require a panel to take more seriously a small risk of violent offending than a larger risk of non-violent offending, an estimate of the likelihood of a violent offence would have been useful. It was not possible to provide such an estimate and members of the Board are informed that the table for serious offending is not a close approximation.

The ROR is a good illustration of the difficulty of using statistical estimates of probabilities in assessing the likely future behaviour of an individual. The advice to Parole Board members is that the ROR is an aid to decision-making. It gives an estimate of the frequency of re-offending to be expected in a large sample of men with roughly the same values for the five variables listed above. It takes no account of subsequent events after sentence which may affect risk in the particular case under consideration. In other words, the person may not be a typical member of that statistical group.

The ROR score is calculated for every male parole applicant, the equivalent female population being too small for the probabilities to be calculated. As mentioned above, the advice to the Board is to treat the estimates of chance of re-offending as one piece of information along with all the other information in the dossier. Probabilities relate to the frequency of certain outcomes in large samples; the Board must assess the risk of an individual, details of whom are greater than the five factors, committing another crime. In general, the advice is correct. There is a sound rule of inference: if there is no further information and the probability of an outcome is given, then the strength of belief that it will happen should be proportional to the probability (a rule which good card players follow when they have no further information). In risk assessment, there are nearly always further facts about the individual and these can provide a reason to depart from the statistical indicator of risk. So, the ROR is treated as one piece of information among many on which a view about the application can be made.

I think that this fails to acknowledge the real difficulties which are met when two different styles or methods of reasoning are used together. The rule of inference mentioned above states strictly that if there is no other *statistically relevant* information, then the strength of belief should be based on the given probability. In some cases it would seem irrational to question relevance. For example: a man is considered for parole with a very low ROR — the chance of his offending on even a two-year licence is approximately two per cent; he is a first-time offender who attacked his wife, inflicting serious injuries, and he has recently written her a letter threatening to attack her again when he is released; the letter indicates a current intention which overrides a prediction based on the ROR. It is hard to imagine, outside an academic setting, someone questioning the legitimacy of ignoring the ROR in this case. However, there are many other cases where the relevance of a factor is disputed and could be settled, if at all, only through a statistical investigation. In general, the only information which can show that some factor is relevant is statistical information.

The Parole Board interview is an opportunity for the Board to ask the prisoner questions which will help it reach a decision. In the past, every parole applicant had the right to be seen by a member of the local review committee. The purpose of the meeting was to enable the parole applicant to add further details to his written representations. The interview was intended to be non-judgmental and to help bring out points in support of the applicant's case. It was recognised that offenders should still have the opportunity to state their case to someone other than prison staff, but the opportunity was taken to make the interview an occasion for exploring further issues which would concern a panel. The interviewing member is responsible for checking the completeness of the dossier and taking steps through the prison parole clerk to get missing documents prior to the interview. He will conduct the interview with directions and training guidance in mind and the Board has agreed a structure to the report itself which ensures that issues bearing on risk are discussed. The prisoner should have his own copy of the dossier and should have had a chance to read it beforehand or had it read to him by an officer.

The training guidance states that the Board should take into account the sentencing judge's comments, and these are rarely included in the dossiers of DCR cases, although they are virtually always in lifer papers. Unless the Board is given the information elsewhere, it will not know that a prisoner is serving a longer-than-normal sentence (see chapter 5). The Board will, presumably, treat each case on its merits at each review, but the judge will have had reasons for imposing the longer sentence, including reasons connected with risk. The Board should therefore take these into account, as it takes account of the reasons for a discretionary life sentence being imposed. However, there is nothing to prevent a man who is serving a longer-than-normal sentence being released at first review. That is a matter for the Board, if the sentence is less than seven years, or the Home Secretary. The Board, in training its members, is careful to insist that it is wrong to re-sentence. The judge has awarded the appropriate sentence and a prisoner cannot be denied parole on the grounds that he has not served enough time. By the same token, there should not be a general rule within the Board that prisoners who receive longer-than-normal sentences cannot have parole or only a short time on licence.

It is a common belief that if a prisoner denies his offence at the time of review, he cannot get parole. My experience is that this is not true. The prisoner who denies that he committed the index offence may, nevertheless, be released on licence, although the Board's practice is to assume, without question, that he is guilty. But the more serious the offence the more difficult it can be to discount the denial.

Recalls to Custody

The Board has been given directions and training guidance for the recall of parolees and lifers on licences. It must consider the extent to which continued liberty will present a *serious* risk to others or the likelihood of an imprisonable offence being committed (in the case of lifers the word 'serious' is not used). When a swift recall seems advisable this can be arranged without reference to the Board. Most recalls are for breaches of one of the conditions of the licence. The standard licence for parolees requires them to keep in touch with their supervisors; to receive home visits from their supervisors if requested; to live and work where 'reasonably approved by supervisors'; not to travel outside the UK without prior permission; and generally to 'be of good behaviour', not taking any action which would jeopardise the objectives of supervision (the last of these conditions is not included in the lifer's licence, probably because the discretion to recall lifers, which lasts until death, is wider). Panel members and supervisors may suggest special conditions for special cases, but this is not encouraged.

Prisoner's Rights

No prisoner has a right to parole, but the consequences of being denied it are so serious that there should be the right to a fair procedure. The changes introduced by the CJA 1991 have led to greater fairness in several respects. Open reporting has enabled the parole applicant to question or correct any statements made. When first discussed this concept of 'openness' was said to lead to blandness, particularly in reports by officers who would have to continue working with the offender after their reports had been read. Opinions vary as to whether that has happened. Probation officers have had longer experience of open reporting, and many claim that there is no evidence that the writers avoided being frank in their assessments. There are reports which the offender should not see because they place others at risk; for example, letters from social services which give details about victims or potential victims, or letters from victims themselves which may have been included in a closed dossier. In discretionary lifer panels, the chairman can rule that a document is not to be shown to the lifer, although his legal representative is entitled to view it. Rules about confidentiality mean that the author of a report must give his permission for it to be included in a dossier. The result is that many past reports, especially medical ones, have been removed from lifers' dossiers, although some of the information may be retained in summary form.

The Parole Board interview is another means of ensuring greater fairness, as it provides the chance for the applicant to respond to negative points in the dossier, and maybe develop better reasons in favour of parole. It is probably too early to know whether the most common perception of the interview among prisoners — that it is a helpful means of promoting their cause, or a trap — is true.

Now that the Board is required to give reasons, the applicant is able to see why the decision was made and can appeal against it. In the first instance, appeals go to the chairman of the Parole Board. If the applicant remains dissatisfied he can apply for judicial review. The scope of the appeal is restricted to whether the correct procedures were followed or whether the decision is irrational given the contents of the dossier or statements before a discretionary lifer panel (DLP). Some information about appeals is given in the Parole Board's *Annual Report*.

In the past, the Parole Board or the Home Office has been criticised for delays. The possibility of early release is so important to nearly all prisoners and their families that the period leading up to the decision is a tense time for them. They can usually also predict when the decision will be sent to the prison. A delay in preparing the dossier, arranging the interview and panel, or sending the decision is unfair; it also creates more problems for the officers on the wing.

Discretionary lifers have greater protection against delays than other cases. They are entitled to a DLP after the tariff period has expired and every two years thereafter: unless they elect not to have a hearing the dates by which each stage of the procedure has to be fulfilled are laid out in the CJA 1991 and Parole

Board Rules. Of greater value to lifers is that they are entitled to a hearing with legal representation before members of the Board. The Act also protects a decision to release from interference by the Home Office. The lifer's release cannot be delayed unless he commits a criminal offence.

Conclusion

The new directions for release on parole have changed the basis of the decision so that it is more difficult for a prisoner to satisfy the Board that he should be released on licence. Parole, as opposed to automatic release on licence, is now restricted to prisoners serving at least four years and it is claimed that these prisoners are more likely to commit violent offences. The new directions have led to more focused reports for dossiers and a report written by a member of the Board. The new statistical indicator is sufficiently refined to be able to see how the probability of offending varies over the months on licence. Discretionary lifer panels enable the Board's members to question both the lifer and those who have written reports and made recommendations. It is too early to know the effect of the new directions and procedures on rates of serious re-offending.

References

Carlisle Report, *The Parole System in England and Wales: Report of the Review Committee* (1988), London: HMSO.

Copas, J., Ditchfield, J. & Marshall, P., 'Development of a new reconviction prediction score', *Home Office Research Bulletin No. 36*, London: Home Office.

Hood, R. & Shute, S. (1993) *Paroling with the New Criteria. Evaluating the Impact and Effects of Changes in the Parole System: Phase One*, Oxford: Centre for Criminological Research, University of Oxford.

Hood, R. & Shute, S. (1995) *Paroling with the New Criteria. Evaluating the Impact and Effects of Changes in the Parole System: Phase Two*, Occasional Paper 16 of the Oxford University Centre for Criminological Research.

Lacey, N., Wells, C. & Meure, C. D. (1990) *Reconstructing Criminal Law*, London: Weidenfeld and Nicholson.

Mitchell, B. (1992) 'Preparing Life Sentence Prisoners for Release', *The Howard Journal*, 31, pp. 224–39.

Report of the Parole Board for 1991 (1992), London: HMSO.

Report of the Parole Board for 1993 (1994), London: HMSO.

von Hirsch, A. (1985) *Past or Future Crimes*, Manchester: Manchester University Press.

White Paper (1990): *Crime, Justice and Protecting the Public*, London: HMSO, 1990.

9

Supervising the Dangerous in the Community

Roger Shaw

The Morality, Politics and Practice of Control

Concluding a workshop on the supervision of dangerous offenders, Prins (1987) observed, 'We were concerned to emphasise the special nature of the work in the field of dangerousness. "Society" through its various agencies expects and emphasises tight control and it expects protection. The worker is thus much more exposed to the public and the media, and his ... (or her) ... professional career can be at stake. But perhaps the essential element is that the worker is embroiled in Society's moral and ethical value systems' (cited in Wedge, 1987).

Supervision of the dangerous in the community immediately raises an important philosophical and practical point: 'How serious does an individual's past behaviour need to be before he or she forfeits the right to be treated as any other case or client of a service or is denied freedoms of privacy and movement permitted other offenders when they have completed their period in hospital or prison?' (Shaw (1992)). Rule 23 of the European Rules on Community Sanctions and Measures, states:

> The nature, content and methods of implementation of community sanctions and measures shall not jeopardise the privacy or the dignity of the offenders or their families, nor lead to their harassment. Nor shall self-respect, family relationships, links with the community and ability to function in society be jeopardised. Safeguards shall be adopted to protect the offender from insult and improper curiosity or publicity.

154

The Rules were adopted by the Committee of Ministers of the Council of Europe in 1992 and published in 1994. They have no force in UK domestic law and are designed to provide a framework for member states in drafting legislation and formulating practice advice. However, definitions of 'privacy', 'harassment', 'links with the community' and 'ability to function in society' become critical if an individual who has been punished for his past demeanours is now, in the interests of public protection, treated to heightened surveillance and control in the community on the basis of what he *might* do.

The Criminal Justice Act 1991 gave emphasis to the work of the probation service in contributing to public protection through its work with potentially dangerous people. A report on an inspection of this area of the service's work (HM Inspectorate of Probation (1995)) made it clear that individuals identified as presenting a risk to public safety should be supervised more strictly and that this aspect of the service's supervisory role takes precedence over the supervision of other offenders. Tight controlling systems are seen as paramount and people who are considered a threat to public safety forfeit some of their individual rights, although it is not articulated in that way by ministers and government officials. Increasing emphasis by the Home Office on aspects of supervision may have the effect of reducing freedom of movement and tightening control of the dangerous offender. However, Coker and Martin (1985) observed, following their study of lifers:

The notion of, or belief in, 'strict' supervision is nonsense. In the absence of any definition of what this term is intended to imply, the probation officer largely imposes his own definition which relies on more frequent contact with the lifer and a more controlling approach. This is likely to be counter-productive. Apart from the practical difficulties, men resent a demeaning style of supervision which may set up a conflict between man and officer, and the man may be unable to voice his resentment directly.

In respect of psychiatric patient violence Grounds (1994) concluded that supervision is inseparable from a relationship with the patient of support, mutual trust and openness; a point which is supported by Hedderman (1995) in her observation that 'safe monitoring depends on establishing and maintaining such a relationship and when it breaks down supervision is no longer possible'.

The philosophical and practical issues would be more manageable if we could accurately foresee the consequences of taking different forms of action: but this is impossible. Walker (1991) observed, 'We do not have and are not likely to have in the foreseeable future prediction tables that would tell us who can be released with little risk to others, nor can we assume that any substantial risk would be greatly reduced by supervision in the community'. Coker and

Martin (1985) concluded from their study of life licencees that supervision in the community does not substantially reduce risk to the public. However, they recognised that life licensees are a highly selective group and that the relatively low incidence of reconviction was, at least in part, a tribute to the selection process and what went on before release. It is important to add that the use of reconviction-rates as a measure is a somewhat blunt instrument and does not necessarily equate with actual re-offending. The British Crime Survey demonstrated that only about four per cent of offences result in conviction or caution (Home Office (1993)). It seems reasonable to suggest that it is not only petty transgressions that are not reported, recorded or traced to their perpetrators; arson, for example, is one of the more damaging crimes, frequently having repercussions far exceeding those intended by the fire-raiser, leading to death, injury, loss of jobs and, in addition, a mistrust of institutions associated with insurance and business upon which much of the structure of society today rests. Yet it is believed that only two per cent of malicious and fraudulent fire-raisers are brought to court (Arson Prevention Bureau (1994)). In her review of the psychiatric literature Barker (1994) concluded that 'arson must be a far more common activity than is ever portrayed in the criminal statistics'. She added that 'a crime such as arson which consumes the evidence of its existence is always likely to be underestimated. It is also probably true to say that the prevalence of such a crime is only ever as high as the index of suspicion for it'. An analysis of fires occurring in 1993, estimated to cost in excess of £50,000 each or causing fatalities which were reported to the Fire Protection Association, found that more than one-third were deliberate arson with a total value exceeding £56 million (Kirby (1995)).

Murder is another serious offence, and the large number of missing persons together with the revelations in Gloucester in 1994, where a number of bodies of missing persons were found buried in a building, begs the question whether this was a unique incident or merely the tip of the iceberg.

Although definitions of dangerousness and high risk have been suggested in the writings of many authors, for instance, Scott (1977) and Prins (1986), precise statements are illusive and subject to varied interpretations. Some working in this field, particularly practitioners, dislike the label 'dangerous', but few would deny that some such offenders exist. Leighton (1990), for instance, observed that 'a review of the more responsible literature on the subject would make it clear that dangerousness cannot be predicted but rather that people can be assigned to probability groups on the basis of their present behaviour, its antecedents and if relevant, a psychiatric diagnosis'. Shaw (1991), reporting on research carried out at Cambridge University's Institute of Criminology into probation service policy and practice in relation to dangerous and high risk offenders, noted that one-third of all probation services in England and Wales had a policy relating specifically to dangerous and high risk offenders, and a further one-third planned to develop or introduce such a policy before the end of 1991. There were, however, considerable differences in the various statements. Not all categories most likely to include offenders whose previous behaviour suggested they might be dangerous in the future were included. For instance, some policies referred only to the protection of staff, or only to people released from prison, or only to the mentally disordered. Many policies ignored individuals subject only to probation orders, whatever their past history might have been, and considered only those on parole, life licence or released from special hospitals. Other services laid great store on the professional ability of individual probation officers to assess a person as dangerous or high risk regardless of their most recent offence or sentence; others used the Butler Report Classification (Home Office and DHSS (1975)). However, in the majority of cases it was clear that a designated senior manager carried responsibility for ensuring that dangerous and high risk offenders were adequately supervised. Sometimes this was undertaken in the normal line management structure, sometimes as a functional responsibility. In some services, special committees or meetings were convened for this purpose and individuals were put on a 'dangerous register' following a decision reached in a meeting. Some services had initiated a policy following a serious incident or inquiry, whilst in others it could be traced to a conference on management issues in relation to dangerous offenders (Wedge (1987)). The initiative of HM Inspectorate of Probation, through its Area Reviews in the 1980s to encourage probation services to formalise policy and practice in relation to dangerousness, was also a factor. It was as much due to those varied reasons, as it was to geography, demography and epidemiology, that there was such wide variation in the response of probation service managements to dangerousness. Shaw (1991) observed:

> What appeared *not* to significantly influence policy was the social work ethos and ideology of the probation service which informs much of its response to other aspects of its work. With dangerous and high risk offenders the emphasis was very much on control, public protection and staff safety. Again, this raises the question, how serious does an individual's past behaviour need to be before he or she forfeits the right to be treated as any other client of the service or denied freedoms of privacy and movement permitted other offenders when they have completed their period in hospital or prison?

Shaw examined all cases designated as dangerous and high risk in five probation areas. These covered a range of licences and court orders (see Table 1).

Table 1

TYPE OF SUPERVISION TO WHICH OFFENDERS CATEGORISED AS DANGEROUS OR HIGH RISK BY FIVE AREA PROBATION SERVICES WERE SUBJECT									
Order or Licence	*No.*	*0%*	*5%*	*10%*	*15%*	*20%*	*25%*	*30%*	
Life licence	122								
Parole licence	131								
Other licence	22								
Voluntary after care	30								
Probation order	62								
Section 53 C&YP Act*	6								
Conditionally discharged restricted patient	66								
Total	439								

*Children and Young Persons Act 1969.

Not all offenders had been placed on the dangerous and high risk register because of the offence for which they were currently subject to supervision. In some probation services minor theft and fraud charges resulting in probation orders had led to the offenders being on the register because they were known pederasts.

Many different offences which could severely injure a person were listed as the most recent crimes committed by persons categorised as dangerous. However, as has just been said, it was sometimes past behaviour, and not the most recent crime, which gave cause for concern. Whilst murder was the most commonly listed offence, the next most frequently encountered was arson, constituting more than 12 per cent of all probation service cases identified as dangerous or high risk (see Table 2).

Table 2

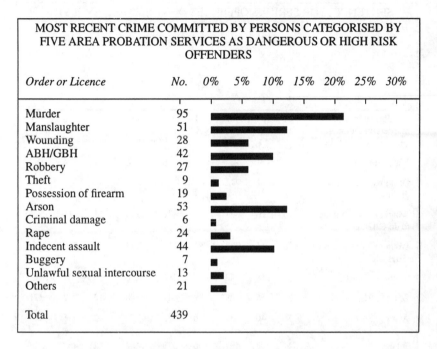

MOST RECENT CRIME COMMITTED BY PERSONS CATEGORISED BY FIVE AREA PROBATION SERVICES AS DANGEROUS OR HIGH RISK OFFENDERS									
Order or Licence	*No.*	0%	5%	10%	15%	20%	25%	30%	
Murder	95								
Manslaughter	51								
Wounding	28								
ABH/GBH	42								
Robbery	27								
Theft	9								
Possession of firearm	19								
Arson	53								
Criminal damage	6								
Rape	24								
Indecent assault	44								
Buggery	7								
Unlawful sexual intercourse	13								
Others	21								
Total	439								

HM Inspectorate of Probation (1995), using different methodology and definition, also disclosed a high proportion of arsonists identified by probation services as dangerous or high risk. However, the Inspectorate's study indicated a larger number and proportion of offenders against children than was evident in Shaw's study five years earlier, probably due to mechanisms set in place in response to public concern about child abuse. The Inspectorate, using figures from the fourth quarter of 1993, demonstrated the high proportion of individuals convicted of 'serious offences of violence' who were subsequently supervised by the probation service. Table 3 is taken directly from the report.

Table 3

SENTENCES FOR SERIOUS OFFENCES OF VIOLENCE, INVOLVING SUPERVISION BY THE PROBATION SERVICE — ENGLAND AND WALES FOURTH QUARTER OF 1993								
	PO	SO	CSO	CO	YOI	Immediate Imprison over 12 months	Hospital order	Detention Section 53	
Murder, attempted murder, threat or conspiracy to murder	18	2	8	1	10	84	3	8	134
Manslaughter	3	—	—	—	6	46	1	4	60
Death by reckless driving	—	1	12	—	11	19	—	—	43
Wounding with intent to do GBH, etc.	15	10	21	9	72	194	11	11	343
Wounding or inflicting GBH, etc.	150	41	333	53	117	173	8	—	875
Robbery	61	118	53	15	289	490	15	32	1073
Sexual offences	221	56	29	22	41	388	12	2	771
Arson	76	40	31	6	33	70	12	6	274
Totals	544	268	487	106	579	1464	62	63	3573

England and Wales fourth quarter of 1993
Information supplied by S1 Division

PO = Probation order
SO = Supervision order
CSO = CS order
CO = Combination order
YOI = Young offender institution

Recently, government has paid increasing attention to the risks posed by offenders released from institutions and those subject to community sentences. Circulars have been issued by government departments, principally the Home Office, containing instructions relating to such matters as incident reporting and risk assessment for the temporary release of prisoners.[1] The precise purpose of these Circulars as instruments of public protection is not always accepted by field staff, since some of the assumptions are seen as unsubstantiated or as having little scientific validity. Discussions with practitioners engaged in the supervision of dangerous offenders disclose that the principal purpose of these

---

[1] See, for example, Probation Circulars 84/1994, 96/1994 and 41/1995.

Circulars is seen as the protection of government departments and the avoidance of embarrassment to ministers when disasters occur, as well as engendering a feeling in the public that supervision in the community is punishment rather than treatment. When instructions are given, blame can be levelled at staff if elements within them are not followed. The growth of instructions, standards and guidelines has been such that it can have a swamping effect and so reduce compliance and effectiveness. A report by HM Inspectorate of Probation on community service, which preceded, by a few months, the report on dangerous offenders, gave a catalogue of examples where standards were not being met, whilst paying very little attention to the high rates of successfully completed orders (HM Inspectorate of Probation (1994)). The Inspectorate's report on the handling of dangerous offenders showed similar shortcomings. This was followed by a study of 'serious incident reports' by 30 probation services covering a six-month period in 1995, which revealed 50 murders by offenders who had at the time been under supervision of one sort or another. A tentative projection suggested that this would be true of 13.5 per cent of murders committed annually (Home Office 1996). It is not clear how many of these murders had ascertainable histories of violence, and (as Nigel Walker observed in chapter 1) a high percentage of serious assaults on members of the public are perpetrated by individuals who have not previously been convicted for such behaviour. Further evidence to support this is found in Shaw's (1991) sample. Less than half of those committing violent or sexual assault on a stranger had previously been convicted for a similar offence; and, when they had, the seriousness of the previous offence, where this was known, was frequently of a much lower standard, for example an incident which, but for the benefit of hindsight, could be described as a fight between young men. Nevertheless, supervisors must be mindful of Prins' (1988) warning that those who supervise offenders known to have committed horrendous acts in the past should be constantly on their guard for behavioural triggers, similar circumstances and unusual signs. If this warning were heeded, some people who became victims might still be alive today. Even though a high proportion of serious assaults are perpetrated by individuals who are not under supervision, there is now an abundance of evidence to indicate that a small proportion of individuals do constitute a serious threat to public safety and that supervision which takes account of Prins' warning should be routine in these cases. It should, therefore, be a matter of concern that HM Inspectorate of Probation (1995) observed:

> The absence of clearly stated, easily assessable statements about risk on case records was matched by a dearth of any comments showing 'developing concerns' that the offender might pose a risk to the public. Many supervising officers recorded only factual information. In some cases this was because

they believed that case records should contain only verified facts. Other supervising officers were concerned that action would be taken against them by offenders who disputed the content of the record. The use of the case record by both supervising officers and their managers appeared to be changing to a simple record of contact rather than a diagnostic tool.

The consequences of having open records, endorsed by the Citizens' Charter and reinforced by guidelines from the Home Office, have far-reaching implications for the supervision of dangerous offenders. There is no doubt that increasing legislation and advice from both Europe and Westminster aimed at safeguarding the rights of individuals is on a collision course with the expectations of other government departments concerned with public safety.

As with other offenders supervised by the probation service, those identified as dangerous can be subject to different types of intervention by probation officers and other agencies with whom they are working in partnership, the aim being to address the particular facets of the offender's behaviour which give rise to damaging consequences. Anger-management groups and courses are undertaken by probation services up and down the country. Individual and group work with sex offenders is now commonplace and sometimes involves psychologists, sex therapists, psychiatrists or others with expertise in a particular field. Whilst many people can be classified as 'sex offenders', this grouping contains an assortment of different individuals with different motivations and different problems, from the heterosexual rapist whose targets are adult women, to the homosexual pederast who is attracted to pre-pubertal boys, and a great range of other individuals. Not surprisingly, therefore, the types of intervention and treatment used vary. However, what is increasingly common in the probation service today is a recognition of two essential features which are shared by many offenders. The first addresses denial. Many offenders deny that the incident took place or that they were the perpetrator, or else maintain that the child or woman encouraged them. Until this denial is broken down little constructive work can be undertaken. In prisons, particularly, there is a tendency for offenders to deny their sexual proclivities in order to survive unharmed in a prison setting, and this denial can be maintained upon release, rendering treatment difficult. The second issue commonly addressed in treatment groups is aimed at enabling the offender to recognise that throughout the process which led to the offence a number of choices could have been made and, if any had been different, the crime would not have been committed. An example is the pederast who arranges to be a babysitter, drinks before he arrives and then seats himself close to the child. At each one of these processes a choice could have been made which would have broken the chain leading to the offence. In attacking denial and addressing choice it is clear that the sexual orientation of the offender is not being challenged but he, and occasionally she, is being better equipped to avoid the circumstances leading to offending in the future. More sophisticated and ambitious interventions are sometimes also attempted.

Occasionally misuse of drugs can give rise to behaviour which causes an individual to be viewed as dangerous, e.g., injection of amphetamines. However, it is the consumption of alcohol which correlates most highly with behaviour which puts the public at risk. Examples are the pederast, already noted, who may not put himself in the position of risk with children until he has had a drink, the violence perpetrated in the home after drinking, and the carnage on the roads caused by the persistent drink-driver. As a result the probation service has mounted alcohol courses and drink-drive courses all over the country. Some of these have been particularly successful, for instance high risk offenders who had completed the Powys Probation drink-drive course were shown by the Transport Research Laboratory to have a reconviction rate of only one-fifth of comparable high risk offenders who had not been through the course.

Probation service work with offenders is governed by a set of National Standards, produced by the Home Office (1995) after some consultation with the probation service, which is revised from time to time. In respect of the supervision of offenders before and after release from custody the aims and objectives are stated in National Standards as:

- the rehabilitation of the offender;
- the protection of the public from harm from the offender;
- the prevention of further offending.

In respect of probation orders the aims and objectives set out in national Standards are very similar and it is clear that, notwithstanding the rhetoric surrounding retribution and punishment which sometimes emanates from politicians, the expectation placed on the probation service is that it will rehabilitate the offender and protect the public from further victimisation. The standards lay down expectations, including how frequently and when offenders released from prison should be seen, what supervision plans should include and how records should be kept. Whilst the constant expansion and tightening of standards and other guidelines can be counter-productive to tight supervision, as has been demonstrated earlier, as far as the protection of the public from the dangerous offender is concerned quality of supervision and safety must go beyond the standard. Probation services and the Inspectorate of Probation acknowledge that public protection is the responsibility of *all* probation staff and not just that of the officer supervising the case.

If an offender fails to comply with the requirements of his licence or probation order he can be taken back before the court. Proceedings in the event of a breach of licence conditions are different according to whether offenders have been sentenced to 12 months and over and less than four years on the one hand, or to four years and over on the other (see chapter 8). They are also different in respect of probation and other court orders. However, for any breach action to succeed the court will need to be satisfied that a condition has not been adhered to. In respect of offenders sentenced to four years and over, National Standards place greater emphasis on the safety of the public than in other sentences. Whilst it is not unreasonable to suppose that an individual sentenced to four years and over has been convicted of a more serious offence than one with a shorter prison sentence or subject to a community sentence, this is not always the case, nor is the lightly sentenced offender necessarily less dangerous.

Section 39 of the Criminal Justice Act 1991 provides the statutory framework for the recall of licencees. Again, protection of the public is paramount and recall is not limited to cases where the licensee has committed a further criminal offence, although the act does not define what constitutes ground for revocation of a licence. After a life licence has been revoked and the licensee returned to prison he must be given reasons in writing for the recall and has a right to make representations to the Parole Board and, in so doing, may seek legal advice. The Parole Board may recommend immediate release; in cases where it does not, the licensee will continue to be detained. When considering these cases the Parole Board is subject to directions from the Secretary of State which hinge on two principal issues: (a) the danger which the individual may represent to members of the public; and (b) the extent to which he has failed to comply with licence conditions and is or is not likely to do so in the future.

Ultimately, the issue most concerning the supervisor, and presumably the public, is whether or not the dangerous offender under supervision in the community re-offends. During the first half of the 1990s there has been increasing interest in exploring what works in reducing criminal behaviour. Some of this is particularly relevant to the more serious offender, for instance McGuire (1993). Although McGuire's report dealt mostly with group work, Trotter (1993) explored a one-to-one programme which appeared to demonstrate impressive effectiveness, with breach rates reduced to between 30 and 50 per cent.

Home Office Statistical Bulletin 18/1994 provides some insight into reconviction, allowing comparisons to be made between life licensees, restricted patients and all other adult prisoners. Two-year reconviction rates for life licencees and restricted patients were found to be very similar: 10 per cent for standard list offences and two per cent for grave offences for life licensees; and 13 per cent for standard list offences and two per cent for grave offences for restricted patients. Two-year reconviction rates for life licensees released from prison and restricted patients discharged from hospital were both much lower than the equivalent reconviction rates for all adult male ex-prisoners, which is about 50 per cent. The close concordance in reconviction between life licensees and restricted patients is interesting but not surprising, given that the decision to place an offender in prison as distinct from hospital is more dependent upon the attitude of the court and the psychiatrist at the time, than it is on the behavioural characteristics of the offender. As West (1995) observed in respect of psychopaths, 'placement of a psychopath in hospital depends more on the attitudes of the psychiatrist and the lawyers than on the patient'.

Andrews *et al* (1990) and Gendreau (1995) suggested that there were two types of risk factors, which they referred to as 'static' and 'dynamic'. Static factors were aspects of the offender's life which maintained his criminality but could not be changed, whereas dynamic risk factors were aspects such as social achievement and interpersonal conflict which could be changed and might therefore lessen recidivism. They included in the dynamic predictors factors such as companions. However, they considered these in relation to peer group influences on the offender's behaviour, whereas it could be argued that since much violent and serious crime is perpetrated against a person known to the offender the role of the victim is critical when he is a companion of the offender rather than merely a partner in a crime against a third party.

The Roles of Victim and Circumstances

It is important to keep in mind that in terms of numbers of people hurt the risks posed by criminals, identified by their previous dangerous behaviour, is very small when compared with the risks posed by, for instance, tired drivers and tobacco.

In addition, reconviction rates for grave offences are low, although the consternation which can result is out of all proportion to the numbers of individuals involved. Currently, risk assessments undertaken by probation services and advice from government departments focus largely on the offender. This is in spite of the fact that in order that a damaging incident can take place, three elements are essential: offender, circumstance and victim. These are not separate, discrete elements but link with each other in order that the event can be acted out and the crime committed. First, the offender will have motive, predisposition, illness or other factors which might be variously described by the observer as 'greed', 'lust', 'aggression', 'sickness', and so forth. Secondly, the suitable circumstance must exist or be created. Thirdly, there is usually a victim who is vulnerable by virtue of the potential he provides for the offender's needs or desires, for example, an offender sexually attracted to small boys is unlikely to be a threat to adult women whatever the circumstances.

The behaviour of some individuals demonstrates their propensity for causing serious harm, and information about their behaviour exists which can be used to alert the supervisor to risk factors. However, many harmful events have not been preceded by convictions, nor even, as far as we know, by dangerous behaviour which failed to result in a conviction. In these cases it is particularly important to question the part played in the occurrence by circumstance and victim. From their study of lifers Coker and Martin (1985) observed, 'They seemed ordinary people. The majority were different only in respect of the offence, which in itself did not necessarily signify personality disorder. This impression gives weight to the largely overlooked situational component of violent behaviour, and acknowledges that violent crime is not solely the product of individual pathology'. In a list of guiding principles seeking to ensure staff safety, HM Inspectorate of Probation (1995) observed, 'Violence is more likely to be situational than inherent in the individual'.

Judges and magistrates, probation officers, social workers, psychiatrists, psychologists and others working with offenders classified as dangerous or high risk are sometimes discouraged from openly considering the role of circumstance or victim for fear of upsetting sensitivities. There are examples of judges being criticised by interest groups and the media for observing that a female victim had been provocative in some way. Such a comment, often taken out of context, is then seen as excusing the behaviour or putting some element of blame on the victim. The important point is thus lost, namely the role that circumstances and/or victim played in the incident, and what can be learnt from that. Increasingly, the role of circumstance and victim is being recognised in the commission of some types of offence. People who leave the doors and windows of their homes open when they are absent are viewed as irresponsible, as are those who leave valuables open to gaze in unattended cars. There is increasing media sympathy for women who have murdered a male partner who had subjected them to long-term violence and abuse. But how vulnerable are those women to committing a similar offence under less severe circumstances? What percentage of the female public would do the same thing if they had been similarly abused? We do not know the answers to these questions, but what is clear is that the circumstance and the victim played as crucial a part in the perpetration of the offence as the offender herself, and had the circumstance or the victim been different the offender might well have lived out her life presenting no threat whatsoever to anyone.[2] Most men are physically stronger than most women, and a violent altercation between a man and a woman

---

[2] There is, of course, a rider to this, which space does not allow time to explore, namely that some women have been so abused throughout their lives and are so disempowered that they replace one battering partner with another, a fact which should not go unnoticed by anyone supervising such a person in the community.

usually results in victory for the man without the use of a weapon or the infliction of serious injury. In order to defend herself in what is usually an unequal struggle a woman will sometimes have recourse to a knife or other weapon. The results are usually more serious than those inflicted by a man's hands and prisons contain a number of women as a consequence. Western culture looks with particular alarm at women who kill or wound and is liable to label them dangerous. But would they be dangerous in any other circumstance?

Violent assaults on children perpetrated by adults are usually viewed very seriously and may well lead to the offenders being labelled 'dangerous'. However, Shaw (1987) cited a case where a nine-year-old boy was attacked in the street by adults, injured and his face rubbed in dog's excreta. His only 'crime' was that he was known to be the son of a sex offender. His attackers, though known, were not even prosecuted and certainly not described as 'dangerous'.

Society has a responsibility to protect its weak and vulnerable members without their having to take the law into their own hands, although it often fails in this respect. It also has an undoubted responsiblity to protect its children from violent or deviant adults. Clear though these statements are, they raise complex issues when an offender who has been labelled 'dangerous' or 'high risk' is being supervised in the community. There is a difficult dividing line between trying to understand the full picture without being accused of looking for excuses, on the one hand, and conceding that some behaviour is so extreme that the cause of it can only be sought within the mind and activity of the perpetrator, on the other. In many cases the latter may give rise to a blinkered and vengeful view which hinders our attempt to understand dangerous criminal behaviour.

There are many examples of behaviour which should cause us to question whether we are right in viewing dangerousness as the product of individual pathology. Consideration of history, even recent history, can demonstrate how circumstance and the vulnerability of potential victims led to the perpetration of a range of behaviours that would, in any other situation, cause the offender to be labelled 'dangerous'. Atrocities against women and children in war, and not necessarily in the heat of battle, give rise to questions such as whether the perpetrators behaved in a similar manner before, whether they would have done so but for those particular circumstances. We may deduce that the veneer of civilisation is so thin and the innate behaviour of human beings so nasty that when codes and laws break down all hell can be let loose and that a threshold, which varies from person to person, exists in us all. Consequently, it can be suggested that whilst there are some very dangerous people, dangerousness is not otherwise a property inherent in a particular individual or a particular behaviour — it is also the property of a particular circumstance and the vulnerability of a particular victim. Feminists may say, 'there is nothing special about men who rape'. It might be more accurate to say 'there may be something special about those who do not'. It may be a disposition of the individual, but it may also be that the circumstances and opportunities have never arisen coincidentally with a vulnerable victim. It is not sufficient to dismiss examples taken from war as 'different' — only the extremes and the breakdown in structure and code are different. The rape, torture or murder of a civilian, which is not even being used for direct military aims such as to extract information, is as heinous a crime in a time of war as it is in a time of peace.[3] In times of breakdown in law and order, civil disturbance and riots, a greater proportion of the population may be sucked into extreme behaviour than would happen at other times. They are not necessarily dangerous, if by 'dangerous' is meant, 'likely to do it again in different circumstances'.

Opportunity is a major factor in some of the more serious crimes committed against people. Terrorists, but for the opportunity to train and be provided with weapons, might otherwise not have committed murder and, indeed, many have no convictions for any other crime. Nevertheless, one man with no previous convictions except for his terrorist activities was open in expressing to the writer how he enjoyed what he did, 'particularly shooting someone in the guts'.

Sometimes it is clear that the demeanour, dress and signals from a woman who is subsequently raped were factors in the event. Whilst these do not remove culpability from the offender, recognition of the factors aids our understanding of the offender's behaviour and may help in deciding more accurately the probability of a repetition and how he should be supervised. Some organisations active in the interests of women, children and other vulnerable groups play down this factor in a crime. This is regrettable because a full understanding of the event and the probability of its occurrence are essential if we are serious about reducing victimisation. It should not be confused with condoning the behaviour of the offender.

In respect of the mentally ill, Purchase (1995) demonstrated how one event, allowed to happen by a supervisor or psychiatrist, can lead to a pattern of deteriorating circumstances resulting ultimately in a violent offence:

---

[3] This is not to suggest that direct military aims can justify such behaviour, but they do provide a reason, albeit an illegal one. It should also be remembered that throughout history conquest has often been followed by rape and pillage.

Failure to attend clinic and no action taken by supervisor/psychiatrist

↓

failure to take medication

↓

deterioration in mental state

↓

failure to sign on for social security

↓

no money

↓

inability to buy food and have accommodation

↓

petty survival offence

↓

more serious offence against the person when confronted

In this scenario the victim is chosen at random, i.e., whoever happens to confront the patient because of his thieving or appearance. It might be a shopkeeper or a police officer. The key factors in the dangerous episode were the deteriorating circumstances of the mentally ill person. To view it simplistically as an offender — victim confrontation would completely miss the cause. The type of medical, probation or social work supervision are the key to reducing the probability of offending in the first place by ensuring regular contact and medication. Supervision records disclose that failure to attend for medication is sometimes allowed to happen by the medical authorities without action being taken.

Dangerous offenders sent to prison tend to be removed from both suitable circumstances and from their victim group. This is particularly marked where the victims are children or females and where crimes have been committed in private and secretive circumstances. On the other hand, violent offences against other males within prison are quite common and the percentage of self-inflicted injuries and suicides in prison exceeds that of the population in the community. Outside prison, total protection is difficult to engineer by supervision and to suggest that it can be undertaken with absolute certainty is as unrealistic as it is to suggest that safety can be ensured by incarcerating all dangerous offenders for most of their lives. Neither the law, the principles of justice nor the public purse would permit this, even if all those at risk could be identified. As a result there will always be an element of risk, and the reasonable expectation of those supervising dangerous and high risk offenders in the community can only be to reduce that risk as much as possible. This must involve serious consideration of the role of circumstance and victim in the offence.

It behoves us to pay much more attention to the elements of circumstance and victim in risk prediction than we do at the moment. We can then use what we know about the offender to give weighting to these two variables with the aim of reducing further victimisation.

Assessing Risk

Walker (1991) suggested a tentative 'typology of dangerousness':

- The individual who harms others only if sheer bad luck brings him into a situation of provocation or sexual temptation.
- The individual who gets into such situations not by chance, but following inclinations.
- Individuals who are constantly on the look-out for opportunities.
- Individuals who do more, and who create opportunities.

Whilst Walker did not refine this further it provides a useful basis upon which to address reduced victimisation. To illustrate this, let us take as an example a worker in a children's home who has been identified as having offended against one of his charges. The question then to be asked is where in Walker's typology does the individual fit. Was it sheer bad luck that brought him into a situation of sexual temptation, initiated by the child, which otherwise would never have arisen? Had he come into the job because he liked to be with and work with children but with no overt intention to offend? Does he seek out work where opportunities for offending exist? Did he seek out this employment in order to create an opportunity for offending? If he fits into the first two categories he might well be amenable to recognising his vulnerability in the child care situation and the advisability of alternative employment. If he fits into the other two categories he would not be likely to respond to that particular type of intervention. The probability of further offending and the likelihood of successful supervision in the community can thus be assessed, at least in part, by where the offender fits in the typology of dangerousness.

Sometimes the offence results from an incident in which the victim and the circumstance are very closely linked. In a particular case a burglar in a highly excited state with his 'adrenalin running high', as he explained later, and who thought himself to be alone in a house he was burgling, discovered a woman who got out of bed to investigate the noise. He tried to make his escape by pushing past the woman in the semi-dark and they fell over. He then raped her. There were no indications that he had ever been involved in any form of sexual assault on a woman before, although he had a number of convictions for burglary. He seemed full of remorse for what had happened and had attempted suicide. He explained the situation, how he felt and how he had never been in such a situation before. Excitement mingled with fear and coupled with proximity appeared to be major factors in this incident. The very nature of the offence and the fact that the woman was abused in her own home at night and that he had a number of previous convictions for burgling dwelling houses led to his being classified as dangerous and a high risk to women. However, regardless of the sentence which an offence of such gravity merits (which is another matter altogether) the probability of a further incident of this nature was probably not high.[4] He had not sought out a woman, he had no history of such behaviour, the vulnerability of the victim, the circumstances and his excited state led to the event. He may therefore belong to the first of Walker's types, an individual who harms others only if sheer bad luck brings him into a situation of provocation or sexual temptation. It is important that this assessment is not seen as somehow condoning his behaviour or suggesting that burglary, even without rape of the occupant, is not a serious matter. However, resources available for the supervision of dangerous people in the community are scarce and it is therefore critical that they are not expended on the wrong persons. Consequently, a full assessment of a case to identify who is and who is not at risk of further offending is essential, and this requires serious consideration of the roles played by both circumstance and victim.

Certain behaviour which is intrinsically dangerous and causes loss of life may not have been aimed at the victim. Examples are drunken and dangerous driving, smoking in an area of high fire risk, deliberate arson for fraudulent purposes, and violation of building and allied regulations. In none of these cases had the victim a part to play in the incident. Consequently, the supervision of the offender in the community, usually following a prison sentence, would be of a different nature to what is needed when the offence involved the selection of a victim or where the victim was, to a certain extent, self-selecting.

Although there is an expectation that risk assessments will be undertaken by supervisors in all cases, there is no doubt that decisions are sometimes made with insufficient information. This includes decisions made in courts where

---

[4] This is, of course, quite separate from the amoral individual who takes what he wants without regard to the consequences, whether it is goods, services or women, and where there is a considerable overlap in his offending.

sentencers and those advising them can be lulled into a false sense of security by viewing the offence in isolation because there appears to be a clear common-sense motive. Arson is a very good example of this. A number of authorities have developed classifications of different types of arson, breaking them down into crimes committed for financial reward, revenge, mental ill-health, attention-seeking, etc., whilst recognising and emphasising a degree of overlap (e.g., Prins (1994), Cooke and Ide (1985)). The overlap was very marked in Shaw's (1991) study and the following four examples demonstrate how factors in the past, which were unknown to investigators and courts at the time, throw a different light on what would otherwise appear to be clear motives and classifications.

Case 1

Offence: A cardboard box factory was burnt down by a burglar using flaming cotton waste to illuminate the darkness after he had dropped his torch and broken it. He denied any intention to raise a fire.
Background: As a young boy under 10 years of age he had placed a petrol can in a bonfire. This shook up the Guy Fawkes party considerably but no one was hurt. On another occasion he had damaged the school laboratory whilst larking about with carbide.

Case 2

Offence: A vengeful man who felt unjustly sacked from his job told the probation officer, 'The boss just fired me, so I fired him'. The defendant had lit a fire in a wastepaper basket before going home on his last day and left it under the boss's desk. No serious damage resulted. He was described by the probation officer as suffering from 'deep-seated unhappiness' and by the psychiatrist as 'a depressive'.
Background: Sometime later it was discovered that as a child he had lit a fire under his baby brother's pram 'to keep him warm' when mother failed to return home from bingo.

Case 3

Offence: Business premises were fired, apparently for insurance purposes, when the owner was in financial trouble.
Background: It was later revealed by his wife that he had burnt down part of his own house whilst renovating it, but no insurance claim was made. He had also burnt himself with a flame-thrower whilst weeding the garden and on another occasion had destroyed the chimney with chemicals he was using to clear the soot away: again, no insurance claim was made.

Case 4

Offence: A pub was fired by a woman to spite her partner. She was depressed, on drugs prescribed by her GP, and had taken alcohol with them.

Background: Later her mother commented that she used to set fire to hayricks as a child and was 'quite a problem in the family as a result'.

The need for thoroughness in investigation and careful consideration of all the facts, particularly past behaviour, social circumstances and the current offence is crucial to the investigation of arson and the treatment of arsonists and other dangerous offenders if further victimisation is to be avoided (Scott (1977)). Added to this is the importance of agencies talking together, learning from one another and recognising that in the final analysis, whether the objective is reducing insurance fraud, protecting the public from harm or simply processing justice, there is need for liaison and recognition of the responsibilities and work of other professionals. Such liaison is often inhibited by the specific responsibilities and roles of the individuals concerned, for instance those tasked to secure a conviction, those associated with insurance and those concerned to reduce the likelihood of a subsequent crime, either by the person concerned or by others who might imitate the incident.

There is increasing evidence of probation, police and other services sharing information in respect of dangerous people. This is particularly so in the field of child protection and in bail information schemes, and is extending to other avenues, including clearing people for work. HM Inspectorate of Probation (1995) recommended the West Yorkshire model, in which decisions are taken jointly in a case conference where information is shared unreservedly but amongst a limited number of staff and within a tightly monitored policy. Agencies have learned to trust one another and to see that their shared responsibility for public protection is more important than the separate objectives they might have.

Probation services' risk assessments are becoming increasingly sophisticated and, as a result, time-consuming. Guidance notes are sometimes quite lengthy as services strive to account for all possible eventualities (see Appendix 1). The Criminal Justice Consultative Council (1995) has been exploring the possibility of a common risk assessment document which might travel with an offender. This would involve heightened need for information sharing. A high probability of occasional minor re-offending should not be allowed to mask the fact that a large number of potentially dangerous people are satisfactorily maintained in the community without further mayhem. Nevertheless, the issue of risk in the management of dangerousness is controversial and it is important that the added emphasis given to it recently through the expectation of risk

173

assessments on all offenders does not confuse the matter, put a further strain on resources and lead to false expectations of assessments of the harm posed by criminals to society. As pointed out in chapter 1 by Walker, the majority of those who commit a serious offence against another person are not currently subject to any form of supervision and many are not known to criminal justice agencies. Of all dangerous people at large in the community the identified few represent only a minute proportion. That proportion can be assigned to high risk groups, but to suggest that we can accurately assess who is likely to offend and who is not, and that, even if we could, it would make a significant difference to the outcome, is unreal. In the Home Office's *Research Findings No. 19*, Hedderman (1995) observed in respect of the supervision of restricted patients in the community that '6.5% of the 183 patients studied, who were released in 1985–87, were reconvicted of serious or potentially serious violence against the person, or of arson, in the 6–7 year follow-up period. Examination of supervisors' reports to the Home Office showed that it was seldom possible, even with hindsight, to identify cases where preventive action could have been taken'. There is some evidence that probation staff may lay themselves open to greater risk of assault when confronting an offender with the consequences of his behaviour, and forcing him to consider its effect on victims ('challenging behaviour' or 'confronting offending behaviour' as it is termed; Shaw (1995)). However, it must be remembered that thousands of people who have previously been convicted of serious offences against the person or of arson are supervised successfully in the community, with only a low incidence of breakdown.[5] Unfortunately, the attention of the media to crime, particularly crime which has sex and violence as its components, details of which are avidly sought after by the public, gives added pressure, stress and visibility to the work of those who are supervising the dangerous in the community and, consequently, makes the task even more difficult than it might otherwise be. Yet, as has been shown earlier in this chapter, better communication and continual assessment of risk factors and triggers must be addressed by those supervising the dangerous. The success rates might be improved further and resources used more appropriately if greater overt attention was paid to examining the part played by circumstance and the part played by the victim.

---

[5] Some evidence is, however, coming to light to suggest that not all supervised offenders who are reconvicted are recorded as having been subject to a community sentence or licence. Although the proportion is probably small, it is likely to become a matter of political and media interest and potential exaggeration if probation services and the Home Office are unable to ensure the demonstrable accuracy of their reconviction statistics.

References

Andrews, D. A., Zinger, I., Hoge, R., Bonta, J., Gendreau, P. & Collen, F. T. (1990) 'Does Correctional Treatment Work?', *Criminology*, 28.

Arson Prevention Bureau (1994) *Arson Investigation Seminar*, London: 25/26 April.

Barker, A. F. (1994) *Arson, A Review of the Psychiatric Literature*, Oxford: Oxford University Press.

Coker, J. B. & Martin, J. P. (1985) *Licensed to live*, Oxford: Blackwell.

Cooke, R. A. & Ide, R. H. (1985) *Principles of fire investigation*, Leicester: The Institution of Fire Engineers.

Council of Europe (1994) *European Rules on Community Sanctions and Measures*, Strasbourg: Council of Europe Press.

Criminal Justice Consultative Council (1995) *Supervising Difficult Offenders in the Community* (CJCC (95) 16), London.

Gendreau, P. (1995) 'What works in community corrections: Promising approaches in reducing criminal behaviour', *IARCA Journal*, 6.

Grounds, A. T. (1994) 'Risk Assessment and Management in Clinical Context', in Crichton, J. M., *Psychiatric Patient Violence: Risk and Response*, London: Duckworth.

Hedderman, C. (1995) *The Supervision of Restricted Patients in the Community*, Research Findings No. 19, London: Home Office.

HM Inspectorate of Probation (1995) *Dealing with Dangerous People: The Probation Service and Public Protection*, London: Home Office.

HM Inspectorate of Probation (1994) *Community Service: Report of the Thematic Inspection*, London: Home Office.

Home Office (1993) *The 1992 British Crime Survey*, London: HMSO.

Home Office (1994) *Statistical bulletin 18/1994*, London: Government Statistical Service.

Home Office and DHSS (1975) *Report of the Committee on Mentally Abnormal Offenders* (Butler Report), London: HMSO.

Home Office (1995) *National Standards for the Supervision of Offenders in the Community 1995*, London: Home Office.

Home Office (1996) *Report of a Seminar on HMIP's Thematic Report on Dealing with Dangerous People*, London: Home Office.

Kirby, J. (1995) 'Some Encouraging Improvements Indicated from our Study of Large Loss Fires', *Arson Intelligence*, April.

Leighton, I. (1990) 'Dangerousness — easy to misuse', *Community Care*, 8 February.

McGuire, J. (1993) 'What works — the evidence', Paper presented to conference *What Works — the challenge for managers*, Loughborough University, October.

Prins, H. (1986) *Dangerous Behaviour, The Law and Mental Disorder*, London: Tavistock.

Prins, H. (1975) 'A Danger to Themselves and Others: Social Workers and Potentially Dangerous Clients', *British Journal of Social Work*, 5, p. 279.

Prins, H. (1988) 'Dangerous Clients: Further Observations on the Limitation of Mayhem', *British Journal of Social Work*, 18, p. 593.

Prins, H. (1994) *Fire Raising — its motivation and management*, London: Routledge.

Prins, H. (1990) 'The Supervision of Potentially Dangerous Offenders — Patients in England and Wales', *International Journal of Offender Therapy and Comparative Criminology*, 34, p. 213.

Purchase, N. (1995) 'Court Diversion Schemes as Indicators of Race and Social Deprivation as Vulnerability Factors for Mentally Disordered Defendants', *British Criminology Conference*, Loughborough University, 18 to 21 July.

Scott, P. D. (1977) 'Assessing Dangerousness In Criminals', *British Journal of Psychiatry*, 131, p. 127.

Shaw, R. (1992) 'Probation Supervision of the Dangerous Offender', *Criminal Justice Matters*, 9, Autumn.

Shaw, R. (1991) 'Supervising the Dangerous Offender: Communication the vital but often missing factor', *NASPO News*, 10, p. 4.

Shaw, R. (1987) *Children of Imprisoned Fathers*, Sevenoaks: Hodder and Stoughton.

Trotter, C. (1993) *The Supervision of Offenders: What Works?* Clayton, Victoria: Monash University (Report to the Australian Criminology Research Council.

Walker, N. (1991) 'Dangerous Mistakes', *British Journal of Psychiatry*, 158, p. 752.

Wedge, P. (1987) *Issues for Senior Management in the Supervision of Dangerous and High Risk Offenders*, Workshop report, HM Inspectorate of Probation/University of East Anglia: 7 to 10 April.

West, D. J. (1995) 'Sex Offenders: Hospital, Prison and/or Treatment', *British Criminology Conference*, Loughborough University, 18 to 21 July.

Appendix 1

This extract from Powys Probation Service Risk Assessment draws heavily on advice from the Association of Chief Officers of Probation, on health service models and on the experience of other probation services. It also aids consideration of the role of victim and circumstance, although the emphasis is on the offender.

Events perpetrated by the subject of the assessment (please ring all appropriate descriptions)

Violence: to persons			Sexual:		
	1.	Death		1.	Rape
	2.	Serious injury		2.	Indecent assault (serious)
	3.	Minor injury		3.	Indecent assault (minor)
	4.	Threat		4.	Buggery
	5.	Kidnap		5.	Gross indecency
	6.	Arson			

Damage: to property			Frequency of events:
	1.	Serious	Years: 1 2 3 4 5 6 7 8 9 10
	2.	Minor	Events: 1 2 3 4 5 6 7 8 9 10
	3.	Threat	

Theft:				
	1.	Robbery/mugging	e.g. ring 5 years and ring 7 events
	2.	House burglary	= In the last 5 years there have been 7
	3.	Industrial burglary	events
	4.	Petty theft	

Person affected

Family/ Relative:			Friends/ Colleagues:		
	1.	Offender		1.	Girlfriend
	2.	Husband		2.	Boyfriend
	3.	Wife		3.	Friend — specify
	4.	Partner		4.	Peer
	5.	Child of offender		5.	Boss
	6.	Child of partner		6.	Work colleague
	7.	Child of former partner			
	8.	Mother	Officials	1.	Police
	9.	Father		2.	Prison Officer
	10.	Grandfather		3.	Probation Officer
	11.	Grandmother		4.	Hostel Warden
	12.	Brother		5.	Supervisor — specify
	13.	Sister		6.	Receptionist
	14.	Uncle		7.	Bus Driver/Conductor/ Taxi Driver
	15.	Aunt		8.	Shopkeeper/Cashier/ Barman
	16.	Mother-in-law		9.	Other official — specify
	17.	Father-in-law			
	18.	Other relative — specify			

Strangers:			Race/ Gender:		
	1.	Children (12 and under)		1.	Black
	2.	Young people (12–18)		2.	White
	3.	Young adults (19–35)		3.	Male
	4.	Middle-aged adults (36–60)		4.	Female
	5.	Older people (61 +)			
	6.	Random victim			

Circumstances (in which the feared event is thought most likely to occur)

Threats:			*Needs:*		
	1.	Arrest		1.	Money
	2.	Eviction		2.	Sexual gratification
	3.	Separation		3.	Revenge
	4.	Unwanted disclosure		4.	Protection
	5.	Custody		5.	Transport
	6.	Illness		6.	Power
	7.	Death		7.	Status
	8.	Rejection		8.	Excitement
	9.	Injury		9.	Other — Specify
	10.	Redundancy			
	11.	Loss of child	*Influence:*	1.	Alcohol
	12.	Loss of parent		2.	Drugs (prescribed)
	13.	Loss of friend		3.	Drugs (unprescribed)
	14.	Loss of partner		4.	Medical/Psychiatric
	15.	Other loss — specify			illness
	16.	Expulsion		5.	Other — specify
	17.	Punishment			

The following are examples of the summaries of risk assessment that might be produced

1. Child Sex Abuse

Events	*Person(s)*	*Circumstances*	*Frequency*
Sexual: indecent assault (serious)	Relatives: Children of offender, partner and former partner	Influence: Alcohol Needs: sexual gratification Threats: loss of partner	3 in last 5 years

2. Arsonist

Events	*Person(s)*	*Circumstances*	*Frequency*
Damage: serious	Officials	Threats: eviction, rejection, loss of partner Needs: revenge Influence: drugs	5 in last 3 years

10

Some Comments

Nigel Walker

In chapter 1 I argued that there could be little doubt about the moral justification for labelling some people as 'dangerous' and imposing on them the minimum of precautions necessary to protect others; but that there would often be doubt about the choice of candidates for such precautions; and that not much help could be expected from actuarial predictions. In chapter 2 Paul Bowden's invaluable review of research showed that certain psychiatric diagnoses are predictive of personal violence, but not strongly. Many false positives must be expected. Most violence, of course, is not attributable to mental disorder, or even abnormality, and this is emphasised in chapter 3 by Elaine Genders and Shona Morrison's study of violent incidents of an everyday kind. It is worth noting, however, that a substantial eight per cent of their sample consisted of a 'hard core', with several convictions for non-trivial violence; and that more than half of their interviewees predicted that if they found themselves in a similar situation they would again respond with violence. In chapter 4 Donald West discusses sexual harm, distinguishing several types of molesters, some more repetitive and damaging than others, and is frank about the possibilities and difficulties of remedial treatments.

John Crichton's commentary in chapter 6 reminds us that admissions to hospitals do not 'take offenders out of circulation' completely, but merely transfer them to smaller communities, as indeed do prison sentences. Unlike prisons, however, hospitals do not have an official code of rules for dealing with anti-social behaviour, of a kind that might provide some protection for both patients and staff — arguably a gap that needs filling. Nicola Padfield's chapter on sentencing (and bailing) offenders who may be dangerous raises issues so important that they will be discussed later. When it comes to considering release — the subject of chapters 7 and 8 — the decision-makers have the advantage over sentencers of fuller and more up-to-date information about the offender and the milieu to which he or she might be entrusted; but as David Hirschmann's and John Gunn's chapters make clear, the task is a complex one. It can be made to seem easier by pretending that 'management' or 'supervision' will reduce risk to an acceptable level; but Roger Shaw, in chapter 9, emphasises the difficulties of this: another point to which I shall return.

Nicola Padfield's chapter makes the sentencer's situation starkly clear. If he is dealing with a violent or sexual offence the Criminal Justice Act 1991 says, in so many words, that the sentence 'shall be [not 'may' be] ... longer than commensurate [with the seriousness of the offence itself]'; but its mandatory wording is deceptive, since it leaves it to the sentencer to decide what extra length is needed for public protection against serious harm. The judge who decided that Mumtaz Ali was dangerous gave him only a three-year instead of a two-year sentence, thus ensuring that — unless he lost time for indiscipline — he would be paroled after 18 months, a period so short that it could scarcely be called a protection for the public. Again, while the offence may be one for which the statute permits a life sentence to be imposed, the Court of Appeal will probably substitute a determinate sentence unless a psychiatrist has called the offender mentally disordered or at least unstable, and unlikely to be safe within a predictable period. Murder apart, 'life' is virtually ruled out, whatever the statutes say and however harmful the offence, for violent or sexual offenders who do not fit this description. This can be contrasted with the position when a hospital order is proposed. The judge can add a restriction order for an indeterminate period, even if the psychiatrists do not think it necessary, and even if the offence itself is not serious. The only consolation for the offender-patient is that he has a better safeguard than a lifer: he can claim early and regular hearings before a Mental Health Review Tribunal.

These contributions raise a complex question. How should a sentencing system be designed if it is to meet the following conditions?

(a)   the public's demand, encouraged by the news media, for secure protection against offenders who have shown themselves capable of serious personal harm;

(b)   the fact that both 'clinical' and 'actuarial' predictions about their future harmfulness or harmlessness involve many false positives and negatives, and that the prospect of reducing such mistakes by refining predictive variables is poor;

(c)   the fact that supervision in the community does not *and cannot be expected to* provide much protection for the public;

(d)   the judiciary's reluctance to use such powers as it has to impose indeterminate detention when there is no psychiatric diagnosis of disorder or instability.

The weak feature of the English system has, for generations, been the legislative attempts at a compromise between determinate and indeterminate prison sentences. Preventive detention, 1908 style, was followed by preventive detention, 1948 style, which was itself followed by the 'extended sentence' in 1967. The pseudo-mandatory longer-than-commensurate sentence which replaced all these in 1991 is merely the latest compromise and, as we have seen, is being used in odd ways. The Court of Appeal has even been known to reduce a 10-year longer-than-commensurate sentence by one year for mitigating reasons, which is as logical as reducing a dose of medicine because it tastes nasty. It is a good example of inability to see when retributive reasoning is inappropriate.

Other expedients have been proposed, or even adopted. Washington State has enacted a statute which allows an offender — with procedural safeguards — to be officially declared a dangerous sexual offender at any stage of his sentence, and even while on parole, thus allowing his detention to be prolonged. Its constitutionality is being challenged in the US Supreme Court. The Netherlands has, for many years, had 'renewable sentences', of lengths specified by the sentencing court, but liable to be extended for one year at a time if a judge is satisfied that this is necessary for the protection of others from serious harm. Twenty years ago in England the Butler Committee proposed a 'reviewable sentence' for offenders — it had in mind chiefly 'psychopathic' men and women — who were dangerous but whom no hospital would accept, usually because they were unlikely to respond to treatment. It is an expedient, however, which might fit a wider category: the offender convicted of an offence which renders him liable to a discretionary life sentence, but for whom the judge decides against this course, either because, without a psychiatric label, the Court of Appeal would not uphold it or because the judge does not trust the system to review the case early or often enough.

The reviewable sentence would be indeterminate, but would differ from 'life' in more than name. Since its purpose would not include retributive punishment it would specify no minimum period to be served. It would have to be reviewed regularly (the Committee thought every two years) by the Parole Board. Release would be on licence, but the need for it, and its conditions, would also be subject to review (again, the Committee thought every two years). It would be a permissible sentence for most of the offences which, at present, carry 'life' as a possibility. The Committee recommended that it should also be permissible for some other offences if committed by a person who had earlier been convicted of an offence for which he could have received a reviewable sentence: a neat but not essential feature.

An expedient of a more Draconian sort was proposed by the Home Secretary at the 1995 Conservative Party Conference. A second conviction for a violent or sexual offence of the most serious kind would leave the judge with no alternative to 'life', unless there was a case for an exception. The White Paper with details had not yet been published when this book went to press; but from what has been made public it seems that the judge would be expected — or required — to specify a minimum term to be served, as he normally does when passing a non-mandatory life sentence. The term could be altered on appeal, but not by the Home Secretary. Once the term had been served it would be for the Parole Board, not the Home Secretary, to decide whether and when the prisoner could be released on licence without too much risk. Legislation seems likely in the 1996–97 parliamentary session.

The unpopularity of the mandatory life sentence for murder (see chapter 5), and the myth that there is some constitutional principle which protects judges' discretion, will ensure a rough passage for legislation on these lines. The Lord Chief Justice and other judges have already declared themselves against it. Yet it is at least an attempt to solve the gratuitous problem created by the Court of Appeal's policy of restricting discretionary life sentences to mentally abnormal offenders, with only a few exceptions. As we have seen, this means passing determinate sentences on offenders whose records demonstrate their propensities for doing grave harm, with the result that the Parole Board must release them by fixed dates, however anxious it may be about their future. The Home Secretary's solution might be more acceptable if it allowed exceptions; and if Parliament does not reject the whole measure it might well force some such compromise.

As for release (whether from a long custodial sentence or a hospital order), two points need to be made, especially since decision-makers seem chary of making them. When it is a question of setting free someone who has been proved capable of serious personal harm the information obtainable may be positive or negative, and the difference is important. Sometimes it is such that it justifies the inference that the offender is no longer capable of doing anything like what he did, or that the only likely victim is now safe (or dead). The offender may have been incapacitated by injury or illness: the only victim may no longer be a child, or may have moved out of reach. But such situations, in which the information is reassuring in a positive way, are uncommon. Usually the information is negative: merely that the offender has said and done nothing to suggest that he is likely to repeat the offence. If, as in most cases, he has not been at liberty, or only at conditional liberty for very short periods, his behaviour is hardly a predictor, and what he says may well have been said for effect. Yet negative information is what most decisions to risk release are based on. This is one of the less acceptable faces of reality.

The second point is that decision-makers often — perhaps usually — invoke the prospect of professional supervision to make the risk seem less.

Occasionally this is realistic. Supervision can sometimes avert a tragedy, whether by recommending immediate recall or by some other sort of intervention; but it can never amount to *surveillance*. With luck it may stop a man or woman from drifting yet again into tempting or provoking situations, but it cannot be expected to control the opportunity-seeker or the opportunity-maker. This is another unacceptable face of reality.

Consequently, nearly every decision to release involves some degree of risk. Sometimes there is pressure to take the risk, for example in an overcrowded hospital. More often the motive is compassion for a man or woman who has spent the best part of his or her life in custody. There is a safer way, however, of showing compassion. Whether an offender is being detained in prison or hospital there nearly always comes a stage at which the only justification for continued detention is the protection of others ('nearly always' because some crimes are regarded by many as deserving life-long incarceration). When that stage is reached the offender can no longer be regarded as 'deserving' the conditions under which he is being forced to live. The quality of his life is being sacrificed because it has been decided, correctly or incorrectly, that others will be safer as a result. The situation calls not for compassionate release but for reparation of some sort. The only sort which seems rational is to make conditions of detention as tolerable as possible. Some prisons and hospitals might claim that they already do this for long-term inmates; others would defend themselves by emphasising the problems of security and the inadequacy of funds, or by pointing out that some inmates would abuse improved conditions. But making conditions as tolerable as possible should at least be a declared objective, and it would be a step towards this to recognise the special status of people whose detention is being prolonged solely for the sake of others.

Index

Index

Index